ISLAM AND SECULARISM IN THE MIDDLE EAST

JOHN L. ESPOSITO
AZZAM TAMIMI
editors

Islam and Secularism
in the Middle East

NEW YORK UNIVERSITY PRESS
WASHINGTON SQUARE, NEW YORK

First published in the U.S.A in 2000 by
NEW YORK UNIVERSITY PRESS
Washington Square
New York, NY 10003

Library of Congress Cataloging-in-Publication Data

Islam and secularism in the Middle East/ Azzam Tamimi, John L. Esposito, editors
    p   cm.
    Includes bibliographical references and index.
    ISBN 0-8147-8260-4 (cloth: alk. paper) — ISBN 0-8147-8261-2 (paper: alk. paper)
      I. Islam and Secularism—Middle East. 2. Islam and politics—Middle East. 3. Middle East
—Politics and government—1979- I. Tamimi, Azzam. II. Esposito, John L. BP190.5.S35 185 2000
322'.1'0956—dc21   00-036065

CONTENTS

NOTES ON THE AUTHORS

JOHN L. ESPOSITO is Professor of Religion and International Affairs and of Islamic Studies and Founding Director of the Center for Muslim-Christian Understanding, History and International Affairs at Georgetown University, Washington, DC. Editor-in-Chief of *The Oxford Encyclopedia of the Modern Islamic World* and *The Oxford History of Islam,* his other publications include: *The Islamic Threat: Myth or Reality?*; *Islam and Democracy* (with John O. Voll); *Islam: The Straight Path*; *Islam and Politics; Political Islam: Revolution, Radicalism, or Reform?*; *The Iranian Revolution: Its Global Impact*; *Islam, Gender and Social Change* and *Muslims on the Americanization Path* (with Y. Haddad); *Voices of Resurgent Islam*; *Islam in Asia: Religion, Politics, and Society*; and *Women in Muslim Family Law.*

AZZAM TAMIMI is Director of the London-based Institute of Islamic Political Thought, and a researcher at the Centre for the Study of Democracy, University of Westminster, London. He has edited *Power-Sharing Islam?,* London 1993; *Musharakat al-Islamiyin Fil-Sultah,* London, 1994; and *Al-Shar'iyah al-Siyasiyah fil-Islam* (Political Legitimacy in Islam), London, 1997. His forthcoming book, based on his doctoral research, is a study of the life and political thought of Rachid Ghannouchi.

JOHN KEANE is a Professor of Politics at the University of Westminster and Director of the Centre for the Study of Democracy. He is the author of *Public Life and Late Capitalism* (1984); *Democracy and Civil Society* (1988); *The Media and Democracy* (1991); *Tom Paine, A Political Life* (1995); and *Reflections on Violence* (1996). He is a contributor to leading journals and newspapers including the *International Social Science Journal, Political Studies* and the *Times Literary Supplement.* He was a senior visiting fellow at the European University Institute in Florence in 1990 and during 1991 was visiting professor at the Central European University in Prague.

PETER L. BERGER is Professor of Sociology and Director of the Institute for the Study of Economic Culture at Boston University.

ABDELWAHAB EL-MESSIRI is Professor Emeritus of English and Comparative Literature at Ein Shams University in Cairo. He has authored several books in both Arabic and English. The Arabic publications include: *Epistemological Bias*; *Zionist Ideology: A Case Study in the Sociology of Knowledge*; *The Earthly Paradise: Studies in American Culture*; *The*

Princess and the Poet: A Story for Children; Secrets of the Zionist Mind; Zionism, Nazism and the End of History: A New Cultural Outlook; The Encyclopedia of the Jews, Judaism and Zionism: A New Explanatory Paradigm (8 vols). His publications in English include: *The Land of Promise, a Critique of Political Zionism; Israel and South Africa: The Progression of the Relationship; The Palestinian Wedding: a Bilingual Anthology of Palestinian Resistance Poetry; A Land of Stone and Thyme, a Collection of Palestinian Short Stories.*

S. PARVEZ MANZOOR is a critic who actively contributes to the Islamic debate in the West. He was editor of the Muslim journal *Afkar-Inquiry* and is currently editor of *The Muslim World Book Review*. His writings have appeared in various books and journals and been translated into Arabic, Turkish, Malay and Urdu. He is currently preparing a study entitled *Faith and Existence: The Problem of Norm, History and Utopia in Islamic Thought.*

RACHID AL-GHANNOUCHI is leader of the Tunisian An-Nahdah (Renaissance) Party. He has published several books (all in Arabic) including *We and the West; Our Way to Civilisation; The Islamic Movement and Modernisation; The Woman Between the Qur'an and Society; The Basic Principles of Democracy and Islamic Government; The Rights of Citizens in the Islamic State; Destiny and Man in Ibn Taymiya's Thought; The Rights of Non-Muslims in the Islamic State* (available in English); and *Public Liberties in the Islamic State.*

HEBA RAOUF EZZAT is a teaching assistant in Political Science at Cairo University, and has worked as a researcher in conjunction with the International Institute of Islamic Thought (Washington). She was a visiting scholar at the Centre for the Study of Democracy, University of Westminster and is currently writing a Ph.D. thesis at Cairo University entitled 'Analysing the Concept of Citizenship in current Liberal Thought'. She is a freelance writer for many Arab journals and magazines on women's issues.

MUNIR SHAFIQ, a Palestinian writer, was until 1992 Director of the PLO's Tunis-based Palestine Planning Centre. Born a Christian, he espoused Marxism at a young age then converted to Islam in the late 1970s. He has authored more than thirty books, all in Arabic, covering a wide range of issues including a critique of Marxism/Leninism, contemporary Islamic political thought and the Palestinian cause.

ABDELWAHAB EL-AFFENDI is a researcher at the Centre for the Study of Democracy at the University of Westminster, London, and Coordinator of its project on democracy in the Muslim World. His publications include *Turabi's Revolution, Islam and Power in Sudan; Who Needs an Islamic State?;* and *Al-Thwarah wal-Islah Al-Siyasi Fil-Sudan.*

AHMET DAVUTOGLU is an Associate Professor of Political Science at Marmara University Istanbul, Turkey. He is chairman of the Foundation for Science and Arts. His publications include *Alternative Paradigms: The Impact of Islamic and Western Weltanschauungs on Political Theory* (1994) and *Civilizational Transformation and the Muslim World*. He has published scholarly articles and research papers in several languages on international relations, political thought and comparative civilizational studies.

ISLAM AND SECULARISM IN THE TWENTY-FIRST CENTURY

John L. Esposito

The world at the dawn of the twenty-first century challenges the 'wisdom' and expectations of the prophets of modernity. Modernisation and development theory had for decades maintained unequivocally that the development of modern states and societies required Westernisation and secularisation. Religion would then become restricted to private life. And if some spoke of the privatisation of religion, others predicted the marginalisation and ultimate disappearance of traditional belief. Harvey Cox's *Secular City* reflected the expectation of theologians as well as political analysts at a time when the writings of theologians like Dietrich Bonhoffer spoke of a secular Christianity and the Death of God school of theology challenged Christian traditions.

The global resurgence of religions in the last decades of the twentieth century, the Islamic reawakening in particular, have challenged, some might say discredited, the belief, indeed dogma, of the prophets of modernity. Some critics talk of the collapse or bankruptcy of secularism and the need to replace it with religiously based states. Others wish to trim its sails, to modify modern secular states.

The confluence of religion, nationalism, ethnicity and tribalism in global politics in the post Cold War period has both threatened the existence and stability of nation states and governments, leading some to warn of a clash of civilisations. Conflicts in Sudan, Rwanda, Somalia, Nigeria, Bosnia, Kosovo, India, Kashmir, Pakistan, Afghanistan, the Central Asian republics, Sri Lanka and Indonesia (to name a few) underscore the fragility of states. Religious nationalisms (Hindu, Muslim, Buddhist, Serbian and Russian Orthodox) demonstrate the variety of ways in which religion has been used to reinforce national identities, to legitimate governments, to mobilise popular support and even to justify actions that have led to ethnic cleansing.

The discrediting and, in some cases, dethronement of secular paradigms has been particularly vivid in the Islamic world. The Iranian

1

revolution, the emergence of new Islamic republics in Iran, Afghanistan and Sudan, and the use of Islam by Muslim governments and opposition movements alike reaffirm the presence and power of Islam in Muslim societies. It directly challenges, some would say threatens, the more secular patterns of development and nation building in many Muslim states.

Religion and nation formation

In many parts of the Muslim world, from North Africa to Southeast Asia, independence movements employed Islamic symbols, slogans, parties and actors to legitimate their struggle (*jihad*) and mobilise popular support. Thus, for example, in North Africa, the Algerian *'ulama* calls for *jihad* and Islamic publications played a prominent role in calling for an end to French rule and the reaffirmation of Algeria's Arab-Islamic heritage. In the Indian subcontinent, Muslim nationalism became the *raison d'être* for the creation of Pakistan with its two wings (West and East Pakistan). However, the post-independence period witnessed the emergence of modern Muslim states whose pattern of development was heavily influenced by and indebted to Western secular paradigms or models. Saudi Arabia and Turkey reflected the two polar positions. Saudi Arabia was established as a self-proclaimed Islamic state based upon the *shariah*, Islamic law. At the opposite end of the spectrum, Atatürk (Mustafa Kamal) created a secular Turkish republic. The vestiges of the Ottoman Empire – the caliph/sultan, the Shari'ah, Islamic institutions and schools – were replaced by European-inspired political, legal, and educational systems.

The majority of Muslim states chose a middle ground in nation building, borrowing heavily from the West and relying on foreign advisers and Western-educated elites. They ranged from the more secular oriented Tunisia and Iran to the Islamic republic of Pakistan. Parliamentary governments, political parties, capitalist and socialist economies and modern (European and American) curricula were the norm. While the separation of religion and politics was not total (as it is not in fact in many secular countries in the West), the role of Islam in state and society as a source of legitimation of rulers, states, and government institutions was greatly curtailed. Most governments retained a modest Islamic facade, incorporating some reference to Islam in their constitutions such as that the ruler must be a Muslim or that the *shariah* was a source of law, even when it was not. The central government also attempted to bring Islamic institutions (mosques, religiously endowed properties or *awqaf*, religious courts etc.) under state control. However, while most Muslim governments replaced Islamic law with legal systems inspired by western secular codes, Muslim family law (marriage, divorce, and inheritance) remained in force. Though family law was regarded as too sacrosanct to replace, it was reformed. In contrast to Islamic tradition, in which law was the province of the *'ulama* (religious scholars), modern reforms were the product of governments and parliaments. In many cases, the *'ulama* played no role or, at best, a marginal one. The pattern of authoritarian modernising governments and Western-oriented elites defining the role and direction of the state and imposing Western models (ideas, values, and institutions) of development seemed an established fact of life. Many concluded that indeed much of the Muslim role would be played on an unremittingly secular stage.

Retreat from the secular path

The Iranian revolution of 1978-9 shattered the illusions of advocates of modernisation/secularisation theory. The spectre of an elderly, bearded religious leader, Ayatollah Khomeini, leading a populist revolution from his exile in a small French village and toppling the government of a modernising Shah of Iran, oil rich, with strong Western allies and a formidable military was beyond the imagination of experts and rulers alike. The resurgence of Islam in Muslim politics in the most modernising of Muslim countries (Egypt, Lebanon, Algeria, Tunisia and Turkey) flew in the face of those who believed religion should be at the margins not the centre of public life. If some were initially content to describe the Islamic revival as a movement of the poor and the marginalised, the alienated and uneducated, the late 1980s and 1990s shattered their beliefs and predictions as it revealed the 'quiet revolution' that had hitherto gone unnoticed. Islam emerged as a presence and force in mainstream society, informing political parties and organisations, social movements and the institutions of civil society. Moreover, in most cases this was an urban not a rural phenomenon; its leaders and supporters were educated professionals. Alongside the secular elite leadership and institutions of many Muslim societies, a new alternative was established, revealing the extent to which Islamic activism had become institutionalised. As governments and their models of economic development (Arab socialism and capitalism) failed and amidst mounting public protests and demonstrations, rulers 'cracked' open the political process and called for elections. A stunned world watched as Islamists emerged as the leading opposition in municipal and parliamentary elections held in the late 1980s and 1990s. In countries like Egypt, Tunisia and Jordan, the Muslim Brotherhood and Tunisia's Islamic Tendency Movement proved effective against governments who controlled the electoral process, financial resources and access to the media.

Algeria and later Turkey proved even more of a challenge to secular visionaries and expectations. In Algeria, a one party Arab socialist state with a secular elite, the Islamic Salvation Front (FIS) swept municipal and parliamentary elections. For the first time in contemporary history, Algeria and indeed the world seemed poised to have an Islamic party come to power through the electoral process. Fears that 'Islamic fundamentalists' would come to power through revolution or bullets were countered by the power of ballots, sending shivers down the collective spines of many Muslim rulers and Western governments. Thus, when the Algerian army intervened, with the approval of their secular elites, cancelled the final round of parliamentary elections and ruthlessly suppressed the FIS, few objected. For many, the replacement of a secular government and orientation by an Islamic alternative was unthinkable. Thus, while it was believable to charge that the FIS was antidemocratic and that Islam (religion) and democracy were incompatible, the military's seizure of power and negation of free and fair elections to preserve a secular option was not accepted.

The second major example of the apparent defeat of secularism occurred in Turkey. Long held up as the only completely secular option in the Muslim world and one of the few examples of democratic governance (albeit if limited), Turkish secularism had seemed impregnable. Indeed, many saw Turkey as providing the paradigm for other parts of the Middle East and broader Muslim world. Discussions about how to contain the spread of Islamic fundamentalism included two major options, repression and decapitation of movements or the promotion of secular Islam. Turkish Islam, often described as Muslim secularism, was touted as a viable and safe alternative to be promoted, particularly in the newly independent Muslim republics of Central Asia. Few worried about the existence of an Islamic party, the Welfare (Refah) Party (RP) under the leadership of Dr Necmettin Erbakan, a prominent Islamist and politician. Welfare's electoral record had not been impressive. Turkey's laic state, with its entrenched secular traditions and elite and its military guardians seemed impregnable.

Two factors seemed to preclude Turkey's being swept up by the Islamic wave in motion across much of the Middle East and broader Muslim world: the revered memory and legacy of Atatürk (1881-1938) with its strong secular (laic) tradition and institutions; and the self-proclaimed role of the army as the 'guardian of the secular republic', defenders of the secular ideology and stability of the state. However, by 1996, secular Turkey had its first Islamist prime minister, Dr Necmettin Erbakan, and thirty of its main cities had elected Islamist mayors in elections in which the Welfare Party garnered up to twenty-one per cent of the vote. By 1997 Erbakan had been forced out of office by the Turkish military.

Welfare used democracy as a yardstick by which to judge the failures of Turkish secularism to be truly pluralistic, to respect the rights of all of its citizens, including their freedom of conscience or right to live according to their religious beliefs. Erbakan had maintained that true secularism (separation of religion from the state) should not only mean state autonomy but religious autonomy. That is, religion also has its autonomy that is to be respected and free from state interference. The state should not intervene in the religious sphere by attempting to regulate dress (the right of women to wear a headscarf or, for that matter, men to wear beards) or religious practice. The Welfare Party wished to amend the definition of secularism to guarantee the right of all people to live in accordance with their religious beliefs. For Turkey's radical secularists, this stance was regarded as a direct threat: 'The radical secularists, comprising the majority of the intelligentsia, including a number of leading journalists, believe this stand on the part of RP is a challenge to the secular premises of the state. They think that the RP is concealing its long-term intention to establish an Islamic state in Turkey.'[1]

Welfare had benefited from what Eric Rouleau has called the 're-Islamisation of the Turkish state'. The reintroduction of religious instruction in state schools in the 1980s and 'government funding of 450 *imam-hatip* religious schools where more than 470,000 adolescents, many future state functionaries, are imbued with Islam; and taxpayer support for the construction of hundreds of new mosques have contributed to the rise of political Islam'.[2] In addition, Turkey in the 1990s adopted a foreign policy which, when convenient, emphasised Islamic solidarity as it attempted to extend its influence in the Central Asian Muslim republics of the former Soviet Union, the Caucasus, and the Balkans.

On 24 December 1995, Welfare won twenty-one per cent of the vote, tripling its performance of 1987, and 150 seats in parliament. It attracted more votes than any other party. However, Turkey's secular political leaders (Motherland's Mesut Yilmaz, True Path Party's Tansu Ciller, and Bulent Ecevit), despite their common desire to keep Welfare out of government, failed to transcend their personal rivalries and animosities and were unable to form a coalition government. Erbakan and the Welfare Party, whose 150 seats constituted the largest bloc in the 550-seat National Assembly, came to power in a coalition with former Prime Minister Tansu Ciller's secular, right-wing True Path Party. With Erbakan and the Welfare's coming to power, many secular Turks and many in the West warned of another Iran, Sudan or Afghanistan. The most secular of Muslim states had its first Islamist prime minister.

While many in Turkey who revered Necmettin Erbakan called him *hodja*, a term reserved for honoured teachers, others vilified him as a deceptive, radical Islamic fundamentalist, a wolf in sheep's clothing. A Western reporter observed that the new prime minister was:

the most interesting politician to have emerged from the Muslim world in many years. He is cultivated and worldly, a master of subtle political manoeuvre,

---

[1] Ayse Saktanber, 'Becoming the "Other" as a Muslim in Turkey: Turkish Women vs. Islamist Women', *New Perspectives on Turkey*, no. 11 (Fall 1994), pp. 43-4.
[2] Eric Rouleau, 'Turkey: Beyond Ataturk', *Foreign Policy*, no. 103 (Summer 1996).

yet has slashed his way through the jungle of Turkish politics with fiery oratory
about Zionist conspiracies, the decadence of the West and the superiority of
Muslim law and culture. He favours elegantly tailored suits and imported silk
neckties and prays five times a day.[3]

During Erbakan's brief tenure as prime minister, Welfare encouraged the
expanded role of religion in society: increasing the number of Islamic
schools, religious foundations, businesses, banks, social services and
media. Both secular Muslims and religious minorities such as Turkey's
Alevi Muslim minority (perhaps a fifth of its ninety-eight per cent
Muslim population), despite the public assurances of Welfare, were
sceptical about its commitment to pluralism. They questioned whether
the Welfare's redefinition of the state would affect its ability to respect
the rights of others – other (non-Welfare) Muslims, non-believers and
religious minorities. Cynics charged that the Welfare, like the FIS in
Algeria, was using the democratic system to come to power in order to
dismantle Turkey's democratic and secular state.

The biggest obstacle to Erbakan proved predictably to be the military.
Staunch secularists, some might say militant secularists, have consistently espoused a role as defenders of Kemalism and reacted allergically
to any form of religion in public life, from female students' right to wear
a headscarf (*hijab*) to Islamist politics. Among the common justifications
for previous coups was the claim that the government had betrayed
Atatürk's principle of secularism. Thus, it took every occasion to signal
its concerns about any compromising of Turkey's secular principles;
there was a new purge of officers who were suspected of being Islamists
(on the grounds, say, that an officer's wife wore a headscarf or that they
prayed at a mosque). When the Iranian ambassador called for implementation of the *shariah* in Turkey, tanks were sent through the streets of
Sincan, a suburb of Ankara and Welfare Party stronghold, where the call
was made. The military kept up the pressure. In Spring 1997, it presented
the Erbakan government with a set of eighteen demands, designed to
stem an Islamist threat to the secular state. These included restrictions
on the wearing of Islamic dress, measures to prevent Islamists from en-
tering the military or government administration, and a mandate that the
Imam-Hatep religious schools, that it believed taught religious propaganda and served as a training ground for Islamists, be closed because
of their anti-secular bias. At the same time, the military demanded that
compulsory secular education be increased from five to eight years.
These concerns seemed ironic since the schools were started and funded
by the government and subject to state regulation and inspection. In
April, General Cevik Bir publicly declared that the military's top priority,

---

[3] Stephen Kinzer, 'The Islamist Who Runs Turkey, Delicately', *The New York Times*,
23 Feb. 1997, p. 29.

greater even than that of its ten-year battle with Kurdish separatism, was the struggle against anti-secular Islamists.[4]

Erbakan and the Welfare Party's short-lived government proved to be a lightening rod for militant secularists, contributing to the increased polarisation of society. Erbakan moderated his rhetoric and previous positions and accommodated the military, so much so that many in his party believed his compromises had undermined the identity, message and credibility of Welfare. This mattered little to Turkey's radical secularists (much of the military, civil service and intelligentsia), whose secularism was based not simply on a belief in the separation of religion and the state but on an anti-religious secular ideology/belief system, which was as rigid, militant and intolerant as it claimed 'Islamic fundamentalism' was. The fear and charges of radical secularists led some to observe that 'there is a neurotic edge to the way many secularists talk about the awkward, rather earnest, just-up-from-the-country sort of people who make up most of Mr Erbakan's following.'[5] As in Algeria, the secularist establishment was willing to compromise Turkey's commitment to democracy to prevent Islamists from participating in politics and society and to preserve their power, privilege and lifestyle rather than allow voters to choose through free and open elections. It was unwilling to take the risk that democracy always involves, one that some leading Turkish secularists had believed possible if democracy was to prevail:

A marriage between Islam and democracy in Turkey can be consummated if the radical secularists stop trying to impose their preferred life-style and set of values upon the Islamists, and if the latter do not attempt to undermine by word or deed the basic tenets of the secular democratic state in Turkey. A critical mediating role can be played by moderate secularists whose numbers are on the increase.[6]

In many ways, the military and radical secularist intellectuals were remaining true to an earlier pattern. As Adnan Adiver noted in the early 1950s, 'The domination of Western thought, or rather of the positivism of the West, was at times so intense that one can hardly call it thought. It should be termed the "official dogma of irreligion".'[7] More recently, Ayse Kadiogl commented, the Republican elite, the political offspring/disciples of Atatürk, were moved by a 'disgust' towards religion even if

---

[4] Kelly Couturier, 'Anti-Secularism Eclipses Insurgency as Army's No. 1 Concern', *The Washington Post*, 5 April 1997.

[5] *The Economist*, 19 July 1997, p. 23.

[6] Martin Heper, 'Islam and Democracy in Turkey: Towards a Reconciliation', *Middle East Journal*, 51, no. 1 (1997), p. 45.

[7] Adnan Adiver, *Interaction of Islamic and Western Thought in Turkey* in *Near Eastern Culture and Society* T. C. Young (ed.), (Princeton University Press, 1951), p. 126.

they sometimes resorted to religious symbols, paying lip service to religion.[8] Sherif Mardin's comparison of this Kemalist attitude to Voltaire's hatred of the church goes a long way toward understanding the source and living legacy of militant secularism in Turkey.[9]

Erbakan and the Welfare Party had to contend with increased pressure from the military, no confidence votes in parliament, and in May 1997 a petition to the Constitutional Court by Turkey's chief prosecutor to ban Welfare for violating the Turkish constitution's articles on secularism and pushing the country towards civil war. The military increased the intensity of its campaign in June by conducting briefings for judges, attorneys and the media on the Islamist threat to the Turkish state. Finally, the Erbakan-Ciller coalition collapsed when it lost its parliamentary majority due to the resignation of several of Ciller's DYP members. Erbakan submitted his resignation on 18 June 1997. On 28 (or 22?) February 1998, Turkey's Constitutional Court issued an order which banned Welfare. Erbakan was expelled from parliament and barred from participation in the political process for five years. Welfare's assets were seized. He and a number of other leaders were tried for sedition. In February 1998 a new law was passed requiring that children first complete eight years of secular education before being permitted to take Qur'an classes. Weekend and summer Qur'an courses were banned. Female students and teachers in Islamic schools were barred from wearing the *hijab*, a ban that already existed in all other areas of education and in government departments.

Atatürk created and shaped modern Turkey as a secular state, the only totally secular state in the Middle East. After his death political realities produced a more fluid history in which Islam and Muslim identity became more visible in Turkish politics and were used at various times by the military and the government to counter communism or to reinforce morality. In the past two decades, Turkey has witnessed the progressive growth and impact of political Islam, culminating in the electoral successes of the Welfare Party. The emergence of Welfare as a key political player precipitated a cultural and political crisis between secular elites and Islamists. As Hakan Yavuz has observed, 'Because secularism did not separate religion and politics, but rather subordinated religion to the political realm, it promoted the politicisation of Islam and struggle between secularists and Muslims for control of the state.'[10] The goal of

[8] Ayse Kadioglu, 'Republican Epistemology and Islamic Discourses in Turkey in the 1990s', *Muslim World*, vol. 84, no. 1 (January 1998), p. 11.

[9] For a discussion of this phenomenon, see Sherif Mardin, 'Ideology and Religion in the Turkish Revolution', *International Journal of Middle East Studies*, 2 (1971): especially pp. 208-9.

[10] Hakan Yavuz, 'Political Islam and the Welfare (Refah) Party in Turkey', *Comparative Politics*, vol. 30, no. 1 (October 1997), p. 65.

Welfare, like many other Islamic organisations, was a more pluralistic state, the creation of a space alongside the Kemalist westernised secular model within the Turkish secular state in which to live their lives in accordance with their Islamic culture and values. For many in the establishment such a course endangered Turkish secularism. Moreover, given their militant secularism, rooted in a nineteenth-century rationalism, the recourse to religion was itself viewed as retrogressive, anti-modern, a retreat to the Dark Ages and a threat to their power and lifestyles.

Algeria and Turkey are but two examples of the presence and danger of 'secular fundamentalism'. In many Muslim countries, as in the West, secularism is not an option but a political dogma or doctrine, not an alternative but an imperative. If secularism is normative and the rational imperative, then to depart from the norm is seen as abnormal and irrational. Those who wish to base a modern state on religion are regarded as extremists, religious fanatics.

Militant secular fundamentalism

Even more insidious is the militant secular fundamentalism of countries like France and Turkey (as well as Tunisia) where secularism is not simply the separation of religion and politics but, as past and current history demonstrate, an anti-religious and anticlerical belief. Thus, both countries have attempted to ban the wearing of the headscarf or discriminated against those who do. France has also rejected multiculturalism and required integration, warning its Muslim population that to be French and welcomed they must become secular Muslims.

In the mid-twentieth century, many Muslims gained independence from European colonialism. Today throughout the Muslim world we are witnessing a domestic war over national/cultural identity. It is a battle to define the very identity and soul of nation states which pits entrenched regimes and elites against new social forces, an alternative sector of society wishing to see its societies modern but Islamic rather than secular in orientation. Increasingly the struggle incorporates calls for greater political participation and democratisation. Ironically the forces of secularism often opt for greater authoritarianism rather than democratisation in order to retain their power and privilege. Western governments more content with short term gains than facing long term realities and strategies quietly acquiesce.

As a result, from a modern secular perspective (a form of 'secular fundamentalism'), the mixing of religion and politics is regarded as necessarily abnormal (departing from the norm), irrational, dangerous and extremist. Those who do so are often dubbed 'fundamentalists' (Christian, Jewish or Muslim) or religious fanatics. Thus, when secular-minded people (government officials, political analysts, journalists and the bulk of the general public) in the West encounter Muslim individuals and groups who speak of Islam as a comprehensive way of life, they immediately dub them 'fundamentalist' with the connotation that these are backward-looking individuals, zealots who are a threat. The attitude of many governments and secular elites in the Muslim world is often similar. Images of militant mullahs and the violent actions of some individuals and groups are then taken as representative and proof of the inherent danger of mixing religion and politics.

Secularisation and modernisation: the dangers of secular fundamentalism

Secular presuppositions which inform our academic disciplines and outlook on life, our Western secular worldview, have been a major obstacle to our understanding and analysis of Islamic politics and have contributed to a tendency to reduce Islam to fundamentalism and fundamentalism to religious extremism. As previously noted, for much of the 1960's, the received wisdom among many, from development experts to theologians, could be summarised in the adage: 'Every day in every way, things are and will continue to get more and more modern and secular.' Integral to definitions of modernisation was the progressive Westernisation and secularisation of society: its institutions, organisations, and actors.[11] This attitude was reflected in analyses that viewed the choices in development in polar dichotomies: tradition and modernity, Mecca and mechanisation. Religion and theology reflected the same presupposition and expectation as theologians spoke of demythologising the scriptures, of a secular gospel for the modern age, of the triumph of the secular city (as distinguished from Augustine's City of God), and a school of theological thought emerged which was dubbed the 'Death of God Theology'.[12] Religious faith was at best supposed to be a private matter. The degree of one's intellectual sophistication and objectivity in academia was often equated with a secular liberalism and relativism that seemed antithetical to religion. Although church or synagogue membership were recognised as useful, most political candidates avoided discussing their faith or religious issues.

[11] See for example, Daniel Lerner, *The Passing of Traditional Society: Modernizing the Middle East*, New York: Free Press, 1958, and Manfield Halpren, *The Politics of Social Change in the Middle East and North Africa*, Princeton University Press, 1963. For an analysis and critique of the factors which influenced the development of modernisation theory, see Fred R. von der Mehden, *Religion and Modernisation in Southeast Asia*, Syracuse, NY: Syracuse University Press, 1988.

[12] See, for example, Harvey Cox, *The Secular City: Urbanization and Secularization in Theological Perspective*, New York: Macmillian, 1965; and *Religion in the Secular City: Toward a Post Modern Theology*, New York: Simon & Schuster, 1984; Dietrich Bonhöffer, *Letters and Papers from Prison*, rev. ed, New York: Macmillan, 1967; and William Hamilton and Thomas Altizer, *Radical Theology and the Death of God*, Indianapolis: Bobbs Merrill, 1966.

Acceptance of this 'enlightened' notion of separation of church and state and of Western, secular models of development relegated religion to the stockpile of traditional beliefs, valuable in understanding the past but irrelevant or an obstacle to modern political, economic and social development. Neither development theory nor international relations considered religion a significant variable for political analysis. The separation of religion and politics overlooked the fact that religious traditions were established and developed in historical, political, social and economic contexts. Their doctrines and laws were conditioned by these contexts. This was certainly true in the history of Islam and even more so in the belief of many Muslims. Ironically, some analysts became like conservative clerics the world over – they treated religious beliefs and practices as isolated, free-standing realities rather than as the product of the interplay of faith and history or, more accurately, faith-in-history.

Religious traditions, while characterised as conservative or traditional, are the product of a dynamic changing process in which the word of revelation is mediated through human interpretation or discourse in response to specific socio-historical contexts. The post-Enlightenment tendency to define religion as a system of belief restricted to personal or private life, rather than as a way of life, has seriously hampered our ability to understand the nature of Islam and many of the world's religions. It has artificially compartmentalised religion, doing violence to its nature, and reinforced a static, reified conception of religious traditions rather than revealing their inner dynamic nature. To that extent, a religion not restricted in this way (a religion that mixes religion and politics) appears necessarily retrogressive, prone to religious extremism and fanaticism, and thus a potential threat. Islam has generally been regarded in the West (and among many secular-minded Muslims) as a static phenomenon doctrinally and socioculturally, and therefore anti-modern and retrogressive. This attitude was supported by the prevailing tendency to emphasise such notions as the closing of the door of religious interpretation (*ijtihad*) or reform in the tenth century.

A second factor that has hindered our analysis of the Islamic dimension and dynamic in Muslim societies and perpetuated images of an inherently retrogressive religion has been its secular elite orientation. Focus on some governments and elites reflects a bias that hampers understanding of the nature of populist movements in general and Islamic movements in particular. It reinforces the notion that religion is the province of the tradition-bound cleric (*mullah*), religious scholars (*'ulama*), and the uneducated or illiterate masses. Thus few scholars of the Middle East or other Muslim societies believed it necessary or relevant to know and meet with religious leaders, to visit their institutions, or to have some idea of their leadership roles in society. Too often the *'ulama* were regarded as irrelevant or of marginal interest. Most Western, as well as

Western-trained Muslim scholars, were more comfortable working and studying with like-minded members of a modern Westernised elite and in urban settings. Much of Western scholarship viewed Muslim societies through the modern prism of a development theory that was secular and Western in its principles, values and expectations. Experts analysed and judged societies as their elite ran them – from the top down. As a result, academic and government analysts and the media often slipped into the same pitfalls: focusing on a narrow, albeit powerful, secular elite segment of society; equating secularisation with progress, and religion with backwardness and conservatism, believing that modernisation and Westernisation are necessarily intertwined. As a result, the options available for the political and social development of Muslim societies were often seen in polarities. More recently, this attitude has been characterised as a clash of civilisations: the tug between tradition and modernity, the past and the future, the *madrasa* (religious college or seminary) and the university, the veil or *chador* and Western dress and values. In fact the battle is not between tradition and modernity but between two competing alternative sectors of society and their visions or models for development. In contrast to the past, alongside secular elites is a new generation of professionals with a modern education but Islamically-oriented. The latter are visible in social and political movements, in the media, in professional associations (lawyers, physicians, journalists), in education and, where not suppressed, in the military.

In the twenty-first century, Muslim governments will continue to struggle with issues of identity, authority and legitimacy. Their future paths will be diverse, dependent upon local contexts and cultural traditions. The failures of alternative ideologies (liberalism, Arab nationalism and socialism etc.) and of many governments will continue to require that local nationalisms be rooted in history and culture. Islamists will be challenged to demonstrate that an Islamic option can be sufficiently pluralistic and tolerant to incorporate diverse religious and political tendencies. At the same time, those who advocate a more secular orientation will be challenged to adopt and adapt a secular option that remains true to the pervasive presence of Islam in society. Both secular and Islamic paths will be challenged to develop modern forms of secularism that foster a true and open pluralism which responds to the diversity of society, one that protects the rights of believers and unbelievers alike.

THE ORIGINS OF ARAB SECULARISM

Azzam Tamimi

Introduction

In the social sciences, one of the commonest theses is the secularisation thesis, which runs as follows. Under conditions prevailing in industrial-scientific society, the hold of religion over society and its people diminishes. By and large this is true, but it is not completely true, for there is one major exception, Islam. In the last hundred years the hold of Islam over Muslims has not diminished but has rather increased. It is one striking counter-example to the secularisation thesis.[1]

The last one hundred years Gellner refers to comprise the period when secularism was introduced to various parts of the Muslim World. This was also the period when, as a reaction, Islamic movements emerged to counter what they saw as a colonial design against Islam and the Muslims in the form of an intellectual and political onslaught aimed at westernising the Muslims and stripping them of their cultural identity.

Secularism, in Arabic *'ilmaniyah* (from *'ilm* – science) or *'alamaniyah* (from *'alam* – world), may be more accurately rendered by the word *dunyawiyah*, meaning that which is worldly, mundane or temporal. It is a concept that came to the Muslim world in the company of other related terms such as modernity, westernisation and modernisation within the context of colonialism. Although secularism is usually taken to imply the liberation of the political from the authority of the religious, it has, together with its related terms, been used in different contexts to describe a process aimed at the marginalisation of Islam, or its exclusion from the process of re-structuring society during both the colonial and post-independence periods. Secularisation in the Middle East has entailed severing society's cultural roots; its objective has been to effect a complete break with the past.

In the English-language literature on secularism and secularisation, political theorists and historians at least agree on one fundamental observation, namely that 'secularism' is a product of Christian society. Whether secularism is defined as a reaction or a protest movement,[2] as a

---

[1] Ernest Gellner, 'Marxism and Islam: Failure and Success' in A. Tamimi (ed.), *Power-Sharing Islam?*, London: Liberty for Muslim World Publications, 1993, p. 36.

[2] *Encyclopedia of Religion and Ethics*, James Hastings and T. Clark (eds), Edinburgh, 1971, vol. II, p. 347. See also the *Blackwell Dictionary of 20th Century Social Thought*, W. Outhwaite & T. Bottmore (eds), 1995.

doctrine or an ideology,[3] whether secularisation's eventual objective is to
deny God and eliminate religion altogether or just to restrict religion to
the private sphere while recognising the existence of a 'god' that has no
say in people's worldly, or secular, affairs, the concept cannot be com-
prehended outside the context of Europe's evolution and its Christian
reform movements. Long before the Renaissance, the term 'secular' was
used to describe functions that were extra-ecclesiastical. The religious
establishment itself sanctioned and requested these functions either
because priests could not or did not perform them, or in response to
changes in social or political circumstances.

In order to survive in the first centuries of its existence, Christianity
had to posit the separation of faith and city; a separation that ran parallel
with the distinction between world and body. Christ's injunction to 'render unto Caesar' – which became extremely important in St Paul's
writing – added a political dimension to Christianity and the already dual
nature of Christ.[4] In the course of religious revival, reform movements
which sought to purge Christianity of cultural, traditional or superstitious
accretions, had an almost explicit secularising impact. Reform movements such as Renaissance Humanism, Lutheranism, Calvinism, Deism
and Unitarianism were all secularising forces within Christianity, purging faith and practice of immanentist conceptions of deity, progressively
applying the canons of reason to doctrine, and reducing mystical, mi-
raculous, sacramental and sacerdotal claims. In the process, religious
institutions ceased to be central in society and religious consciousness
diminished.[5]

Coined by George Jacob Holyoake (1817-1906), the term secularism
described a nineteenth-century movement that was expressly intended
to provide a certain theory of life and conduct without reference to a
deity or a future life. Politically, it sprang from the turmoil which pre-
ceded the passing of the Reform Bill in 1832.[6] Secularism's search for
human improvement by material means alone arose at a period when
the relationship between science and religion (in Europe) was beginning
to be regarded as one of sharp opposition. Secularism proclaims the independence of 'secular' truth, arguing that secular knowledge is founded
upon the experience of this life and can be tested by reason at work in
experience. Just as mathematics, physics and chemistry are 'secular'
sciences, it would be equally possible to establish a secular theory of the
conduct and meaning of life, and provide instruction for the conscience

---

[3] *The Encyclopedia of Religion*, Mircea Eliade (ed.), Macmillan, New York, 1987, vol.
13, p. 159.

[4] Renee Fregosi, 'From the Secular to the Politico-Religious', *Contemporary European
Affairs*, vol. II, no. 4, 1989, p. 21.

[5] *The Encyclopedia of Religion*, vol. 13, p. 162.

[6] *Encyclopedia of Religion and Ethics*, vol. II, p. 347.

alongside instruction in the sciences.[7] In its mildest forms, secularism deals with the known world interpreted by experience, and neither offers nor forbids any opinion regarding another life. It follows, at least theoretically, that unless religious dogma actively interfered with human happiness, secularism was content to leave it to flourish or perish as it may.[8]

However, throughout its course, secularism has been intermingled with atheism. Charles Bradlaugh (1833-91), an associate of Holyoake, considered that secularism was bound to contest theistic belief and that material progress was impossible so long as 'superstition' so powerfully manifested itself. Bradlaugh's partisans shold that he was more consistent than Holyoake and find confirmation in this in secularism having been most vigorous when linked with anti-religious views. This position is further bolstered by the assumption that the attempt to ignore, rather than deny, religion is impractical because religion embraces both secular and spiritual concerns. It is also argued that it is impossible to maintain that there is a God infinitely remote from material existence. The assumption that a secularism lacking a firm anti-religious basis was bound to fail, encouraged the complete denial of God.[9]

The intellectual revolution of the nineteenth century, symbolised by the contributions of Freud, Marx and Nietzsche, involved an advocacy of atheistic thought that effected a significant change in the interpretation of Man's place in the world.[10] It has been argued that even though not all traces of eschatology were eradicated in secular thought, and even though teleology remained at the heart of certain 'materialist' views of the world and society, the suppression of the ultimate divine basis of things did produce a fundamental break. Henceforward, at the heart of secular thought was the view that the 'disenchantment of the world' took place via the agency of critical thought.[11]

The French equivalent of secularism, *laïcisme*, has a much more radical connotation than the English term. If the latter is a crystallisation of Holyoake's idea, the former may be considered an application of Bradlaugh's concept. *Laïcisme* is conceived of as a doctrine of complete freedom from, and non-interference by, religion. It involves the belief that functions previously performed by a priesthood should be transferred to the laity, especially in the judicial and educational spheres.[12] In France, by early this century, *laïcisme* had accomplished the complete

---

[7] *Ibid.* p. 348.

[8] *Ibid.*

[9] *Ibid.*

[10] Renee Fregosi, 'From the Secular', p. 21.

[11] *Ibid.* p. 22.

[12] *The Dictionary of Political Thought*, Roger Scruton (ed.), 1983, p. 253.

constitutional separation of church and state. Religious instruction in state schools was abolished in 1882 and replaced by general ethical instruction.[13] In its extreme form *laïcisme* demanded anti-clericalism and the advocacy of a *Kulturkampf* (the repressive political movement against the Roman Catholic Church, instigated in 1871 by Bismarck, with the intention of wresting all educational and cultural institutions from the church, and conferring them instead upon the state).[14] In Turkey, the Kemalists (followers of Kemal Atatürk (1880-1938) who abolished the Ottoman Caliphate and founded the modern secular Turkish republic in a spirit of Turkish nationalism) regarded radical secularism as an essential part of the process whereby modern political institutions could be constructed.[15] Tunisia and Algeria are two Arab North African countries where *laïcisme* is advocated or adopted with varying intensities.

Muslim critics of secularism maintain that in the Western tradition secularism is not only justifiable but has even had positive aspects. It is justifiable in the West due to the nature of the Christian religion. Christianity in medieval Europe, it is argued, was responsible for the emergence and success of secularism in the West for it already recognised the division of life into what belonged to God and what belonged to Caesar, lacked a system for the legislation and regulation of mundane affairs, and had for many centuries been associated with despotic regimes and with oppressive theocracies. Furthermore, medieval Christianity entertained the existence of a special class of people, the priests, who claimed to be God's representatives on earth, interpreting what they claimed were his words and using their religious authority to deprive members of the community of their basic rights. In other words, the Christian theocratic establishment constituted a major obstacle to progress and development, and consequently to democracy. In contrast the rise of secularism in the Muslim world occurred in completely different circumstances. Until the beginning of the nineteenth century, and specifically until just before Napoleon invaded Egypt in 1798, the entire Arab region was Islamic in norms, laws, values and traditions. During the Western colonial era, inaugurated by the French campaign, the Arab world witnessed gradual intellectual, social and political changes as a result of the impression left by the modes of thought and conduct brought to the area by the Western colonialists.[16]

[13] *Dictionary of 20th Century Social Thought*, Outhwaite and Bottmore (eds), Oxford: Blackwell, 1995, p. 573.

[14] *The Dictionary of Political Thought*, p. 250.

[15] *Ibid.*, p. 253-4.

[16] R.S. Ahmad, *Al-Din Wal-Dawlah Wal-Thawrah* (Religion, State and Revolution), Al-Dar Al-Sharqiyah, 1989, p. 31.

The Rise of Arab Secularism

Although, since the sixteenth century, Europe had been climbing the ladder of scientific discovery, intellectual innovation, political institutionalisation and economic development and the Arab world had been sliding down, it was not until the middle of the nineteenth century that Europe began to have a tangible cultural impact on the Arab region. At that point secularism entered the intellectual debate in the Arab world, and from then on a new cultural model began to be quietly introduced by enthusiasts and admirers of the West, or more forcefully imposed by the colonial authorities. Here was a new set of standards alien to the Islamic ones upon which local culture was based. Although European colonial powers, such as France and Britain, were intruders with imperialist ambitions in the Muslim world, they were admired by an elite, composed mainly of Western-educated intellectuals, for their scientific and cultural progress.

The early Arab debate on secularism centred mainly on the relationship between religion and state, and on matching European successes in science, technology and governance. 'Secularism' was translated into Arabic either as *'ilmaniyah*, a neologism derived from *'ilm* (science or knowledge) or as *'alamaniyah*, derived from *'alam* (world or universe). It has been suggested that the use of any other translation, such as *la diniyah*, that implied the exclusion or marginalisation of religion, would have met with outright rejection by Muslims. It was therefore necessary to introduce it through a term that implied knowledge and success, which Islam not only encouraged but also demanded.

Nevertheless, the meaning of *'ilmaniyah* or *'alamaniyah* in the Arabic literature is no less varied and confused than it is in the Western literature. In his four-volume encyclopedia on secularism, Elmessiri lists eighteen different definitions of 'secularism' collected from modern Arabic literature. For this reason, Elmessiri distinguishes between secularism as a concept, secularism as a movement and secularism as a paradigm or sequence.[17]

The decline of Islamic civilisation prompted a number of Arab intellectuals, including some already exposed to European culture and impressed by the accomplishments of Europe, to call for radical reform. As a consequence of the intellectual debate aroused within the Arab world by European advancement, an opposition was drawn between *din* (religion) and *'aql* (reason), *asalah* (nobility) and *mu'asarah* (modernity), *din* and *dawlah* (state) and *din* and *'ilm* (science or knowledge). Two trends were initially distinguishable among the intellectuals engaged in the debate, one Islamic and the other Christian.

---

[17] A. Elmessiri, *Tafkik al-Khitab al-'Ilmani* (Deconstructing Secular Discourse), a 4-volume Encyclopedia in Arabic, forthcoming, Cairo, Summer 2001.

Islamic modernists

The leaders of the Islamic trend believed that modernisation and progress should be sought but without relinquishing the accomplishments of Islamic civilisation. Their objective was to create an Islamic Renaissance that could deliver the Arabs from the state of backwardness while protecting them from the European colonial campaign that had been taking place since Napoleon set foot in Egypt.[18]

Rifa'a Al-Tahtawi (1801-73) was the first to campaign for interaction with European civilisation with the aim of borrowing elements not in conflict with the established values and principles of the Islamic *shari'ah*. A graduate of Al-Azhar, the Islamic university in Cairo, he was appointed imam (leader of prayers and adviser on religious matters) to the Egyptian regiment that was dispatched by Muhammad Ali to France. Although sent there as an imam and not as a student, he was a scion of a scholarly family and threw himself into study with enthusiasm and success. He acquired a precise knowledge of the French language and read books on ancient history, Greek philosophy and mythology, geography, arithmetic and logic and, most importantly, the French thought of the eighteenth century – Voltaire, Rousseau's *Social Contract* and other works.[19] Returning home after five years, he diagnosed the illness of the *ummah* as being due to the lack of freedom and suggested multi-party democracy as a remedy. He criticised those who opposed the idea of taking knowledge from Europe saying: 'Such people are deluded; for civilisations are turns and phases. These sciences were once Islamic when we were at the apex of our civilisation. Europe took them from us and developed them further. It is now our duty to learn from them just as they learned from our ancestors.'[20]

In 1834, shortly after his return to Cairo from Paris, Tahtawi published his first book *Takhlis al-Ibriz Ila Talkhis Bariz*, which summarised his observations of the manners and customs of the modern French[21] and praised the concept of democracy as he saw it in France and as he witnessed its defence and reassertion through the 1830 revolution against King Charles X.[22] Tahtawi tried to show that the democratic concept he was explaining to his readers was compatible with the law of Islam. He compared political pluralism to forms of ideological and jurisprudential pluralism that existed in the Islamic experience:

[18] R.S. Ahmad, *Al-Din Wal-Dawlah*. p. 33.

[19] A. Hourani, *Arabic Thought in the Liberal Age 1798-1939*, Cambridge University Press, 1991, p. 69.

[20] R.S. Ahmad, *Al-Din Wal-Dawlah*. p. 34.

[21] Hourani, *Arabic Thought*, p. 70-1.

[22] M. S. Al-Dajani, *'Tatawur Mafahim al-Dimuqratiyah fil-Fikr al-Arabi al-Hadith' Azmat al-Dimuqratiyah fil-Watan al-'Arabi*, Arab Unity Studies Centre, Beirut, 1984, p. 121.

Religious freedom is the freedom of belief, of opinion and of sect, provided it does not contradict the fundamentals of religion. An example would be the theological opinions of the *al-Asha'irah* and the *al-Matiridiyah*; another would be the opinions of leading jurists within the doctrine of the branches. For by following any one of these schools, a human feels secure. The same would apply to the freedom of political practice and opinion by leading administrators, who endeavour to interpret and apply rules and provisions in accordance with the laws of their own countries. Kings and ministers are licensed in the realm of politics to pursue various routes that in the end serve one purpose: good administration and justice.[23]

Other nineteenth-century Islamic reformists, also referred to as Muslim modernists – including Khairuddin Al-Tunisi (1810-99), Jamal Al-Din Al-Afghani (1838-97), Abdel Rahman Al-Kawakibi (1854-1902) and Muhammad Abduh (1849-1905) – followed the model of Tahtawi in stressing that Muslims could benefit from European successes without undermining Islamic values or culture.[24] Indeed, many important ideas attributed to Europe were not alien to those brought up in the tradition of Islamic political thought: that man fulfills himself as a member of society; that a good society is directed by the principle of justice; that the purpose of government is the welfare of the ruled.[25]

One important landmark in this regard was the contribution of Khairuddin Al-Tunisi, leader of the nineteenth-century reform movement in Tunisia. In 1867, he formulated a general plan for political reform in the Arab world in a book entitled *Aqwam al-Masalik fi Taqwim al-Mamalik* (The Straight Path to Reformation of Governments). He appealed to politicians and scholars to explore all possible means to improve the status of the community and develop its civility, and cautioned the general Muslim public against shunning the experiences of other nations on the misconceived basis that all the writings, inventions, experiences or attitudes of non-Muslims should simply be rejected. He further called for an end to absolutist rule, which he blamed for the oppression of nations and the destruction of civilisations.[26] Khairuddin Al-Tunisi believed that kindling the *Ummah*'s potential liberty through the adoption of sound administrative procedures and enabling it to have a say in political affairs would put it on a faster track toward civilisation, would limit the rule of despotism, and would stop the influx of European civilisation that is sweeping every thing along its path.[27]

[23] Faruq Abdessalam, *al-Ahzab al-Siyasiyah fil-Islam*, Qalyoob Publishing House, Cairo, 1978.

[24] R. Ghannouchi, *al-Hurriyat al-'Ammah fil-Dawlah al-Islamiyah*, Arab Unity Studies Centre, Beirut, 1993, p. 252.

[25] Hourani, *Arabic Thought*, p. 70.

[26] Al-Dajani, *Tatawur Mafahim*, p. 122-3.

[27] Khairuddin Al-Tunisi, *Aqwam al-Masalik fi Taqwim al-Mamalik*, Tunis, 1972, p. 185.

Jamal Al-Din Al-Afghani called for adheremce to Islamic fundamentals and insisted that it was not necessary for Muslims to take up where
the Europeans ended. He criticised those who believed in aping the
European model without modification or reservation and accused them
of posing a threat to the sovereignty of the *ummah*. In his search for the
causes of decline in the Muslim world, Al-Afghani's diagnosis was the
absence of *'adl* (justice) and *shura* (council) and the government's non-
adherence to the constitution.[28] One of his main demands was that the
people be allowed to assume their political and social role by participating in government through *shura* and elections.[29] In an article, 'The
Despotic Government', published in the journal *Misr* on 14 February
1879, Al-Afghani attributed the decline to despotism, which, he stressed,
was the reason thinkers in the Muslim countries of the Mashriq could not
enlighten the public about the essence and virtues of 'republican government'.

For those governed by a republican form of government, it is a source of happiness and pride. Those governed by it alone deserve to be called human; for a
true human being is only subdued by a true law that is based on the foundations
of justice and that is designed to govern man's moves, actions, transactions and
relations with others in a manner that elevates him to the pinnacle of true
happiness.[30]

To Al-Afghani, republican government was a 'constricted' government,
a government accountable to the public, and thus the antithesis of absolutism. It would consult the governed, relieve them of the burdens laid
upon them by despotic governments and lift them from the state of decay
to the first level of perfection.[31]

Abdel Rahman Al-Kawakibi authored two books, *Taba'i' al-Istibdad*
(The Characteristics of Tyranny) and *Umm al-Qura* (The Mother of Vil-
lages). The first was dedicated to defining despotism in its various forms,
particularly political despotism. He discussed the 'inseparable tie'
between politics and religion and the relationship between religion and
despotism. While stressing that Islam as a religion was not responsible
for the forms of despotic government that had emerged and reigned in
its name, Al-Kawakibi concluded:

'God, the omniscient, has intended nations to be responsible for the actions of
those by whom they choose to be governed. When a nation fails in its duty, God
causes it to be subdued by another nation that will govern it, just as happens in a
court of law when a minor or an incompetent is put under the care of a curator.

---

[28] Al-Dajani, *Tatawur Mafahim*, p. 123.
[29] Ahmad, *Al-Din wal-Dawlah*, pp. 44-7.
[30] Abdulbasit Hasan, *Jamal Al-Din Al-Afghani,* Cairo, 1982, pp. 267-8.
[31] *Ibid.*

When, on the other hand, a nation matures and appreciates the value of liberty, it will restore its might; and this is only fair.[32]

The entire book was an attempt to account for the decline of the Muslim *Ummah* that had become easy prey for nineteenth-century colonial powers. Like Al-Afghani, Al-Kawakibi attributed the success of the Western nations to 'the adoption of logical and well-practised rules that have become social duties in these advanced nations which are not harmed by what appears to be a division into parties and groups, because such a division is only over the methods of applying the rules and not over the rules themselves.'[33]

In *Umm al-Qura*, Al-Kawakibi constructed a series of fictional dialogues between thinkers from prominent towns in the Muslim world. He imagined that all these figures were summoned to a conference organised in Mecca (known as Umm al-Qura) during the *hajj* (pilgrimage) season to discuss the causes of the Muslim *Ummah*'s decline. In the words of one character, Al-Baligh Al-Qudsi: 'It seems to me that the cause of tepidity is the change in the nature of Islamic politics. It was parliamentary and socialist, that is perfectly democratic. But due to the escalation of internal feuds, after the *Al-Rashidun* (the four rightly guided caliphs) it was transformed into a monarchy restrained by the basic rules of *shari'ah*, and then it became almost completely absolute.' Ar-Rumi, another character, comments: 'The calamity has been our loss of liberty.' The conferees finally agree that progress is linked to accountability while regress is linked to despotism.[34]

Finally, Muhammad Abduh, while pressing for reforms, believed that a modern legal system should develop out of *shari'ah* and not in independence and he favoured an equal partnership, rather than separation, between those who governed and the guardians of the law.[35] He stressed above all that no conflict existed between Islam on the one hand and logic or science on the other. Shocked by the magnitude of backwardness in the Arab world, he scorned those who blindly imitated the old and resisted the new. He believed that Islam's relationship with the modern age was the most crucial issue confronting Islamic communities. In an attempt to reconcile Islamic ideas with Western ones, he suggested that *maslaha* (interest) in Islamic thought corresponded to *manfa'ah* (utility) in Western thought. Similarly, he equated *shura* with democracy and *ijma'* with consensus. Addressing the question of authority, Abduh denied the existence of a theocracy in Islam and insisted that the authority of the *hakim* (governor), *qadi* (judge) or *mufti*, was civil. He strongly believed

[32] A. Al-Kawakibi, *Taba'i' al-Istibdad*, Mofam Publications, Algiers, 1988, p.187.

[33] *Ibid*. p. 169.

[34] A. Al-Kawakibi, *Umm al-Qura*, Dar Al-Shuruq Al-Arabi, Beirut, 1991, pp. 33-6. See also Al-Dajani, p. 124.

[35] Hourani, *Arabic Thought*, p. 70.

that *ijtihad* should be revived because 'emerging priorities and problems, which are new to Islamic thought, need to be addressed.'[36] He was a proponent of the parliamentary system; he defended pluralism and refuted the claims that it would undermine the unity of the *ummah*, arguing that the European nations were not divided by it. 'The reason,' he concluded, 'is that their objective is the same. What varies is only the method they pursue toward accomplishing it.'[37]

Christian modernists

The Christian trend was dominated by a group of Christian Arabs who had received their education at the Syrian Protestant College and then settled in Egypt. Important figures included Shibli Shumayyil (1850-1917), Farah Antun (1874-1922), Georgie Zaidan (1861-1914), Ya'qub Suruf (1852-1917), Salama Musa (1887-1958) and Nicola Haddad (1878-1954).[38] The publications *Al-Muqtataf* and *Al-Hilal* founded respectively in 1876 and 1892, were used by writers and thinkers belonging to this group. They strove to propagate the transcendence of ideas like love of country and fellow countrymen over all other social ties, even those of religion.[39]

Through their copious writings, these thinkers succeeded in consolidating the foundations of secularism in the Arab world. Praising the liberal thought of France and England during the eighteenth and nineteenth century and condemning the hegemony of tradition over the human mind, they stressed that reason should set the standard for human conduct. For modernisation to take place, they demanded that only traditions which were compatible with this objective should remain.[40] The main aim of these intellectuals was to lay the basis of a secular state in which Muslims and Christians could participate on a footing of complete equality.[41]

Shibli Shumayyil, who after graduation from the Syrian Protestant College went to Paris to study medicine, is reputed to have first introduced the theories of Darwin to the Arab world through his writings in *Al-Muqtataf*. He belonged to the late nineteenth-century movement which saw science as the key to unlock the secret of the universe, even as a form of worship. He believed that the religion of science necessitated a declaration of war on older religions. To him social unity, which was essential for a general will to exist, involved the separation of religion

[36] Ahmad, *Al-Din wal-Dawlah*, pp. 48-50.
[37] Abdessalam, *al-Ahzab al-Siyasiyah fil-Islam*, p. 28.
[38] *Ibid.*, p. 51.
[39] Hourani, *Arabic Thought*, pp. 246-7.
[40] Ahmad, *Al-Din wal-Dawlah*, p. 51.
[41] Hourani, *Arabic Thought*. pp. 256-7.

from political life since religion was a cause of division. He insisted that nations grew stronger as religion grew weaker, and pointed out that this was true of Europe, which had only become powerful and truly civilised once the Reformation and the French Revolution had broken the hold of religious leaders on society.[42] He condemned both *shuyukh* (Islamic scholars) and priests for resisting progress and development.[43]

Farah Antun (1874-1922) who migrated from Tripoli to Cairo in 1897 chose to propagate his views through a study of the life and philosophy of Ibn Rushd. He was influenced by the works of Ernest Renan to such an extent that Hourani calls him Antun's master. Antun believed that the conflict between science and religion would be solved, but only by assigning each to its proper sphere. He dedicated his book to what he called 'the new shoots of the east':

those men of sense in every community and every religion of the east who have seen the danger of mingling the world with religion in an age like ours, and have come to demand that their religion should be placed on one side in a sacred and honoured place, so that they will be able really to unite, and to flow with the tide of the new European civilisation, in order to be able to compete with those who belong to it, for otherwise it will sweep them all away and make them the subjects of others.[44]

Hourani explained that what attracted Antun to Ibn Rushd was the same as had attracted Renan: the assertion that prophecy was a kind of understanding, that prophets were philosophers, that there was one truth which was dressed by the prophets in religious symbols for the masses but which the elite could contemplate in itself. But like that of Shumayyil and other Lebanese writers of the time, Antun's aim was to lay the intellectual foundations of a secular state in which Muslims and Christians could participate on a footing of complete equality. His emphasis was on proving the invalidity of what he termed 'the inessential part of religion': the body of laws. His second condition for secularism was the separation of temporal and spiritual authorities, suggesting that the separation of the two powers in Christianity made it easier for Christians to be tolerant than for Muslims. He added that if European countries were now more tolerant, that was not because they were Christian but because science and philosophy had driven out religious fanaticism, and the separation of powers had taken place.[45]

Salama Musa (1887-1958) called for separating the sphere of science and the sphere of religion, insisting that religion, due to the influence of religious institutions and clergymen, had lost its progressive nature and

[42] *Ibid.*, pp. 250-2.

[43] Ahmad, *Al-Din wal-Dawlah*, p. 53.

[44] Hourani, *Arabic Though*, pp. 254-5.

[45] *Ibid.*, pp 256-7.

become a heavy burden. He tried to emphasise that Islam and Christianity have identical stands with regard to the freedom of thought and emancipation of the mind. He strongly believed that 'society cannot advance or progress unless the role of religion in the human conscience is restricted; progress is the new religion of humanity.'[46]

The second generation of modernists

The next generation of thinkers, mostly Muslim followers of Abduh, branched into two conflicting schools of thought.

Rashid Rida (1865-1935) pursued what may be described as a *salafi* (traditional Islamic) approach. He suggested that the reason for the backwardness of the *ummah* lay in the fact that the Muslims had lost the truth of their religion, and that despotic political rulers had encouraged this. 'For true Islam involves two things, acceptance of *tawhid* [the creed of monotheism] and *shura* [consultation] in matters of state, but despotic rulers have tried to make Muslims forget the second by encouraging them to abandon the first.'[47] He stressed that the greatest lesson the people of the Orient could learn from the Europeans was to know what government should be like.[48] In his book *Al-Khilafah* (The Caliphate) he stressed that Islam comprised guidance, mercy and social-civic policy, a term he seems to use as a synonym for politics.

As for the social-civic policy, Islam has laid its foundations and set forth its rules, and has sanctioned the exertion of opinion and the pursuit of *ijtihad* in matters related to it because it changes with time and place and develops as architecture and all other aspects of knowledge develop. Its foundations include the princples that authority belongs to the *ummah*, that decision-making is through *shura*, that the government is a form of a republic, that the ruler should not be favoured in a court of law over the layman – for he is only employed to implement *shari'ah* and the wish of the people – and that the purpose of this policy is to preserve religion and serve the interests of the public.[49]

Other disciples of Abduh, like Qasim Amin and Ahmad Lutfi Al-Sayyid formed the second group. They had been influenced by the Christian pioneers of the secularist school of thought and began to work out the principles of a secular society in which Islam was honoured but was no longer the arbitrator of law and policy. Seeking to reconcile secularist ideas with Islam, they went so far as to develop Abduh's emphasis on the legitimacy of social change into a *de facto* division between the two realms of religion and society, each with its own norms.[50]

[46] Ahmad, *Al-Din wal-Dawlah*, p. 53.
[47] Hourani, *Arabic Thought*, p. 228.
[48] Al-Dajani, p. 124-5.
[49] Rida, *Al-Khalifah*, Al-Zahra Publications, Cairo, 1988, p. 9.
[50] Hourani, *op. cit.*.

Qasim Amin (1865-1908), known as the emancipator of women, suggested that the problem with the Muslims was a lack of science. He stressed that it was useless to hope to adopt the sciences of Europe without coming within the radius of its moral principles. The two, he believed, were indissolubly connected, and 'we must therefore be prepared for change in every aspect of our life.' He wrote:

Perfection is not to be found in the past, even the Islamic past; it can only be found, if at all, in the distant future. The path to perfection is science, and in the present age it is Europe which is most advanced in the sciences and therefore also on the path to social perfection. Europe is ahead of us in every way, and it is not true that while they are materially better than us we are morally better. The Europeans are morally more advanced; their upper and lower classes, it is true, are rather lacking in sexual virtue, but the middle class has high morals in every sense, and all classes alike have the social virtues.[51]

Ahmad Lutfi Al-Sayyid (1872-1963) was a leading member of this group. Although he was a close associate of Abduh, Islam played an insignificant part in his thought. He was not concerned, like Al-Afghani, to defend it, nor, like Abduh, to restore to Islamic law its position as the moral basis of society. Religion, whether it be Islamic or not, was relevant to his thought only as one of the constituent factors of society.[52]

The official abolishment of the *Khilafah* (Caliphate) in 1924 aroused a debate among thinkers of the time over the importance of the *Khilafah* and the response of Muslims to its abolishment. Ali Abdel Raziq (1888-1966), a graduate of Al-Azhar and Oxford, contributed to the debate with a book published in 1925 that turned to be one of the most controversial works in modern Islamic history: *Al-Islam wa Usul al-Hukm: Bahth fil-Khilafah wal-Hukumah fil-Islam* (Islam and the Fundamentals of Governance: A Thesis on Caliphate and Government in Islam). Abdel Raziq claimed there was no such thing as Islamic political principles, a theory believed to have been drawn mainly from the opinions of non-Muslim writers on Islam. He denied the existence of a political order in Islam and claimed that the Prophet had never established one and that it had not been part of his mission to found a state. His work has been a main source of ammunition in the vigorous campaign launched by 'secularists' in later times against the validity of Islamic law or *shari'ah*. The book pioneered the idea of rejecting conventional interpretations and replacing them with innovations based mostly on orientalists' opinions and writings on Islam.[53]

[51] Hourani, *Arabic Though*, pp. 164-9.

[52] *Ibid.*, pp. 170-2.

[53] M. Al-Bahiyy, *Al-Fikr al-Islami al-Hadith wa-Silatuhu bil-Isti'mar al-Gharbi* (Modern Islamic Thought and its Link to Western Colonialism), Maktabat Wahbah, Cairo, 12th edn, 1991, pp. 206-9.

The Islamic critique

The pioneers of Arab secularism are criticised by contemporary Islamic thinkers for having founded the principles of their thought on a number of incorrect assumptions. Islam was likened to Christianity and was assumed to be just another religion that could, or even should, be restricted to the spiritual sphere of human life. Islam was assumed to have a spiritual authority, or clergy, that hindered progress and prohibited freedom of thought, and should therefore be prevented from interfering in temporal matters. The assumptions about Islam's conflict with logic or science were merely extrapolations from the Euro-Christian context. The presupposition that Islam and Christianity held identical positions on the freedom of thought and the emancipation of the mind led to the conclusion that as Europe had rid itself of the influence of religion as a prelude to progress, the Arabs needed to constrain Islam. Furthermore, while no clear distinction was made between secularisation and modernisation, westernisation was said to be the sole means of modernisation.

Islamic thinkers maintain that Arab secularism represents a declaration of war against Islam, a religion that, perhaps unlike any other, shapes and influences the lives of its adherents, a religion whose values and principles are aimed at liberating mankind, establishing justice and equality, encouraging research and innovation and guaranteeing freedom of thought, expression and worship. Therefore, secularism is entirely unnecessary in the Muslim world; Muslims can achieve progress and development without having to erect a wall between their religious values and their livelihood.[54] Like nineteenth-century Muslim modernists, many contemporary Islamic thinkers insist that the scientific and technological underpinnings of modern Western civilisation are reducible to categories of knowledge and practice that Muslims can learn and benefit from without having to give up their cultural identity.[55]

Some contemporary Arab secularists support the notion that Islam is different and unique, but seek to offer their own interpretation of its objectives. In contrast to the long-term struggle between science and the grip of a powerful Church, Islam has not witnessed such a struggle, according to Husein Amin. He stresses that 'after all there was and is no Church in Islam, nor a clerical hierarchy provided for by the faith. No distinction was made in the scripture (Qur'an) between temporal and spiritual affairs. Nothing in the Qur'an is opposed to earthly or temporal good, and there is no religious authority set up in order to subjugate temporal institutions in Islam.' However, he insists that Islam acquired an

---

[54] R. Ghannouchi, 'Al-Harakah al-Islamiyah wal-Mujtama' al-Madani' (The Islamic Movement and Civil Society), paper presented at Pretoria University, South Africa, August 1994.

[55] R. Ghannouchi, 'Islam and the West', a lecture at the Centre for the Study of Democracy, University of Westminster, October 1992.

elaborate, powerful class, or caste of interpreters of the religious law, the *shari'ah*, as powerful in their desire to control the community of the faithful and as opposed to change brought about by human sciences as any Christian clergy in medieval Europe ever was.[56]

Shari'ah, the body of laws and regulations without which Islam loses its purpose, has been the primary target of secularists. Some of them deny its existence altogether, some deny its divine origin and some claim they have the right to interpret it the way they deem fit. A popular theory among secularists in Egypt for instance is that *shari'ah* as understood by Islamic scholars and Islamic movements is alien to Egyptian society and is the product of Saudi influence on migrant Egyptian workers. Ebrahim Eissa, an editor of *Rose al-Yusuf*, explains that a folk Islam is in the making due to the impact on society of what he calls 'petro-Islam' imported from Saudi Arabia and other Gulf countries.[57] Fuad Zakariya is known to have made similar claims despite the fact that Saudi and other Gulf authorities have complained that Islamism was imported into their societies from Egypt, the birth place of the largest and most influencial Islamic group, the Muslim Brotherhood.[58] Acknowledging the overwhelming support for *shari'ah* in Egypt, Zakariya says:

Despite its broad base support, the current call for implementing *shari'ah* is a new and alien phenomenon to the rational and calm Egyptian religiosity. Like any other alien phenomenon, we should locate its causes in incidental factors such as repression and intellectual or political hegemony. [...] In my opinion, the broad mass support for a principle cannot be used as a measure of the success of this principle, except in one case, when the awareness of the masses has reached maturity, full maturity.

Zakariya's verdict that the people in Egypt are not mature, and thus should not be consulted, was repeated by Arab secularists in other Arab countries to justify the suppression of democratic trends. Their attitude toward the aborted Algerian legislative elections is illustrative. The victory of the Islamic Salvation Front (FIS) was a clear indication that the majority of the Algerian people sought a change after three decades of enforced secularisation. Free democratic elections have proven secularisation to be unpopular with the masses. Fearing defeat, contemporary secularists appealed to the army to intervene, allegedly to protect democracy from its enemies. They cheered as tanks crushed the ballot boxes and as thousands of citizens were apprehended and jailed in detention camps set up in the desert. They claimed they were protecting democracy from the majority, because according to them the majority could not be trusted.

---

[56] P.J. Vatikiotis, *Islam and the State*, Routledge, 1991, p. 77.

[57] E. Eissa, interview with First Take (TV production company), London, 1994.

[58] Y. Al-Qaradawi, *al-Islam wal-'Ilmaniyyah Wajh li-Wajh* (Islam and Secularism Face to Face), Al-Risalah, 1990.

Secularism as advocated by Arab secularists has been proven to be in-compatible with Islam. If secularism was justifiable in the West due to the nature of religion there, it is entirely unnecessary in the Muslim world. Muslims can progress and develop without having to create a wall be-tween their religious values and livelihood. Secularisation of Muslim societies, though short-lived, has been possible only through force as wielded by despotic governments.

Secularism was turned into a religion by its advocates, and they in-stalled themselves as an authority very much resembling the Church in medieval Europe. A proof of the failure of secularism is the reluctance of secularists to accept the verdict of the people through free democratic elections. Results of elections held so far, at parliamentary, municipal or trade unionist level, clearly show secularists to be unpopular with the masses. The major challenge to them has been the Islamists' commit-ment to the values of democracy, pluralism, civil liberties and human rights, which contemporary Arab secularists claim to uphold but fail to respect.

THE LIMITS OF SECULARISM

John Keane

A provocative question: could it be that the democratic ideal of secular-ism is a dogma that threatens the freethinking pluralism of democracy as we currently experience it? One possible answer: suspicion of secularism is warranted by the fact that most contemporary secularists unthinkingly sacralise secularism. 'No secularism; no democracy' is for them a sacred equation. Secularists suppose that during the past few generations reli-gious illusions have gradually disappeared, and that this is fortunate since the extrusion of religious sentiments from such domains as law, government, party politics and education – the separation of church and state – releases citizens from irrational prejudices and promotes open-minded tolerance, itself a vital ingredient of a pluralist democracy. Secularists further suppose that the void left by God's departure from the world can be filled by the conviction that the separation of church and state and the confinement of religious belief to the private sphere are substitutes for God. The modern quest for personal meaning and salva-tion can be transformed into the 'invisible religion' (Thomas Luckmann) of 'self-expression' and 'self-realisation'. Secularising trends, secularists conclude, are indeed becoming facts of modern life which enable citi-zens everywhere to live less prejudiced, more rational lives, helping them to cope with a world stripped of religiosity, ensuring that they are free to run their own lives face-to-face with earthly experiences.

Despite mounting challenges to its hegemony, the conventional doctrine of secularism remains confident, no doubt in part because its intellectual roots run deep. Surprisingly, a comprehensive scholarly genealogy of these roots remains unwritten, yet it is clear that the belief that the modern world is irreversibly destroying its religious foundations in favour of secularity is a child of mid-nineteenth-century Europe, while the concept of 'the secular', which is unique to European civilisation, is far older. Ever since the adoption under Constantine of Christianity as the official religion of the Empire, the relationship between spiritual and temporal secular power has been controversial. As far back as the late thirteenth century, the adjective 'secular' (from the Latin *saecularis*) was first used in English to distinguish clergy living and working in the wider medieval world from 'religious' clergy who lived in monastic se-clusion. William of Ockham and John Wyclif, writing in the next century, strengthened this sense of the word secular by distinguishing institutions concerned with civil, lay and temporal matters from others that were clearly religious or 'spiritual'. It was in this same sense that the earliest references were made to 'the secular arm' (from the Latin *brachium secu- lare*) of civil power invoked by the Church to punish offenders, and to the figure of the 'secular abbot', a person who was the beneficiary of the title of abbot and enjoyed part of the revenues, but who was himself neither a monk nor entitled to exercise the functions of an abbot.

During the sixteenth century these originally negative connotations of 'the secular' as the temporal domain of 'the worldly' not subject direc- tly to religious rule – the domain of the non-ecclesiastical, non-religious, or non-sacred – weakened. The term 'secular' began to lose its asso- ciation with profanity or outright Godlessness. It also underwent modernisation. To 'secularise' (from the French *seculariser*) meant to make secular, to convert something or somebody from ecclesiastical to civil use or possession, while 'secularisation' connoted a *process* of re- ducing the influence of religion, as when the term was used in legal and ecclesiastical circles to describe the transfer of religious institutions or property to lay ownership or temporal use. This is the sense in which Dr Johnson's *Dictionary* (1755) defined secularity as 'Worldliness; attention to the things of the present life', 'secularise' as 'to convert from spiritual appropriations to common use' and 'to make worldly', and 'secularisation' as the 'act of secularising'.

Although these neologists did not know it, they were preparing the intellectual ground for the seeds of secularist belief that took root in mid- nineteenth-century Europe and has flourished till today: that the Church and the world are caught up in a historic struggle in which slowly and irreversibly worldliness is getting the upper hand. Early examples of this intellectual trend included Feuerbach's insistence that religion itself teaches atheism, since religion 'in its essence believes in nothing else than the truth and divinity of human nature'; Nietzsche's account of the madman, lantern in hand in broad daylight, rushing to a town market- place, shouting in a loud voice that God has been murdered; Herbert Spencer's remark (in *Data of Ethics*) that 'now that moral injunctions are losing the authority given by their supposed sacred origin, the seculari- sation of morals is becoming imperative'; and the strikingly original doctrine of secularism of George Holyoake, Charles Bradlaugh and others, according to whom the decline of religion should be reinforced by efforts to ensure that morality is concerned with the well-being of human beings in the present life, to the exclusion of all considerations drawn from belief in God and the afterlife.

It is easy to see in retrospect that the early protagonists of secularism typically leavened their case with equal measures of presumption, prediction and prescription that in turn have fed academic and literary conclusions of the kind caricatured strikingly by T.S. Eliot in *Choruses from 'The Rock'* (1934): 'But it seems that something has happened that has never happened before: though we know not just when, or why, or how, or where. Men have left GOD not for other gods, they say, but for no god; and this has never happened before.' While such conclusions have undoubtedly bred fear and loathing among believers, secularists, aided by large quantities of academic research, have powerfully pointed to the empirical findings in their favour. Look at the evidence for the oldest parliamentary democracy, they say. Almost half of the adult population in Britain and fully three-quarters of its younger people never go to church at all; two-thirds of its citizens think that religion is generally in decline; a mere quarter of them consider this 'bad in any way'; while the proportion (currently one-third) affirming that Jesus was 'just a man' is on the rise, as is the sizeable majority (currently three-quarters) who deny the existence of the devil.

Contemporary political theorists who favour secularity typically cite such evidence to refine their case for secularity by pointing to the political advantages of the secularisation of modern life. Charles Taylor, for example, has recently argued for the complementarity of secularity and democracy by highlighting the etymology of the word *saeculum*, which although of uncertain origin is regularly used in classical Latin texts to mean 'of or belonging to an age or long period', as in descriptions of so-called 'secular games' (from the Latin *ludi saeculares*) that lasted three days and three nights and were celebrated once in every 'age' or period of 120 years. In Christian usage, Taylor points out, *saeculum* connoted 'the temporal' and, hence, the world as opposed to the church. He tries to develop this theme, insisting that the modern experience of secular time stands opposed to the logic of divine time – God's time, time as eternity, the gathering of time into a unity based on a founding act that dictates the meaning of subsequent events. The positing of time as profane, such that events otherwise unrelated by cause or substantive meaning are linked together by virtue of their occurrence at the same point in a single time line, militates against the idea of society as constituted by metasocial principles, such as the Will of God. Secular time instead nurtures the political principle, vital for public life in a democracy, that the interaction of speaking and acting citizens within a worldly public sphere is primary, overriding all other competing foundational principles.

A different, but parallel case for secularity has been put recently by Richard Rorty, who defends a version of what he calls the Jeffersonian compromise. Modern democracies, he argues, should 'privatise religion without trivialising it'. The religious experience is appropriate for 'what we do with our aloneness' and citizens living together within an open society are certainly entitled to freedom of religious worship. But the problem is that religion usually functions, especially outside the religious community to which believing citizens belong, as a 'conversation stopper'. Communication among citizens is threatened by the silence, antagonism, bigotry and threats of violence nurtured by the dogmatic reference to religious fundamentals. A democratic polity thus has no choice but to enforce a pact: religious believers must be guaranteed their freedom to worship their God in private in exchange for non-believers' entitlement to live without religious bigotry and deception within the public domains of civil society and the state.

Rorty's defence of secularism is vulnerable to the *tu quoque* objection that in certain contexts the proposed Jeffersonian compromise is itself a conversation stopper; Taylor's rarefied description of the logic of the modern public sphere is similarly exposed to the historian's objection that in every known case religious discourse was a basic precondition of the rise of early modern public spheres, which correspondingly displayed strong traces of Christianity in such matters as blasphemy laws, religious holidays and public prayers. Such queries can be set aside to consider instead the more consequential objection that contemporary defenders of the doctrine of secularism exaggerate the durability and open-mindedness of 'secular' ideals and institutions and fail therefore to provide a more democratic understanding of religion and politics because they cannot see that the principle of secularism is itself self-contradictory and, hence, unable in practice to provide relatively stable guidelines for citizens interacting freely within the laws and institutions of democratic civil societies and polities.

It is true that contemporary secularism is not about to collapse under the weight of its own contradictions, in no small measure because it has nurtured a shared sense among citizens and representatives that the bigotry and bloodshed of the old Judeo-Christian struggles for power necessarily belong to the past. Yet despite this important success, secularist ideals and institutions tend to produce a string of difficulties that check their viability and even provoke demands for terminating secularism. The most obvious example is the self-contradictory effects of freedom of religious association. It is commonly said by secularists that democracy requires the separation of church and state and the confinement of organised religion and religious discourse to the civil domain. Secularisation requires that citizens be emancipated from state and ecclesiastical diktat; they should be free to believe or to worship according to their conscience and ethical judgements. Render unto Caesar the things that are Caesar's means: Caesar has no direct business in things that are not Caesar's. In practice, such religious freedom presupposes an open and tolerant civil society within whose plural structures and spaces citizens are required to avoid bitterness and bloodletting so that each can enjoy freedom *from* others' dogmatic beliefs and codes of conduct. In other words, secularity requires citizens to agree to disagree about religion, which ultimately means, as Voltaire spelled out in *Traité sur la Tolerance* (1763), that there must be at least some civil spaces in which religion plays little or no role at all. Religious freedom requires religious indifference. Citizens must tolerate each others' different religious dispositions by accepting that every sect is a moral and political check upon its neighbour, and that peaceful competition, civility and indifference towards the passions of others is as wholesome in religion as in the world of commerce and exchange.

The implied agnosticism and potential atheism of secularism is a godsend to religioners. Convinced that secularisation potentially marginalises or destroys religiosity, they take advantage of the freedom of association provided by civil society to protest against the perceived decline of religion. Some, emphasising that religion has to do with the whole of life, warn that Christians should not become like the rich man who pretended not to know the beggar Lazarus lying at his gate. The life of Christ should instead be imitated: ethical concern must be extended to the hungry, the needy, the homeless, those without proper medical care, above all, to those without hope of a better future. Others, moved by Christ's comment to Pilate that His kingdom is not of this world, emphasise the importance of spiritual outreach, faith and zeal. These new religioners lay stress on such principles as the Bible as revelation, the atoning sacrifice of Jesus on the cross, and the imminent second coming of Christ, and each of these tenets is linked in turn to the importance of preserving the family, morality, and country. Private belief is not enough; believers are called to witness before others in public, through such forums as 'house churches' and public spectacles, in which the born-again discard their dark glasses, rise from their wheelchairs and proclaim the glory of God.

Such 'puffs of the Zeitgeist' (in the words of Hannah Arendt) and public reaffirmations of religious ethics are nowadays commonplace in open societies, not least because secularising civil societies display a second contradiction: their propensity to replace religiosity with existential uncertainty prompts the return of the sacred in everyday life. Modern civil societies comprise multiple webs of 'fluid' social institutions whose dynamism and complexity prevent citizens from fully comprehending, let alone grasping the social totality within which they are born, grow to maturity and die. Citizens' consequent sense of uncertainty about such matters as investment and employment, the quality of schooling and the shifting patterns of personal identity and household obligations makes them prone to stress and confusion, and, hence, prone to involvement in shock-absorbing institutions, of which churches, sects and crusades remain leading examples, especially in times of personal crisis. In a stressed and strained world, religious institutions serve as reminders of the importance of solidarity among the shaken. They help to preserve emotional contact with invented traditions such as 'family life' and, in a world dominated by secular time, religious institutions heighten the sense of mysterious importance of life's rites of passage by baptising such events as birth, marriage and death in the waters of theological time, thereby reminding mortal human beings that, existentially speaking, life is an inevitable defeat. And since the members of civil societies typically experience at least something of what Heinrich von Kleist called the 'fragile constitution of the world', they are prone to experience (and take comfort in) the feeling of absolute dependence upon another, larger order of existence which is anterior to human reflection, speech and interaction. It is this experience of wonder and reverence for the world ('the assurance of things hoped for, the conviction of things not seen' [Hebrews 11.1]) that Friedrich Schleiermacher (in *Uber die Religion* [1799]) considered to be the quintessence of religion, and that nowadays fuels such religious initiatives as the Sea of Faith network and Reconstructionist Judaism, and helps to account for the surprising opinion poll findings in the most secular countries that clear majorities (around seventy-five per cent in Britain) believe in 'religion' and the afterlife.

Perhaps the most strikingly contradictory, self-paralysing feature of secularism is its theoretical and practical affinity with political despotism. Secularists will likely consider this remark blasphemous for they insist that secularity conventionally implies openness to reason, willingness to compromise, freedom from bigotry and the institutional separation of church and state. With some justification, scholars such as John Neville Figgis have traced the roots of the doctrine of secularism to the justified fears of late medieval religioners – William of Ockham's *Octo quaestiones de potestate papae* (1334-47) is a path-breaking example – that matters of religion and conscience were slipping into the hands of political classes who themselves refused to allow that their power merely existed on sufferance of the spiritual powers. Yet one trouble with the view that the struggle for secularity was a struggle for toleration of differences is its failure to spot the inherent dogmatism of secularism. It is not only that various political attempts (in France, Turkey and elsewhere) to institutionalise secularism have been riddled with such violence and coercion that they qualify as experiments in 'internal colonialism' (Catherine Audard); or, at the level of principle, that the early (Christian) advocates of secular freedoms typically denied others – Jews (children of the Devil) and Roman Catholics (members of the body of a prostitute), for instance – such freedoms. It is as if otherwise benign secularists have suffered a temporary failure of imagination, courage or will in extending their own universal principles to others. The problem actually runs deeper, for the principle of secularism, which 'represents a realisation of crucial motifs of Christianity itself' (Bönhoffer), is arguably founded upon a sublimated version of the Christian belief in the necessity of deciding for non-Christian others what they can think or say or even whether they are capable of thinking and saying anything at all.

The inbuilt hostility towards Muslims of the normative ideal of secularism is the most worrying contemporary example of such dogmatism. There are two obvious clues to this extant hostility. One is that many otherwise 'unreligious' and tolerant citizens of countries such as the United States, France, and Germany treat the growing numbers of Muslims – over 20 million in the European Union alone – who now permanently reside within the old democracies with quiet aversion, deep suspicion or even thuggish belligerence; it is as if tolerant secularists must always prevaricate or become bigots when confronted with veil-wearing, *halal* meat, talk of apostasy (*riddah*) and violent martyrdom. Another clue is the heated confusion continually sparked by the term 'secularism' within the Arabic, Farsi and Turkish language communities. Symptomatic is the absence of a term in Arabic to describe the secular, secularity, or secularism. The chosen neologism *'alamaniyah*, a response to the French term *laïcisme*, first appeared at the end of the nineteenth century in the dictionary *Muhit al-Muhit* written by the Christian Lebanese scholar Boutrus Al-Bustani. *'Alamaniyah* was derived from *'alam* (world) because the literal translation, *la diniyah* (non-religious) would have been rejected outright by Muslims, for whom (according to the principle *al-Islam din wa-dawlah*, Islam is religion and state) the division between the temporal and the spiritual is literally unthinkable.

The word 'secularism' subsequently became an insult in the ears of many Muslims not only for etymological reasons but also because secular Europeans – supposedly open to the world and to openness itself – normally harboured anti-Muslim prejudices that stemmed back to the times when Christians first perceived the newly converted Saracens, or Arabs, as little better than a plague. Especially with the advance of the Ottoman Empire into the Balkan region of Christian Europe, words like 'secular' and 'secularisation' became caught up in the struggle against the sinister 'Turk', whose virulent hatred of 'civilisation' was to be met with what was often called a *bellum contra barbaros*. Sometimes prejudices softened into ambivalence, as in Voltaire's intellectual vacillation between treating Mohammed as a profound political thinker and founder of a rational religion and as a prototypical impostor who enslaved souls by resorting to religious fables. And sometimes those who spoke the new language of secularity noted the Ottomans' tolerance of religious minorities and expressed curiosity in the supposedly 'exotic' qualities of the Islamic world, which they pictured as a fabulous phantasmagoria of gaudy colours and magnificent fabrics, of veiled women living at the disposal of men who dined while seated on mats, of palaces decorated with gold, silver and marble, a world whose growing poverty seemed only to add to its charm, sealing off its own specificity from the rest of the world. Such concessions to the world of Islam were hardly concessionary, for they typically functioned as the friendly smile of an ugly hostility towards Muslims in general. Among those who embraced the newfangled doctrine of secularism, free reign was given to 'the ignorance of triumphant imagination' (R.W. Southern) directed at imaginary Muslims, who could be easily eliminated on paper. The Muslim world was also treated as a veritable spring of luxury goods – ivory, precious fabrics, spices, minerals, olive oil – to be exploited for Christendom's benefit, by stealth or violence. Then there were those who favoured appeasement, typically by calling for an end to the persecution of pagans who were said to be what they were because they had so far missed out on the privilege of hearing Christ's message and sharing in the benefits of Christian-style secularity – a call for peace absurdly reminiscent of the latter-day Ulster clergyman who moralised about the need for Zionists and Palestinians to live together in harmony by embracing the teachings of Jesus Christ.

Today's 'secular' hostility towards Islam – the very word itself suggests domination, violence, ignorance, misogyny, fanaticism, international conspiracy – is obviously a restatement and variation on the old theme of the satanism of Islam and it helps explain why most contemporary Muslim scholars mistrust or reject outright the ideal of secularism. 'Secularism is Satan imitating God', the leading Turkish Islamist Ali Bulac told me recently, echoing the widespread impression that European talk of secularity is hubris, and that it has always been a cover for hypocrites who think Muslims can progress only by following the path marked out by the West, which includes the renunciation of religion. Some Islamist scholars, Muhammad Mahdi Shams Al-Din and Rachid Al-Ghannouchi for instance, acknowledge that in the European context the doctrine of secularism certainly helped to tame Christian fundamentalism and to nurture the values of civility and power-sharing. But they also insist that the attempted secularisation of the twentieth-century Muslim world has produced dictatorship, state-enforced religion, the violation of human and civil rights and the weakening or outright destruction of civil society. In a word, secularity has won a reputation for humiliating Muslims – humiliating them through the exercise of Western double standards in Kuwait, Algeria and Palestine, through the corrupt despotism of comprador governments, and through the permanent threat of being crushed by the economic, technological, political, cultural and military might of the American-led West.

The militant Islamic rejection of secularism within the geographical crescent stretching from Morocco to Mindanao understandably worries many in the West. The material stakes are high and the concern that anti-secularism will prove to be a cover for brutal power-grabbing instead of benign power-sharing remains poignant, although largely untested by events. Anxiety centres on Hama – the name of a town in Syria which is remembered with as much fear as it is left unspoken, a terrifying symbol of what happens when the armed forces of secularism drown their throat-slitting opponents in a blood bath. For citizens living in the old democracies, such conflict should serve as a reminder that secularism shelters violent intolerance and, more generally, that we live in times marked by religious protest, the return of the sacred, and the general *desecularisation* of political and social life.

It is strange that so few scholars – Reinhold Bernhardt's *Zwischen Grossenwahn, Fanatismus und Bekennermut*, Gilles Keppel's *La Revanche de Dieu*, and Ronald Thiemann's *Religion and Public Life* are recent exceptions – are reflecting imaginatively on these trends. Public ignorance or outright denial of their significance, especially by hardline secularists, is also widespread. But here and there can be found pockets of genuine public unease about the cramping effects of secularism; calls for a new political philosophy which is rid of fictions about the withering away and privatisation of religion; and, within NGO and government circles and courts of law, practical efforts to fashion new policy compromises – such as employers' provision for festive and prayer times, believers' exemptions from certain civil laws, the proposed admission of Muslim schools into the state-subsidised voluntary-aided sector in Britain – which seek to accommodate better the preferences of non-believers *and* believers alike. Hence the need for more provocative questions about the limits of secularism: is the nineteenth-century doctrine of secularism, still cherished by most democrats a century later, in fact a conflict-producing ideology that, for democracy's sake, ought to be jettisoned? If so, does this imply that the inherited secularist categories of church and state, together with the corresponding notion of their 'separation', need to be abandoned, if only because the terms 'church' and 'state' are insufficiently complex to deal with the growing diversity of religious practices and governmental regulations of morality? Should we from hereon stop searching for universal principles (like secularism) of how to regard religion? Must we instead give priority to context-bound judgements that recognise that all morality including secularism and religious discourse arises in particular contexts, that the secularist view that religioners are like Ixion copulating with clouds and breeding monsters applies equally to secularists, and that therefore a new *desecularised* compromise between non-believers and believers is now required? Are we thus left with no other option but to seek new ways of maximising the freedom of non-believers *and* believers alike – with special emphasis being given to those who currently suffer the injustices produced by a doctrine whose universalist pretensions are no longer credible?

SECULARISM IN RETREAT *

Peter L. Berger

A few years ago the first volume to come out of the Fundamentalism Project landed on my desk. The Fundamentalism Project was generously funded by the MacArthur Foundation and chaired by Martin Marty, the distinguished church historian at the University of Chicago. While a number of very reputable scholars took part in it, and although the published results are of generally excellent quality, my contemplation of this first volume evoked in me what has been called an Aha! experience.

Now, the book was very big. Sitting there on my desk, massively, it was of the 'book-weapon' type, the kind with which one could do serious injury. So I asked myself: why would the MacArthur Foundation pay out several million dollars to support an international study of religious fundamentalists? Two answers came to mind. The first was obvious and not very interesting: the MacArthur Foundation is a very progressive outfit; it understands fundamentalists to be anti-progressive; the Project, then, was a matter of knowing one's enemies. The second was a more interesting answer: so-called fundamentalism was assumed to be a strange, difficult-to-understand phenomenon; the purpose of the Project was to delve into this alien world and make it more understandable.

But here came another question: who finds this world strange, and to whom must it be made understandable? The answer to that question was easy: people to whom the officials of the MacArthur Foundation normally talk, such as professors at American elite universities. And with this came the Aha! experience: The concern that must have led to this Project was based on an upside-down perception of the world. The notion here was that so-called fundamentalism (which, when all is said and done, usually refers to any sort of passionate religious movement) is a rare, hard-to-explain thing. But in fact it is not rare at all, either if one looks at history, or if one looks around the contemporary world. On the contrary, what is rare is people who think otherwise. Put simply: the difficult-to-understand phenomenon is not Iranian mullahs but American university professors. (Would it, perhaps, be worth a multi-million-dollar project to try to explain the latter group?)

The point of this little story is that the assumption that we live in a secularised world is false: the world today, with some exceptions attended to below, is as furiously religious as it ever was, and in some

* This chapter has been reprinted, with permission. © *The National Interest*, no. 46, winter, 1996/8, Washington, D.C.

places more so than ever. This means that a whole body of literature written by historians and social scientists over the course of the 1950s and 1960s, loosely labelled as 'secularisation theory', was essentially mistaken. In my early work I contributed to this literature and was in good company so doing – most sociologists of religion had similar views. There were good reasons for holding these views at the time, and some of these writings still stand up. But the core premise does not.

The key idea of secularisation theory is simple and can be traced to the Enlightenment: modernisation necessarily leads to a decline of religion, both in society and in the minds of individuals. It is precisely this key idea that has turned out to be wrong. To be sure, modernisation has had some secularising effects, more in some places than in others. But it has also provoked powerful movements of counter-secularisation. Also, secularisation on the societal level is not necessarily linked to secularisation on the level of individual consciousness. Thus, certain religious institutions have lost power and influence in many societies, but both old and new religious beliefs and practices have nevertheless continued in the lives of individuals, sometimes taking new institutional forms and sometimes leading to great explosions of religious fervour. Conversely, religiously-identified institutions can play social or political roles even when very few people believe or practise the religion supposedly represented by these institutions. To say the least, the relation between religion and modernity is rather complicated.

Rejection and adaptation

The proposition that modernity necessarily leads to a decline of religion is, in principle, 'value-free'. That is, it can be affirmed both by people who think it is good news and by people who think that it is very bad news indeed. Most Enlightenment thinkers and most progressive-minded people ever since have tended toward the idea that secularisation is a good thing, at least insofar as it does away with religious phenomena that are 'backward', 'superstitious', or 'reactionary' (a religious residue purged of these negative characteristics may still be deemed acceptable). But religious people, including those with very traditional or orthodox beliefs, have also affirmed the modernity/secularity linkage, and have greatly bemoaned it. Some have defined modernity as the enemy, to be fought whenever possible. Others have, on the contrary, seen modernity as an invincible worldview to which religious beliefs and practices should adapt themselves. In other words, rejection and adaptation are two strategies open to religious communities in a world understood to be secularised. As is always the case when strategies are based on mistaken perception of the terrain, both strategies have had very doubtful results.

It is possible, of course, to reject any number of modern ideas and values theoretically, but to make this rejection stick in the lives of people is much more difficult. To do that, one can try to take over society as a whole and make one's counter-modern religion obligatory for everyone – a difficult enterprise in most countries in the contemporary world. Franco tried in Spain, and failed; the mullahs are still at it in Iran and a couple of other places; in most of the world such exercises in religious conquest are unlikely to succeed. And this unlikelihood does have to do with modernisation, which brings about very heterogeneous societies and a quantum leap in intercultural communication, two factors favouring pluralism and not favouring the establishment (or re-establishment) of religious monopolies. Another form of rejection strategy is to create religious subcultures so designed as to exclude the influences of the outside society. That is a more promising exercise than religious revolution, but it too is fraught with difficulty. Where it has taken root, modern culture is a very powerful force, and an immense effort is required to maintain enclaves with an airtight defence system. Ask the Amish in eastern Pennsylvania, or a Hasidic rabbi in the Williamsburg section of Brooklyn.

Notwithstanding the apparent power of modern secular culture, secularisation theory has been falsified even more dramatically by the results of adaptation strategies attempted by religious institutions. If we really lived in a highly secularised world, then religious institutions could be expected to survive to the degree that they manage to adapt to secularity. That, indeed, has been the empirical assumption of adaptation strategies. What has in fact occurred is that, by and large, religious communities have survived and indeed flourished to the degree that they have not tried to adapt themselves to the alleged requirements of a secularised world. Put simply, experiments with secularised religion have generally failed; religious movements with beliefs and practices dripping with 'reactionary supernaturalism' (the kind utterly beyond the pale at self-respecting faculty parties) have widely succeeded.

The struggle with modernity in the Roman Catholic Church nicely illustrates the difficulties of various rejection and adaptation strategies. In the wake of the Enlightenment and its multiple revolutions, the initial response by the Church was militant and then defiant rejection. Perhaps the most magnificent moment of that defiance came in 1870, when the First Vatican Council solemnly proclaimed the infallibility of the Pope and the immaculate conception of Mary, literally in the face of the Enlightenment about to occupy Rome in the shape of the army of Victor Emmanuel I. The disdain was mutual: the Roman monument to the Bersaglieri (the elite army units that occupied the Eternal City in the name of the Italian Risorgimento) places the heroic figure in his Bersaglieri uniform so that he is positioned with his behind pointing exactly toward the Vatican. The Second Vatican Council, almost a hundred years later, considerably modified this rejectionist stance, guided as it was by the notion of *aggiornamento* – literally, bringing the church 'up-to-date' with the modern world. (I remember a conversation I had with a Protestant theologian, whom I asked what he thought would happen at the Council, this before it had actually convened; he replied that he did not know, but that he was sure that they would not read the minutes of the first Council meeting.)

The Second Vatican Council was supposed to open windows, specifically the windows of the anti-secular Catholic subculture that had been constructed when it became clear that overall society could not be re-conquered. (In the United States this Catholic subculture was quite impressive right up to the very recent past.) The trouble with opening windows is that you cannot control what comes in through them, and a lot has come – indeed, the whole turbulent world of modern culture – that has been very troubling to the Church. Under the current pontificate the Church has been steering a nuanced course between rejection and adaptation, with mixed results in different countries.

If one looks at the international religious scene objectively, that of the Roman Catholics as well as virtually all others, one must observe that it is conservative or orthodox or traditionalist movements that are on the rise almost everywhere. These movements, whatever adjective one may choose for them, are precisely those that rejected an *aggiornamento* as defined by progressive intellectuals. Conversely, religious movements and institutions that have made great efforts to conform to a perceived modernity are almost everywhere on the decline. In the United States this has been a much commented-upon fact, exemplified by the decline of so-called mainline Protestantism and the concomitant rise of Evangelicalism; but the United States is by no means unusual in this. Nor is Protestantism.

The conservative thrust in the Roman Catholic Church under John Paul II has borne fruit in both the number of converts and in the renewed enthusiasm among native Catholics, especially in non-Western countries. Following the collapse of the Soviet Union, too, there occurred a remarkable revival of the Orthodox Church in Russia. The most rapidly growing Jewish groups, both in Israel and in the diaspora, are Orthodox groups. There have been similarly vigorous upsurges of conservative religion in all the other major religious communities – Islam, Hinduism, Buddhism – as well as revival movements in smaller communities (such as Shinto in Japan and Sikhism in India).

Of course, these developments differ greatly, not only in religious content (which is obvious), but also in their social and political implications. What they have in common, though, is their unambiguously religious inspiration. In their aggregate they provide a massive falsification of the idea that modernisation and secularisation are cognate phenomena. Minimally, one must note that counter-secularisation is at least as important a phenomenon in the contemporary world as secularisation.

Two revivals . . .

Both in the media and in scholarly publications these religious movements are often subsumed under the category of 'fundamentalism'. This is not a felicitous term, not only because it carries a pejorative undertone, but because it derives from the history of American Protestantism, where it has a specific reference that is distortive if extended to other religious traditions. All the same, the term has some use if one tries to explain the aforementioned developments: it suggests a combination of several features – great religious passion, a defiance of what others have defined as the *Zeitgeist*, and a return to traditional sources of religious authority. These are indeed common features across cultural boundaries. And they do reflect the presence of secularising forces, since they must be understood as a reaction against them. (In that sense, at least, something of the old secularisation theory may be said to hold up, albeit in a rather back-handed way.) Clearly, one of the most important topics for a sociology of contemporary religion is precisely this interplay of secularising and counter-secularising forces. This is because modernity, for fully understandable reasons, undermines all the old certainties; uncertainty, in turn, is a condition that many people find very hard to bear; therefore, any movement (not only a religious one) that promises to provide or to renew certainty has a ready market.

While the aforementioned common features are important, an analysis of the social and political impact of the various religious up-surges must take full account of their differences. This becomes clear when one looks at what are arguably the two most dynamic religious upsurges in the world today: the Islamic and the Evangelical. Comparison also underlines the weakness of the category 'fundamentalism' as applied to both.

The Islamic upsurge, because of its more immediately obvious political ramifications, is the better known of the two. Yet it would be a serious error to see it only through a political lens. It is an impressive revival of emphatically religious commitments. And it is of vast geographical scope, affecting every Muslim country from North Africa to Southeast Asia. It continues to gain converts, especially in sub-Saharan Africa, where it is often in head-on competition with Christianity. It is becoming very visible in the burgeoning Muslim communities in Europe and, to a much lesser extent, in North America. Everywhere it is bringing about a restoration not only of Islamic beliefs, but of distinctively Islamic lifestyles, which in many ways directly contradict modern ideas – such as the relation of religion and the state, the role of women, moral codes of everyday behaviour and, last but not least, the boundaries of religious and moral tolerance.

An important characteristic of the Islamic revival is that it is by no means restricted to the less modernised or 'backward' sectors of society, as progressive intellectuals still like to think. On the contrary, it is very strong in cities with a high degree of modernisation, and in a number of countries it is particularly visible among people with Western-style higher education; in Egypt and Turkey, for example, it is often the daughters of secularised professionals who are putting on the veil and other accoutrements expressing so-called Islamic modesty.

Yet there are also very great differences. Even within the Middle East, the Islamic heartland, there are both religiously and politically important distinctions to be made between Sunni and Shi'a revivals – Islamic conservatism means very different things in, say, Saudi Arabia and Iran. As one moves away from the Middle East, the differences become even greater. Thus in Indonesia, the most populous Muslim country in the world, a very powerful revival movement, the Nahdatul-Ulama, is avowedly pro-democracy and pro-pluralism, the very opposite of what is commonly viewed as Muslim 'fundamentalism'. Where the political circumstances allow it, there is a lively discussion about the relationship of Islam to various modern realities, and there are sharp disagreements between individuals who are equally committed to a revitalised Islam. Still, for reasons deeply grounded in the core of the tradition, it is probably fair to say that, on the whole, Islam has had a difficult time coming to terms with key modern institutions – such as pluralism, democracy and the market economy.

The Evangelical upsurge is just as breathtaking in scope. Geographically that scope is even wider than that of the Islamic revival. It has gained huge numbers of converts in East Asia – in all the Chinese communities (including, despite severe persecution, in mainland China) and in South Korea, the Philippines, across the South Pacific, throughout sub-Saharan Africa (where it is often synthesised with elements of traditional African religion) and apparently in parts of ex-communist Europe. But the most remarkable success has occurred in Latin America; it is estimated that there are now 40-50 million Evangelical Protestants south of the US border, the great majority of them first-generation Protestants.

The most numerous component within the Evangelical upsurge is Pentecostal, combining Biblical orthodoxy and a rigorous morality with an ecstatic form of worship and an emphasis on spiritual healing. Especially in Latin America, conversion to Protestantism brings about a cultural transformation – new attitudes toward work and consumption, a new educational ethos, a violent rejection of traditional machismo (women play a key role in the Evangelical churches). The origins of this

worldwide Evangelical upsurge are in the United States, from where the
missionaries were first dispatched. But it is very important to understand
that virtually everywhere, and emphatically in Latin America, the new
Evangelicalism is thoroughly indigenous and is no longer dependent
on support from US fellow-believers. Indeed, Latin American Evangelicals have been sending missionaries to the Hispanic community in the
US, where there has been a comparable flurry of conversions.

Needless to say, the religious contents of the Islamic and Evangelical
revivals are totally different. So are the social and political consequences
(of which more below). But the two developments also differ in that the
Islamic movement is occurring primarily in countries that are already
Muslim or among Muslim emigrants (as in Europe); by contrast, the
Evangelical movement is growing dramatically throughout the world in
countries where this type of religion was previously unknown or very
marginal.

... and two exceptions

The world today, then, is massively religious, and it is anything but the
secularised world that had been predicted (be it joyfully or despondently)
by so many analysts of modernity. There are two exceptions to this proposition, one somewhat unclear, the other very obvious.

The first apparent exception is in Western Europe, where, if nowhere
else, the old secularisation theory seems to hold. With increasing modernisation there has been an increase in the key indicators of secularisation:
on the level of expressed beliefs (especially such as could be called
orthodox in Protestant or Catholic terms); dramatically on the level of
church-related behaviour (attendance at services of worship, adherence
to church-dictated codes of personal behaviour, especially with regard
to sexuality, reproduction, and marriage), and finally, with respect to re-
cruitment to the clergy. These phenomena had been observed for a long
time in the northern countries of the continent; since the Second World
War they have quickly engulfed the south. Thus Italy and Spain have
experienced a rapid decline in church-related religion, as has Greece (thus
undercutting the claim of Catholic conservatives that Vatican II is to be
blamed for the decline). There is now a massively secular Euro-culture
and what has happened in the south can be simply described (though not
thereby explained) as the invasion of these countries by that culture. It is
not fanciful to predict that there will be similar developments in Eastern
Europe, precisely to the degree that these countries too will be integrated
into the new Europe.

While these facts are not in dispute, a number of recent works in the
sociology of religion (notably in France, Britain and Scandinavia) have
questioned the term 'secularisation' as applied to these developments.

There is now a body of data indicating strong survivals of religion, most of it generally Christian in nature, despite the widespread alienation from the organised churches. If the data hold up to scrutiny, a shift in the institutional location of religion, rather than secularisation, would be a more accurate description of the European situation. All the same, Europe stands out as quite different from other parts of the world. It certainly differs sharply from the religious situation in the US. One of the most interesting puzzles in the sociology of religion is why Americans are so much more religious as well as more churchly than Europeans.

The other exception to the desecularisation thesis is less ambiguous: there exists an international subculture composed of people with Western-type higher education, especially in the humanities and social sciences, which is indeed secularised by any measure. This subculture is the principal 'carrier' of progressive, Enlightenment beliefs and values. While the people in this subculture are relatively thin on the ground, they are very influential, as they control the institutions that provide the 'official' definitions of reality (notably the educational system, the mass media, and the higher reaches of the legal system). They are remarkably similar all over the world today as they have been for a long time (though, as we have seen, there are also defectors from this subculture, especially in the Muslim countries). Why it is that people with this type of education should be so prone to secularisation is not entirely clear, but there is, without question, a globalised elite culture. It follows, then, that in country after country religious upsurges have a strongly populist character: Over and beyond the purely religious motives, these are movements of protest and resistance against a secular elite. The so-called 'culture war' in the US emphatically shares this feature.

Questions and answers

This somewhat breathless *tour d'horizon* of the global religious scene raises several questions: What are the origins of the world-wide resurgence of religion? What is the likely future course of this religious resurgence? Do resurgent religions differ in their critique of the secular order? How is religious resurgence related to a number of issues not ordinarily linked to religion? Let us take these questions in turn.

As to the origins of the world-wide resurgence of religion, two possible answers have already been mentioned. The first is that modernity tends to undermine the taken-for-granted certainties by which people lived throughout most of history. This is an uncomfortable state of affairs, for many an intolerable one, and religious movements that claim to give certainty have great appeal by easing that discomfort. The second is that a purely secular view of reality has its principal social location in an elite culture that, not surprisingly, is resented by large numbers of people who are not part of it but who nevertheless feel its influence (most troublingly, as their children are subjected to an education that ignores or even directly attacks their own beliefs and values). Religious movements with a strongly anti-secular bent can therefore appeal to people with resentments that sometimes have quite non-religious sources.

But there is yet another answer, which recalls my opening story about certain American foundation officials worrying about 'fundamentalism'. In one sense, there is nothing to explain here. Strongly felt religion has always been around: what needs explanation is its absence rather than its presence. Modern secularity is a much more puzzling phenomenon than all these religious explosions – and the University of Chicago is a more interesting topic for the sociology of religion than are the Islamic schools of Qom. In other words, at one level the phenomena under consideration simply serve to demonstrate continuity in the place of religion in human experience.

As to the likely future course of this religious resurgence, it would make little sense to venture a prognosis with regard to the entire global scene, given the considerable variety of important religious movements in the contemporary world. Predictions, if one dares to make them at all, will be more useful if applied to much narrower situations. One, though, can be made with some assurance: There is no reason to think that the world of the twenty-first century will be any less religious than the world is today.

There is, it must be said, a minority of sociologists of religion who have been trying to salvage the old secularisation theory by what may be called the last-gasp thesis: modernisation does secularise, and movements like the Islamic and the Evangelical ones represent last-ditch defences by religion that cannot last. Eventually, secularity will triumph – or, to put it less respectfully, eventually Iranian mullahs, Pentecostal preachers and Tibetan lamas will all think and act like professors of literature at American universities. This thesis is singularly unpersuasive.

Nonetheless, one will have to speculate very differently regarding different sectors of the religious scene. For example, the most militant Islamic movements will have difficulty maintaining their present stance *vis-à-vis* modernity should they succeed in taking over the governments of their countries (as, it seems, is already happening in Iran). It is also unlikely that Pentecostalism, as it exists today among mostly poor and uneducated people, will retain its present religious and moral characteristics unchanged as many of these people experience upward social mobility (this has already been observed extensively in the US). Generally, many of these religious movements are linked to non-religious forces of one sort or another, and the future course of the former will be at least partially determined by the course of the latter. Thus in the US, for instance, the future course of militant Evangelicalism will be different if some of its causes succeed – or continue to be frustrated – in the political and legal arenas.

Finally, in religion as in every other area of human endeavour, individual personalities play a much larger role than most social scientists and historians are willing to concede. Thus there might have been an Islamic revolution in Iran without the Ayatollah Khomeini, but it would probably have looked quite different. No one can predict the appearance of charismatic figures who will launch powerful religious movements in places where no one expects them. Who knows, perhaps the next religious upsurge in America will occur among disenchanted postmodernist academics!

Do the resurgent religions differ in their critique of the secular order? Yes, of course they do, depending on their respective belief systems. Cardinal Ratzinger and the Dalai Lama will be troubled by different aspects of contemporary secular culture. What both, however, will agree upon is the shallowness of a culture that tries to get by without any transcendent points of reference. And there, certainly, they will have good reasons for criticism.

The religious impulse, the quest for meaning that transcends the restricted space of empirical existence in this world, has been a perennial feature of humanity. (This assertion is not a theological statement but an anthropological one – an agnostic or even an atheist philosopher may well agree with it.) It would require something close to a mutation of the species to finally extinguish this impulse. The more radical thinkers of the Enlightenment, and their more recent intellectual descendants, of course hoped for just such a mutation. Thus far this has not happened and it is unlikely to happen anytime in the foreseeable future. The critique of secularity common to all the resurgent movements is that human existence bereft of transcendence is an impoverished and finally untenable condition.

To the extent that secularity today has a specifically modern form (there were earlier forms, for example, in versions of Confucianism and Hellenistic culture), the critique of secularity also entails a critique of at least these aspects of modernity. Beyond that, however, different religious movements differ in their relation to modernity.

As noted, an argument can be made that the Islamic resurgence has a strong tendency toward a negative view of modernity; in places it is downright anti-modern or counter-modernising (as in its view on the role of women). By contrast, the Evangelical resurgence is positively modernising in most places where it occurs, clearly so in Latin America. The new Evangelicals throw aside many of the traditions that have been obstacles to modernisation (machismo, for one, also the subservience to hierarchy that has been endemic to Iberian Catholicism), and their churches encourage values and behaviour patterns that contribute to modernisation. Just to take one important case in point: in order to participate fully in the life of their congregations, Evangelicals will want to read the Bible and be able to join in the discussion of congregational affairs that are largely in the hands of lay persons (indeed, largely in the hands of women). The desire to read the Bible encourages literacy, and, beyond this, a positive attitude toward education and self-improvement. The running of local churches by lay persons necessitates training in various administrative skills, including the conduct of public meetings and the keeping of financial accounts. It is not fanciful to suggest that in this way Evangelical congregations serve (inadvertently, to be sure) as schools for democracy and for social mobility.

How does the religious resurgence relate to a number of issues that are not usually linked to religion? First let us take international politics. Here one meets head on with the thesis, eloquently proposed by Samuel Huntington, to the effect that, with the end of the Cold War, international affairs will be affected by a 'clash of civilisations' rather than by ideological conflicts. There is something to be said for this thesis. The great ideological conflict that animated the Cold War is certainly dormant for the moment, though I, for one, would not bet on its final demise. Nor can one be sure that new and different ideological conflicts may not arise in the future. Indeed, to the extent that nationalism is an ideology (more accurately, each nationalism has its own ideology), ideology is alive and well in a long list of countries.

It is also plausible that, in the absence of the overarching confrontation between Soviet communism and the American-led West, cultural animosities suppressed during the Cold War period are resurfacing. Some of these animosities have themselves taken on an ideological form – as in the assertion of a distinctive Asian identity by a number of governments and intellectual groups in East and Southeast Asia. This particular ideology has become especially visible in debates over the allegedly ethnocentric/Eurocentric character of human rights as propagated by the US and other Western governments and NGOs. But it would probably be an exaggeration to see these debates as signalling a clash of civilisations. The closest thing to a religiously defined clash of civilisations would come about if the radical Islamic interpretation of the world came to be established within a wider spectrum of Muslim countries, and actually became the basis of their foreign policies. As yet, this has not happened.

Religion in world politics

To assess the role of religion in international politics, it would be useful to distinguish between political movements that are genuinely inspired by religion and those that use religion as a convenient legitimation for political agendas based on non-religious interests. Such a distinction is difficult but not impossible. Thus there is no reason to doubt that the suicide bombers of the Islamic Hamas movement truly believe in the religious motives they avow. By contrast, there is good reason to doubt that the three parties involved in the Bosnian conflict, which is commonly represented as a clash between religions, are really inspired by religious ideas. I think it was P.J. O'Rourke who observed that these three parties are of the same race, speak the same language and are distinguished only by their religion – in which none of them believe. The same scepticism about the religious nature of an allegedly religious conflict is expressed in the joke from Northern Ireland (which also worked perfectly in the context of the Lebanese civil war): a man walks down a dark street in Belfast, when a gunman jumps out of a doorway, holds a gun to his head, and asks: 'Are you Protestant or Catholic?' The man stutters, 'Well, actually I'm an atheist.' 'Ah yes,' says the gunman, 'But are you a Protestant or a Catholic atheist?'

It would be very nice if one could say that religion is everywhere a force for peace. Unfortunately, this is not the case. While it is difficult to pinpoint a frequency distribution, very probably religion much more often fosters war, both between and within nations, rather than peace. If so, that is hardly new in history. Religious institutions and movements are fanning wars and civil wars on the Indian subcontinent, in the Balkans, in the Middle East, and in Africa. Occasionally, religious institutions do try to resist warlike policies or to mediate between conflicting parties. The Vatican mediated successfully in some international disputes in Latin America. There have been religiously inspired peace movements in several countries (including the US, during the Vietnam War). Both Protestant and Catholic clergy have tried to mediate the conflict in Northern Ireland, with notable lack of success. But it is probably a mistake to focus simply on the actions of formal religious institutions or groups. There may be a diffusion of religious values in a society that could have peace-prone consequences even in the absence of formal actions by church bodies. For example, some analysts have argued that the wide diffusion of Christian values played a mediating role in the process that ended the apartheid regime in South Africa, despite the fact that the churches themselves were mostly polarised between the two sides of the conflict (at least until the last few years of the regime, when the Dutch Reformed Church reversed its position on apartheid).

Relatedly, a religious resurgence may well have important implications for economic development. The basic text on the relation between religion and economic development is, of course, Max Weber's *The Protestant Ethic and the Spirit of Capitalism*. Scholars have been arguing over the thesis of this book for over ninety years. However one comes out on this (I happen to be an unreconstructed Weberian), it is clear that some values foster modern economic development more than others. Something like Weber's 'Protestant ethic' is probably functional in an early phase of capitalist growth – an ethic, whether religiously inspired or not, that values personal discipline, hard work, frugality, and a respect for learning.

The new Evangelicalism in Latin America exhibits these values in virtually crystalline purity. Conversely, Iberian Catholicism, as it was well established in Latin America, clearly does not foster such values. But religious traditions can change. Spain experienced a remarkably successful period of economic development beginning in the waning years of the Franco regime, and one of the important factors was the influence of Opus Dei,[1] which combined rigorous theological orthodoxy with market-friendly openness in economic matters. Islam, by and large, has difficulties with a modern market economy – especially with modern banking – yet Muslim emigrants have done remarkably well in a number of countries (for instance, in sub-Saharan Africa), and there is a powerful Islamic movement in Indonesia – the aforementioned Nahdatul-Ulama – that might yet play a role analogous to that of Opus Dei in the Catholic world. For years now, too, there has been an extended debate over the part played by Confucian-inspired values in the economic success stories of East Asia; if one is to credit the 'post-Confucian thesis' (and also allow that Confucianism is a religion), then here would be a very important religious contribution to economic development.

One morally troubling aspect of this matter is that values functional at one period of economic development may not be functional at another. The values of the 'Protestant ethic', or a functional equivalent thereof, are probably essential during the phase that Walt Rostow called 'the take-off'.[2] It is not at all clear that this is the case in a later phase. Much less austere values may be more functional in the so-called post-industrial economies of Europe, North America and East Asia. Frugality, however admirable from a moral viewpoint, may now actually be a vice, economically speaking. Undisciplined hedonists have a hard time climbing out of primitive poverty but, if they are bright enough, they can do very well in the high-tech, knowledge-driven economies of the advanced societies.

Finally, there is the effect of the religious resurgence on human rights and social justice world-wide. Religious institutions have, of course,

---

[1] The title of a Roman Catholic society, founded in 1928, to promote the exercise of Christian virtues by individuals in secular society. In some countries and at certain periods (e.g. Spain in the mid-twentieth century) it acquired a measure of political power. [Editor's note]

[2] Former adviser to President J.F. Kennedy (1931-63) and President Lyndon B. Johnson (1966-9). Professor of Economic and History at Texas University and author of many books, particularly relating to questions of economic growth, he is best known for his theory that societies pass through five stages of economic growth. [Editor's note]

made many statements on human rights and social justice. Some of these have had important political consequences, as in the civil rights struggle in the US or in the collapse of communist regimes in Europe. But, as has already been mentioned, there are different religiously articulated views about the nature of human rights. The same goes for ideas about social justice; what is justice to some groups is gross injustice to others. Sometimes it is very clear that positions taken by religious groups on such matters are based on a religious rationale, as with the principled opposition to abortion and contraception by the Roman Catholic Church. At other times, though, positions on social justice, even if legitimated by religious rhetoric, reflect the location of the religious functionaries in this or that network of non-religious social classes and interests. To stay with the same example, most of the positions taken by American Catholic institutions on social justice issues other than those relating to sexuality and reproduction fall into this category.

This mixed analysis is emblematic of what must be our general conclusion. Those who have great hopes for the role of religion in the affairs of this world and those who fear this role must both be disappointed by the factual evidence, which, in the final analysis, points in not just one but several directions simultaneously. In assessing this role, there is no alternative to a nuanced, case-by-case approach. But one statement can be made with great confidence: those who neglect religion in their analyses of contemporary affairs do so at great peril.

SECULARISM, IMMANENCE
AND DECONSTRUCTION

Abdelwahab Elmessiri

The definition of secularism as the separation of church and state has gained currency, becoming more or less the dominant paradigm in the literature dealing with this subject. It undoubtedly has the advantage of clarity and definiteness; it focuses our attention on, and sharpens our awareness of, the impact of secularising processes on the realms of the political and the economic, and on that area of our activity that takes place in what is now called 'public life'.

Its clarity and definiteness notwithstanding, this definition implies that secularism is not a total world-outlook, a *Weltanschauung*. Instead, the separation of church and state paradigm draws a sharp line of demarcation between the realm of the secular (and worldly or profane) on the one hand, and the realm of the religious (and otherworldly or sacred) on the other. It implies that processes of secularisation are explicit and quite identifiable, and that man's private life (his dreams and nightmares, his tastes, his aesthetic sensibility, etc.) can be hermetically sealed off and left free from secularising processes. It also implies that many aspects of public life are left for the citizens to decide upon. The human individual, in a world of an all-pervasive mass media and iron-fisted ferocious bureaucracies and multinationals, can nevertheless, according to this paradigm, maintain his integrity and protect his autonomy, living in the church of his choice, leaving the state to Caesar and his soldiers and technocrats, and the workplace to the corporations. The rest is at best sweetness and light and free choice, and at worst, neutrality, indifference and mere process.

One glance at life in the modern West demonstrates the weak explanatory power of this paradigm. Secularism is no longer a mere set of ideas that one can accept or reject at will, it is a world-outlook that is embedded in the simplest and most innocuous cultural commodities, and that forms the unconscious basis and implicit frame of reference for our conduct in public and in private. The state, far from operating exclusively in a few aspects of public life, has actually dominated most, and at times all of them, and has even penetrated to the farthest and deepest concerns of our private lives. Even though the nation-state has been weakened by the process of globalisation, it has been replaced by the equally ferocious multinational corporations and pleasure industries (movie and fashion industries, entertainment magazines, talk shows, tourism, night clubs, commercials, etc.) which have infiltrated our dreams, have shaped our images of ourselves, and have controlled the very direction of our libidos. Dreaming is no longer a spontaneous or private activity, for it is now controlled and engineered by a hundred different institutions that employ full-time 'experts' in human nature and 'specialists' in man's motivations and drives who exercise so much influence over our lives, and whose minds are not contaminated by any sense of absolute moral or human values. Their ultimate commitment is to the maximisation of pleasure and profit, to buying at the cheapest price and selling at the dearest, and to serving the interests not of the community or even the polity, but rather that of the corporation they happen to belong to. They reshape our lives through a complex process that ostensibly begins with the attempt to discover empirically what are man's 'real' desires and drives, yet actually ends up dictating to us what we should and should not desire, defining our dreams and visions, packaging them, flashing them endlessly on TV screens, videos and supermarkets, till we, or at least our children, internalise them, and act according to them.

To describe this process, and similar processes, that disseminate a definite world-outlook and an attendant set of values and norms, innumerable terms are used (see below). But the very diversity of the terms and their apparent unrelatedness suggest a certain absence, which in turn implies the need for a paradigm that would synthesise all these terms, showing their ultimate relatedness (for they all refer to different aspects of the same phenomenon).

This paper will argue that the term 'secular', if defined in a complex way, would have a high explanatory power, and would reveal the underlying overall unity between the terms used to describe modernity. The current paradigm of secularism as separation of church and state should be replaced by a more complex paradigm that sees secularism as a comprehensive world-outlook that operates on all levels of reality through a large number of implicit and explicit mechanisms. Accordingly, secularism is seen as the underlying and over-arching paradigm in modern Western civilisation, and for that matter all modernities.

This argument is not entirely new, but is implicit in the works of many authors. Max Weber, for one, assumes some kind of relatedness, if not synonymity at times, between terms such as 'secularise', 'modernise', 'rationalise', 'de-sanctify', and 'disenchantment'. In other words, he, like many other sociologists, assumes the existence of some kind of a unified 'secular' world-outlook.

Samuel Huntington, in his essay *The Clash of Civilisations*,[1] quotes various statements (from the works of a number of authors) which imply a comprehensive and a complex paradigm of secularism. There is for

---

[1] Samuel P. Huntington, 'The Clash of Civilizations', *Foreign Affairs*, vol. 72, no. 3, Summer 1993, pp. 22-49.

instance George Weigel's statement about 'the un-secularisation of the world', Bernard Lewis's reference to 'our secular present', and Kemal Atatürk's attempt to build 'a modern, secular, Western nation-state'.

Fouad Ajami, in his response in *Foreign Affairs* to Huntington's essay, is only too aware of the comprehensiveness of the paradigm, lumping modernity and secularism together and thereby assuming their synonymity.[2] The statement by Naipaul[3] (also quoted by Huntington), that modern secular Western civilisation is the 'universal civilisation that fits all men', is of course somewhat comic, but what matters from the standpoint of this paper is the implicit view that secularism is not merely a separation of church and state; it is a total world-outlook.

The clash of civilisation's debate is clearly taking place within the framework of a comprehensive and complex paradigm of secularism. However, Huntington himself falters in the middle of his essay, speaking of 'Western ideas of individualism, liberalism, constitutionalism, human rights, equality, liberty, the rule of law, democracy, free markets, the separation of church and state'. In other words, after using the term 'secularism' to refer to a world-outlook, his discourse fragments into a mere catalogue of terms – 'secularism' being just one among many – confined to the level of the political and economic.

One can argue that a similar situation obtains in the social and human sciences in the West, namely, an implicit view of secularism as a total world-outlook, and an explicit, more dominant, view of secularism as the separation of church and state. The same view, or variations thereon, has been espoused by social scientists in the rest of the world. Consequently, a unified complex paradigm of secularism has not been developed, sharpened, focused, and enriched through repeated application and testing. Instead, different aspects and phases, and various phenomena of modern life, have been described, one at a time, generating a plethora of independent terms. Some unity is sensed, for, as indicated earlier, all terms are used to refer to the same social and cultural configuration, but nevertheless, each term remains encapsulated in the specific phenomenon it describes, and is never integrated into a higher paradigm that would encompass all the apparently discrete phenomena and unrelated terms. Some of these terms are positive (growth, rationalism, progress,

---

[2] Fouad Ajami, 'The Summoning', *Foreign Affairs*, September/October, 1993.

[3] Sir V.S. Naipaul, Trinidadian novelist born in Chaguanas in 1932. He was educated at Queen's Royal College, Port of Spain, then left the Caribbean for England in 1950 to study at Oxford. He has been criticised for his orientalist views on Islam. For instance, in two of Naipaul's novels: *Guerrillas* and *A Bend in the River* (1979), Islam is 'made to cover everything that one most disapproves of from the standpoint of civilised, and Western, rationality.' See Edward Said, *Covering Islam*, London: Routledge & Kegan Paul, 1981, p. 7. Naipaul's famous works include: *An Area of Darkness: An Experience of India* (1964), *Among the Believers: An Islamic Journey* (1981), *Finding the Centre* (1984), *The Enigma of Arrival* (1987) and *A Way in the World* (1994). [Editor's note]

mobility, conquest of nature, knowledge of the law of necessity, etc.) and some are more or less neutral (value-free outlook, objectivity, modernisation, imperatives of the free market, convergence, end of history, etc.). However, many are quite negative (the price of progress, quantification, mechanisation, standardisation, instrumental value, free rationalisation, alienation, the domination of utilitarian values, anomie, the Americanisation of the world, Cocacola-isation, commodification, reification, fetishism, consumerism, instantaneous gratification, disenchantment of the world, etc.).

The history of secularism is fragmented in the same fashion, for it was monitored by the Western social sciences in a piecemeal diachronic fashion: first humanism and/or the Reformation, the Enlightenment, rationalism, and utilitarianism; then the counter-Enlightenment, Romanticism, and Darwinism; then positivism, existentialism, phenomenology; and finally came the end of history and post-modernism. Racism, imperialism and Nazism were all seen as mere aberrations, having a history of their own, distinct from the history of secularism and modernity. The history of Western philosophy assumes a certain autonomy and it too is dissolved into schools and phases and is seen as an endless oscillation between subject and object. The overall unity is merely glimpsed but hardly ever fully articulated into a comprehensive paradigm. Had we developed a unified and complex paradigm of secularism, we would probably have seen some kind of a relationship between the Enlightenment and deconstruction; between modernisation, modernism, and post-modernism; between Nietzscheanism and Hitler, pragmatism and Eichmann; between rationalism, imperialism, and the Holocaust.

To account for the fact that such a complex and more explanatory paradigm of secularism (that would integrate the various terms, historical phases, different aspects, etc.) has not been fully articulated, then given the centrality it deserves, some of the following reasons may be given:

1. The humanist illusion of the possibility of asserting the primacy of the human over the natural within a materialistic frame of reference seemed too real. Western man operated in terms of two outlooks: man-centred and nature-centred (see below). Rather than see the unity of the overarching paradigm, he saw a duality that fed the hope of a heroic humanist materialism and transcendence.

2. The division persisted in another form, namely, the capitalist/socialist dichotomy where the revolutionary forces of humanism raised the banner of socialism with man as a self-transcending secular absolute inscribed on it.

3. As indicated earlier, secularism as a phenomenon was emerging as it was being monitored and described by Western man. He saw one aspect then another, and therefore he named one aspect after the other. The phenomenon never stood in its wholeness in front of him and the

totality was never clear to him, for the paradigmatic sequence was still unfolding. The perception of the phenomenon of secularism was diachronic, and so was the process of naming. The piecemeal terminology was not integrated into one unified paradigm.

4. Moreover, Western social science itself was being gradually secularised, till it more or less completely assimilated many, if not all, of the 'metaphysical' or *a priori* tenets of secularism such as the belief in progress and in the autonomy of man and nature. The disappearance of the concept of human nature as an ultimate point of reference in the human sciences is a dramatic manifestation of the level of their secularisation.

5. A decisive factor that contributed to the failure of Western man to develop a comprehensive paradigm of secularism is the fact that Christianity persisted, even after having been separated from the state. It provided Western secular man with the ethics and metaphysics necessary to run his personal life, and even some aspects of his social or public life. Thus the Hobbesian problem of a society based on mere self interest and rational calculation was avoided, where man is merely and exclusively a wolf to his brother man, where all human relationships are contractual, and where the state stands guard against warring tribes and individuals. Christianity provided Western man with a conscience and a purpose and a basis for a moral outlook.

Actually, it could be said that secular humanism appropriated for itself some of the non-material categories of Christianity, superficially secularised them, then added them to its materialist system, even though they have no basis in its metaphysics of immanence. This is quite clear in Marxist writings, which are littered with expressions and terms such as 'human essence', 'alienation', and even 'transcendence'. Nor is the liberal version of humanism free from this quasi-religious jargon. The concept of the dignity of man is a case in point; it is a religious creed or idea that makes a good deal of sense within a religious context, but makes very little sense in a naturalistic one, for if there is no God, then man's dignity, self-begotten and self-bestowed as it is, has a very shaky foundation. Secular humanism, as illustrated later, revolves around the concept of natural man, and natural man is reducible to natural matter, thus any talk of dignity has no basis in this natural reality that levels everything. Once stripped of its metaphysical underpinnings, the dignity of man becomes unreal, and to fight for it would be indeed a loveless task. Be that as it may, some secularised Christian symbols and values did persist and slow down the realisation of the secular paradigmatic sequence.

6. The secular myth of a public life controlled by a state (separate from the church), and a private life that represents the realm of freedom for the individual, was largely true till very recently, not because the secular state refrained from invading the individual's privacy, as might be assumed by

some, but on account of various reasons that pertain to the world of state, society, and individual conscience:

i) The secular (central national state) in its early stages of development was not yet all that powerful, and had not yet developed its modern 'security' systems of political control and social engineering.

ii) The pleasure industries and the media, till very recently, were not completely free from morality, had not yet been fully integrated in the free market economy, and had not yet assumed the independence they currently have, nor the sheer power they presently wield.

iii) On the individual level, Christianity, as indicated earlier, persisted in the conscience and consciousness of Western man for much longer than was expected or hoped for, thereby making him more immune and less vulnerable to the onslaughts of the state and the pleasure industries. Western man lived in a largely secularised society, but still dreamt, loved, got married and died in a Christian or a quasi-Christian way.

But all of this has changed considerably. The realm of private life has been gradually eroded over the years by the increasing power of the state and the pleasure industries and the diminishing power of Christian norms and ideals. The humanist illusion of self transcendence and of an ethics without a metaphysics, or an ethics based on a metaphysics of immanence, has been dealt an almost deadly blow by two world wars, environmental disasters, the increase of some negative social phenomena (crime, suicide, pornography, teenage pregnancy, etc.), and our increasing realisation of the impossibility of imperialist control of ourselves or our environment. The socialist illusion lies dead in the ashes of the Soviet Union and its obituary is writ large by the syndicates of organised crime that control many Russian cities. The convergence of socialist and capitalist societies, predicted by 'bourgeois' social scientists, was achieved long before the final disintegration of the socialist camp. The talk of a phoenix-like return of socialism is merely the hope of old-line socialists who need something to clutch at for the rest of their individual lives. As for the secularised categories of Christianity, and the remnants of Christian belief, I argue elsewhere (see my forthcoming study *Comprehensive Secularism: A New and Alternative Paradigm*),[4] that the 1960s marked a decisive point in the history of secularisation, for it was then that secularisation moved on from the realm of general ideas (philosophy) and general dreams and desires (literature and art) to the realm of private fantasies and personal conduct. Public and private life started almost to correspond, and the one-dimensional (natural, rationalised) man became a dominant reality. The ravages of secularism are now evident and its total reality is clearer than ever. It is time to modify our paradigm to make it more comprehensive and complex.

---

[4] To be published by Dar al-Shuruq in Cairo. Expected early 2001. [Editor's note].

In the second part of this paper, an attempt is made to outline some
of the basic and salient characteristics of secularism. I begin off by defining the basic terms I use in this paper such as 'immanence' as opposed
to 'transcendence', 'the nature-matter paradigm', 'duality' as opposed
to 'dualism' and 'monism'. Then I shall try to describe the differences
between two varieties of secularism, partial and comprehensive. I shall
argue that the first can coexist with moral, human and even religious
values, whereas the second is a form of immanentisation that leads to
the dominance of the nature-matter paradigm and the subversion of the
category of man. Western modernity is based on a metaphysics of immanence, and therefore it is almost synonymous with comprehensive
secularism. The last part of the paper tries to establish how immanentisation (modernisation – comprehensive secularisation) leads to the total
deconstruction of man and of his cultural achievements.

Immanence and transcendence

Philosophical outlooks are usually divided into the 'idealistic' or
'materialistic'. I prefer to classify them, for the purposes of this paper,
as 'transcendent' and 'immanent' or 'pantheist'. 'Immanence' derives from
the Latin verb *immanere* which means 'to dwell'. 'Immanent' means 'indwelling', 'inherent', 'operating from within'. Therefore, anything that
is said to be self-contained, self-operating, self-activating, and self-
explanatory could be described as 'immanent', since its laws are inherent
to it and its operating force is internal. The world of immanence, therefore, is a highly unified organic world, with no space separating one of
its constituent parts from the others. It is a monistic universe, with no
dualities or complexities, for everything in it can be reduced to (or
explained in terms of) the activity of one element, an operating force
or an organising principle.

The terms 'immanence' and 'pantheism' are almost synonymous, for
the difference between them is not fundamental; it is actually confined to
the way the organising principle in the universe is named. We can talk
of 'spiritual' pantheism and 'materialistic' immanence. In the case of
pantheism, the organising principle is named 'God' or 'Spirit'. Ancient
paganisms are a good case in point. God, man (the nation – the chosen
people) and nature (the motherland) form an organic unity with the national God (the organising principle) as the ultimate point of reference,
even though He has no existence separate from man and nature. In the
case of immanence, the same organic unity obtains, but the organising
principle is named 'nature', 'natural laws', 'laws of necessity' or any
element latent in matter.

There are many ways in our modern discourse to express an immanentistic outlook. When we say that 'the world (man and nature) is subject to

the laws of nature, immanent in matter', that 'man's existence is determined not by anything beyond this world, but rather by his physical or
social environment', that 'man is defined in terms of production (Adam
Smith and Marx) and/or reproduction (Freud)' that 'blood and soil
determine natural characteristics and destiny', that 'history is subject
to certain laws immanent in matter', that 'science is value-free, deriving
its values from the laws of matter', etc., we are assuming, consciously or
unconsciously, a highly organic, unified, self-sufficient, self-referential,
self-explanatory, self-activating monistic universe, with the material
element as the ultimate point of reference.

There is an intermediate or rather indeterminate stage between the two,
where the organising principle assumes at once a quasi-spiritual and quasi-
material form and name. It is then called *Geist, animus mundi, élan vital,*
'Absolute Mind', 'Absolute Idea', and a highly romanticised 'Nature'
that is supposed to be suffused with the spirit of God. It also passes under
names such as 'spirit of history', 'laws of history', *eros*, or *eros* and *thanatos*.[5]
But the main trait of the organising principle, no matter what name or
form it assumes, is that it liquidates all dualities and that everything is
reduced to it, producing a tight organic unity, a complete monism.

Despite their near synonymity, I prefer to use the term 'pantheism'
when the organising principle dwelling in man and/or nature assumes
the name of God, or any variations thereon, since it contains the suffix
'theism' from *theos*, meaning 'God'. I use the term 'immanence' when
the organising principle assumes a materialist or a quasi-spiritual
name. It is this last variety that interests me most in this paper.

Immanence is a comprehensive, coherent and consistent account of
reality (God, man and nature) as a whole. It represents a view of the
underlying, self-sufficient principle of the existence of all things, the non-
dependent and fully self-determining being, upon which all things depend
for their existence. That is why we talk of a 'metaphysics of immanence'.

'Immanence' is always opposed to 'transcendence', which is derived
from the Latin verb *transcendere* (*trans* means 'across' and 'beyond';
scandere means 'to climb'). Transcendence is going beyond what is given
to our ordinary experience and beyond that which falls within the grasp
of scientific explanation. In other words, transcendence (unlike immanence) always implies a duality, that which is given to the senses, as well
as that which is beyond them.

Even though the immanence/transcendence antithesis is of universal
validity, cutting across many cultures and religious systems, I will first
use some terms from the Islamic lexicon to explore and further clarify
this antithesis, since it is crucial for the argument of this paper.

---

[5] *Eros*, in Greek mythology, is the god of love, whom the Romans called Cupid. *Thanatos*, also in Greek mythology, is death and the personification of death, the offspring
of *Nyx*, night and the Goddess of night, called *Nox* by the Romans. [Editor's note].

According to the Islamic *tawhidi* monotheistic paradigm, the one absolute, indivisible, transcendent God, after having created the world (both man and nature) *ex nihilo*, did not dwell in either of them, nor did He abandon them completely. God cares for the world but maintains a distance from it, a space that separates creator from created. This has resulted in a basic God-man duality, not dualism. In dualism, there are two principles (forces, gods, demons, etc.) that are of equal status and power, yet diametrically opposed to each other. There can never be any interaction between them. They are indeed locked in an eternal struggle (like the Gods of darkness and of light in some ancient paganisms). It is worth noting that one element in the dualism eventually triumphs, absorbing the other, thereby dissolving dualism into a monism.

The God-man duality of the *tawhidi* monotheistic outlook is echoed in many other dualities (man-nature, body-soul, male-female, etc.). These dualities never become dualisms because of the presence of a higher category (God), and because one element in the duality is not completely equal to or identical with, the other element. The space separating the one transcendent God from His creatures (man and nature) might set limits to man's will and freedom, placing moral burdens on him, but it is these very limits that create a human space, where man has the freedom to fulfil or abort his human essence and potential. Through the limits imposed on him by this space, man passes from the simple monistic state of nature to the complex state of culture; from simple innocence, that knows not good or evil, to complex experience that recognises their existence; from a world of material surfaces devoid of value, meaning and sanctity, to a world suffused with meaning, significance and sanctity; from a pure monist 'spirituality' that has no material substance, or a pure monistic 'materiality' that has no spiritual dimensions, to a world that has both material reality and spiritual dimensions; from being an organic part of a larger whole to being an integral, yet autonomous, part of a larger whole; and finally, from a world that oscillates in a dualistic fashion between limitlessness and complete determinism, to a world of boundaries and limits yet with possibilities of moral action and freedom.

Beside terms describing transcendental monotheism, the Islamic lexicon contains a number of terms which describe different aspects or stages of the immanentistic/pantheistic outlook. I will single out the following because of their particular relevance to this paper: *wahdat al-wujud* (literally 'unity of being'), *hulul* (literally, 'indwelling'; can also be translated as 'union') and *fanaa* (literally 'annihilation'). I argue that whereas *hulul* is a process, a gradual unfolding of a sequence, *wahdat al-wujud* is the final point and moment where the sequence reaches its complete realisation. The outcome in so far as man is concerned, is *fanaa*, the complete absorption of the human into the divine, resulting in the former's annihilation.

The transcendent creator is perceived in Islam as being very near (*qarib*) to his creations (man and nature), but does not merge with them. In the Arab Muslim folk tradition, children are referred to as *ahbabullah* ('the beloved of God'). This means that they are very 'near' to God, which implies a touch of immanence, but nevertheless, there are two substances or essences in the world. An unbridgeable, though at times very narrow, space exists between creator and created. The space could be so narrow that God is described in the Quran as 'nearer to man than [his] jugular vein' (Sura Quaf, 16). But no matter how narrow, the space is always there, for 'there is nothing like Him' (Sura Shura, 11). (The space could actually widen, turning into a gap, even an abyss, if man, by forgetting God distances himself from Him.) Even the Prophet Muhammad (peace be upon him) is kept at a distance, in the very moment of divine revelation, when the *logos* is communicated to him. The Quran tells us that 'he approached and came closer, and was at a distance of but two bow-lengths or [even] nearer. So did Allah convey the inspiration to his Servant, conveyed what He [meant] to convey' (Sura An-Najm, 8-10).

The Prophet's relation to God is definitely not *wahdat wujud*. We can call it *taquarrub*, getting closer to God. This kind of nearness can be readily accommodated within the frame of reference of transcendental monotheism. Most strains of Islamic mysticism belong to this kind of *taquarrub*; hence the insistence on the distinction between the divine and the human in Sufi poetry, and the continuous assertion that the talk of 'union', when and if it occurs, is simply figurative

The same painstaking attempt to assert the independence of the divine from the human manifests itself in the distinction between *wahdat al-wujud* and *wahdat al-shuhud* (literally, 'unity of witnessing', namely 'unity of consciousness'). *Wahdat al-shuhud* puts awareness in the place of existence. The moment of *wahdat al-shuhud* is not an ontological union with God, it is rather a psychological or an epistemological condition, a heightened awareness of a unity that encompasses man and the world, with God as the unifying principle who dwells in nature and beyond it.

Yet, in some extreme Sufi trends, the level of *hulul* (of the divine in the temporal) increases, and God, instead of getting nearer to His creations, literally dwells (*immanenre*) in them and is completely identified with them. They, in turn, dissolve completely in Him. This is the final moment of the unity of being, *wahdat al-wujud* resulting in *fanaa* annihilation. God becomes one with the universe, completely immanent in it, no space separating Him from His creations. He is incarnate in one element (man), and/or in another (nature), which creates an initial dualism. But then the dualism is liquidated, for God runs through all creations, suffusing them with the same sanctity and to an equal degree, thereby equalising the sacred with the profane, the holy and timeless with the unholy and temporal, the high with the low, good with evil, the relative with the absolute, everything with everything else, and eventually everything with *nihil* (nothing). Man is levelled down, becoming part of a larger entity, completely lost in it, with no space separating him from other creations. The universe becomes one organic whole, one essence, self-sufficient, self-activating, and self-explanatory. All phenomena, human or non-human, no matter how varied, are reduced, in the last analysis, to the one principle immanent in the world. This is the state of complete monism where all complexities are liquidated, where will, conscience and the possibility of transcendence are denied. In other words, we have moved from the complex world of dualities (God-man, man-nature, etc.) to the less complex world of dualism, only to land eventually in the organic simple world of monism, where the whole world can be reduced to (or experienced in terms of) one single principle.

To further clarify my point I shall use more general terminology. I compare the state of immanence to what I call 'the embryonic state' (as opposed to the state of full human complexity which implies both duality and the possibility of transcendence). In his pre-natal days, the human being exists as an embryo in the womb, literally an organic part of it, having no physical or emotional existence separate from his mother. He depends on her entirely for his sustenance and survival, and lives *in* the womb and *on* it (a state of *wahdat wujud* and *fanaa*). Something akin to this pre-natal condition continues for a few months after birth, when the human infant depends completely on his mother's breast for his physical and emotional sustenance and survival. When hungry, he is immediately gratified, with no space separating him from the womb or the breast. The embryonic state is organic in the literal sense of the word, where all constituent parts (embryo and womb) form one closely knit whole, an organic monism.

Even though what I have just described is a psycho-biological fact, it could also be used as a metaphor of human growth and maturity. Many people fail to grow up, staying psychologically in this embryonic state (or a variation thereon). They go on thinking that the world is an extension of their ego, existing merely to fulfil their desires and answer their demands. Man deems himself self-sufficient and self-referential, a veritable solipsist with no limits or boundaries separating him from the world of nature and things. Such a solipsist lives in a monist world with his ego as the organising principle, the centre of immanence. Given this solipsist frame of reference, given this Faustian imperialist state of mind, man develops an urge to expand and engulf the whole world. This generates an initial man versus nature dualism.

The embryonic state is made up of two ostensibly diametrically opposed aspects, which I call 'stages'. I have just described the first stage of embryonicity with its imperialist Faustian solipsism, and man versus nature dualism. But the dualism proves to be more apparent than real. For when there is no space separating man from his surroundings, he becomes part of something larger than himself, thereby losing his identity, separate selfhood, consciousness, and sense of responsibility. If he is part of nature, he loses his ability to transcend his natural (material) surroundings, because he is 'nothing but' a part of a whole. His human essence dissolves, merging into the natural material world. The imperialist solipsist gets completely reified and objectified, and he who claimed to be a self-referential, autonomous, absolute and irreducible category, is reduced to the world of nature and matter. Ostensible dualism gives way to latent real monism.

In the fully human state, on the other hand, there is a space that separates man from larger entities (the womb – nature – God – the world of things, etc.). So man is limited, but through these very limits, he gains freedom, dignity, identity, separate selfhood, irreducible complexity, consciousness and the ability to choose and transcend. He is never lost in non-human (sacred or profane) entities larger than himself, remaining an autonomous, irreducible, ultimate category.

The space that separates man from nature or God creates a human space and generates dualities. The organic cannot be the mode, for the organic admits no gaps or discontinuities or *tadafu'* (interplay, gentle conflict). The fully human state is a complex state of spirit and matter, and of soul and body, and of culture and nature. Even though man is part of nature, he is not reduced to it, for he is capable of growing up, of transcending, of reaching to a more complex world that lies behind the immediate world of the five senses and instantaneous gratification.

The nature-matter paradigm

Having argued that underlying the immanentistic pantheistic outlook (*wahdat al wujud* and the embryonic state) is a monist paradigm that denies transcendence and that ultimately results in *fanaa*, the annihilation of man as a distinct category in nature, let me apply my thesis to one of the most central concepts in the Western philosophical tradition and a key idea in the philosophical discourse of modernity, namely, the concept of nature.

'Nature' has been variously defined as 'the essence of things' or 'the essential character of a thing'. The Greeks saw it as the world unmodified by man. Medieval Christianity saw nature as 'the world freshly created by God' and, as far as man was concerned, it meant 'man before the fall'. The concept of nature vacillated between the idea of 'physical nature' and 'human nature', and some philosophers even spoke of universal truth as truth rooted in human nature. One can go on listing other meanings (Lovejoy, in his celebrated essays, lists 66).[6] I will confine myself

---

[6] A.O. Lovejoy, 'Nature as Static Norm', *Essays in the History of Ideas*, Baltimore: John Hopkins University Press, 1948.

in this study to one meaning only, namely, nature as 'the general cosmic order'.

A religious outlook views this order as divinely ordained, which means that behind natural law, immanent in matter, there is a higher order, that transcends the world of matter and that bestows meaning on it and provides it with purpose. Man, God's vice-gerent, exists in the world of nature, yet is different from it, for he is aware of the higher order, and can transcend nature and his natural self. In the context of this man-nature duality, it is man, distinguished by his awareness and his reason, who has primacy; he is indeed the centre of the universe.

In the philosophical discourse of modernity, nature as a cosmic order is defined differently. The following are some of its most important traits from a secular standpoint.

1. Nature is eternal, self-existent, self-contained, self-dependent and self-sufficient. It is also self-activating, self-regulating, self-operating, self-directing and even self-transforming. Finally it is self-referential and therefore self-explanatory. (It arrogates for itself all the traits that traditional theology attributes to God.)

2. The laws of nature are immanent in matter; and nature, the totality of objects, events and processes that exist in space and time, is the only level of reality with nothing beyond it. It is a whole that subsumes everything, and that allows no gaps or spaces, discontinuities, specificities, dualities, hierarchies, ultimate purpose, irreducible entities, or even totalities. In other words, the system of nature is monist.

3. The system of nature, being independent of any transcendent entity, is determined only by its own character and is reducible to a set of causal, immutable, uniform laws, immanent in it. Those laws cannot be interfered with, violated, suspended, or intruded upon. They determine and explain everything and nothing determines or explains them. This means that nothing can transcend natural laws, or free itself from them. It also means that 'nature' is the ultimate and final irreducible category that cannot be transcended by, or reduced to, something more fundamental than itself.

4. Even though the basis of all natural phenomena is (solid) matter and (fluid) energy, nature is never fixed; it is a continuous flux that keeps on evolving higher and more complex forms of life and intelligence. But no matter how high or complex, they are all reducible, in the last analysis, to nature.

5. Natural processes are indifferent to the parts (including man). All parts, *qua* parts, from the standpoint of nature, are of equal value and significance because nature knows of no values or significance. Therefore material laws, indifferent to specificities and hierarchies, apply indiscriminately to all phenomena, physical or human.

The universe of the nature paradigm, as defined by Western modernity, is reductive and monist, for all dualities are liquidated and transcendence denied. In other words, it has all the traits of immanentistic paradigms.

What about the fate of man in this universe? We will notice the pattern, detected earlier in immanentistic paradigms, namely, an initial apparent dualism (man versus nature) to be followed by a tight (naturalist) monism.

1. Man is first seen within the framework of the modern concept of nature and of the cosmic order, as a free, limitless element, partaking of all the essential traits of nature, yet capable of conquering and engulfing it.

2. But man, with no gap or space separating him from nature, or its laws immanent in matter, is merely an organic part of nature, having no control over it. He is an ordinary, even incidental, natural material, event, attributable in *all* aspects to the ordinary operations and processes of nature. When he engulfs nature, he actually merges with, and is reduced to, it.

3. Man's knowledge is limited to natural events and the relations holding between them. Material reality is all there is; and man's mind has no causal efficacy, nor is it necessary for the functioning of nature.

4. Human behaviour may be more complex than that of other animals, but in the final analysis, it can be explained in terms of, and seen as related to, theirs. Man in other words can be fully explained in terms of nature and natural laws, and can be reduced to them.

5. Man's ethical values, compulsions, activities, and restraints can be justified on natural grounds, his highest good pursued and attained under natural conditions and determined by natural law.

The laws of nature, immanent in matter, are both neutral and immutable and contain all the cognitive and moral systems that man needs. Hence there is no room for choice and moral discrimination. Man loses his specific boundaries as an autonomous, morally responsible agent capable of transcending his immediate natural Self. In other words, man who is initially seen as a free, limitless agent, controlling and dominating nature, becomes merely an organic part of it, subject to its laws. Any initial dualism of man and nature, dissolves into a 'naturalistic monism', referred to in the modern Western lexicon as simply 'naturalism'.

Naturalism is a reductive philosophical outlook that has been defined in different ways. Nevertheless, most definitions agree that there is some kind of close relationship, if not synonymity and identity, between naturalism and materialism. Naturalism has been variously defined as 'the dependence of social, and more general human, life upon nature, i.e. materialism' – 'the belief that the universe (nature) is the only reality' – 'a species of philosophical monism according to which whatever exists or happens is natural [......] in the sense of being susceptible to scientific explanation.' Naturalism, like materialism, is the application of the nature paradigm, as defined above, to the whole being of man.

Therefore, I argue that rather than use the term 'nature', we should use a compound word, 'nature-matter', and talk of 'the nature-matter paradigm'. In this way we might decode many of the apparent mysteries and contradictions of the philosophical discourse of modernity and secularism. Rather than 'natural man' we should speak of a 'natural-material man', determined by the laws of nature, *ergo* laws of natural-matter; his being is intimately bound up with natural processes, *ergo* natural-material processes, and all his attributes are natural, *ergo*, natural-material attributes. In this way, we can place natural man (a central concept in the humanities in the West) in his proper philosophical context, and can better understand his epistemological and axiological systems. Man in the state of nature exists exclusively in nature, totally reduced to it and to the laws immanent in it, shorn of his autonomy, complexity, and of the power of transcendence and moral discrimination, with no distinct status in the cosmic order.

The reductive monist nature-matter paradigm as defined above is not a modern invention. The pre-Socratic philosophers believed that the basic stuff of nature is sufficiently active and refined to account for all its phenomena, including consciousness. The followers of Diogenes of Sinope,[7] the Cynics, were believers in the nature-matter paradigm, which meant abandoning everything that human intelligence had invented or discovered. Houses, clothing, cooked foods, social organisation were not natural, and hence Diogenes lived in a wine jar, wrapped a single strip of cloth around his body in lieu of fur, feathers, or scales, lapped up water like a dog, and withdrew from all social duties. In other words, he led a truly embryonic natural life, at once completely free and completely determined. Materialist or naturalist monism has always been an important and philosophical trend since the time of Adam. But it remained marginal, for all societies revolved around some kind of belief in a *logos* and *telos* that have some existence beyond the flux of nature and the movement of atoms. Social and ethical norms were based on this belief.[8]

---

[7] Greek Cynic philosopher and moralist (c.412-c.323 BC). Born in Sinope, Pontus, Asia Minor, he moved to Athens as a young man and became a student of Antisthenes, with whom he founded the Cynic sect, preaching an austere asceticism and self-sufficiency. Legendary for his unconventional behaviour and ostentatious disregard for domestic comforts, he was said to have lived in a tub 'like a dog' (Greek *kyon*), the origin of the term 'Cynic'. When Alexander the Great visited him and asked what he could do for him he answered, 'you could move away out of the Sun and not cast a shadow on me'. According to another story he would wander around Athens by day with a lamp 'looking for an honest man'. Later he was captured by pirates while on a sea voyage and was sold as a slave to Xeniades of Corinth. He was soon freed, was appointed tutor to Xeniades' children and remained in Corinth for the rest of his life. [Editor's note].

[8] *Logos* from the Greek, of great breadth of meaning, primarily signifying in the context of philosophical discussion the rational, intelligible principle, structure, or order which

Things changed in the West with the rise of Western modernity. The nature-matter paradigm left the periphery and started gaining currency. For the first time in history, a cultural formation based on the nature-matter paradigm came into being; human society and man himself are perceived as operating exclusively in terms of the laws of nature-matter (called 'natural laws', 'laws of motion', 'laws of necessity', 'laws of objective reality', etc.). So society was seen, at least on the paradigmatic level, as made up, on the one hand, of completely free autonomous individuals (natural men), but on the other, it was seen as completely controlled by self-generating, self-activating, and value-free processes governed by immutable natural laws, immanent in matter.

Secularism, partial and comprehensive

There is a general agreement that modern culture is nothing if not secular. However, as indicated earlier, the current definition of secularism as the separation of church and state is weak from a heuristic point of view. To clarify the term, I wish to distinguish between what I call 'partial secularism' and 'comprehensive secularism'. Partial secularism is just that; it is a view of the world that does not claim any comprehensiveness, confining itself to the realms of politics and perhaps economics. This view of secularism is implicit in the familiar definition of secularism as 'the separation of church and state'. 'Church' means organised religion with its clergy and official hierarchy. The definition maintains complete silence regarding absolute or permanent values (moral, religious, or otherwise) and does not address itself to ultimate things, such as the origin of man, his destiny, the purpose of life, etc. The 'state' mentioned in the definition refers mainly to the state apparatus, and to politics in an immediate and narrow sense of the word. It probably refers to economic activity and some aspects of public life, but it leaves out the whole of man's private life and many aspects of public life. The term 'state' does not in any way pretend to cover man's private joys and sorrows, his moral and philosophical outlooks, his conscience, the ultimate questions in his life, etc. In other words, partial secularism never reaches the deeper and more fundamental aspects of man's life, and does not pretend to answer any of the ultimate questions facing him.

When people use the term 'secular' they usually have in mind 'partial secularism'. This partial secularism can coexist with absolute moral values, and even with religious values, as long as they do not interfere with the political process in the narrow sense referred to above. Many religious thinkers, Christian and Muslim, are perfectly willing to coexist

---

pervades something, or the source of that order, or giving an account of that order. *Telos* is another Greek word meaning the end or purpose, hence teleology, which is the study of the end, goal or purpose of something. [Editor's note].

and cooperate with this variety of secularism. Some would even welcome it, because it frees religion from the inevitable pragmatism and wheeling and dealing of the world of daily politics and economics.

Comprehensive secularism, on the other hand, is a completely different outlook. It aims not merely at the separation of church and state and some aspects of public life, but at the separation of all values (be they religious, moral, human) not only from 'the state', but also from public and private life, and from the world at large. In other words, it strives for the creation of a value-free world. If we probe a little deeper, however, we will discover that it operates in terms of the nature-matter paradigm; it is nothing but a variation on naturalistic materialistic monism, and the metaphysics of immanence.

Like most, or probably all, world outlooks, comprehensive secularism revolves around three elements: God, man, and nature. The attitude to God (is He transcendent or immanent; is He above nature and man and history or immanent in them?) is what defines the status of man in the universe and his relationship to nature-matter. But the secular attitude to God is neither clear nor simple. Comprehensive secularism might not be explicitly or consistently atheistic, as some people claim. More often than not, it is largely deistic, and therefore it circumvents the whole issue of theism, and rather than denying God's existence, it simply marginalises Him, for once marginalised, He ceases to interfere in the formulation of our epistemological, ethical, aesthetic, and signifying systems.

The process of marginalisation takes two extreme forms that seem to be diametrically opposed:

1. God as a Force is seen as too transcendent and distant from man and nature, completely indifferent to them.

2. God as a Force is seen as completely immanent in both man and nature (or in either), and therefore has no separate existence from them. In Spinoza's philosophy, the identification of God and nature is so complete that he talks of *deus sive natura* (God, namely nature). This is the God-nature of eighteenth-century materialists and nineteenth-century romanticists.

This sharp dualism (of extreme transcendence and extreme immanence) could be seen in the Western view of God since the Reformation: an inscrutable, implacable God whose ways cannot be fully understood by man, and whom no human deeds can placate, on the one hand, and on the other, a very comfortable (and accommodating) God who could become at times the 'inner voice' of the believer.

The common element between these two polar opposites is that they marginalise God in so far as our concrete and complex human lives are concerned. They both 'free' the world from the divine, the transcendent and the sacred and therefore from all dualities and complexities. A God too far removed from our lives becomes irrelevant, and man therefore can run his life without any reference to Him, for after all He is unreachable and inaccessible. If God descends and becomes man's inner voice, then man can also run his life without any reference to Him, for after all He is deeply and completely imbedded in man's heart, or mind, or any part of his anatomy he may deem fit.

The same applies to nature, a God too removed from nature and indifferent to it, or a God so close to nature as to be identical with it, means that nature is self-contained, self-dependent and self-explanatory.

Both forms of marginalisation are found in our secular outlook, but the more dominant form at the present time is the second, namely, gradual immanentisation of God till He loses all transcendence and becomes one with man and nature.

Having dealt with the secular view of God, we can now turn to the secular view of nature and man. Even though the category of man is hypothetically separate from the category of nature within the discourse of secularism, I argue that the separation is temporary, for the two categories, sooner or later, converge. Therefore they will be dealt with simultaneously. The pattern of an initial sharp dualism giving way to a thorough monism, which we have just outlined, could be detected in the secular attitude to man and nature. The materialist outlook, as indicated earlier, does not subscribe to the idea of a transcendental God or *logos*. The unifying principle of the universe is immanent in it, and the world, therefore, has within it what is necessary for its full understanding and utilisation. The human mind, within this materialist frame of reference, is so equipped that it could reach all the knowledge necessary for a full understanding of nature.

The materialist, immanentist outlook, on account of its immediacy, definiteness, clarity, and simplicity, has proved quite attractive. Both cause and effect are quite clear, and the mind can find security in tangible data. But this simplicity conceals a deep contradiction that all materialists, be they ancient Greek materialists or modern Western secularists, face, namely, how does the *logos*, the centre of the world, being immanent in it, manifest itself in the processes of nature, or in the mind of man? The materialist outlook, in other words, assumes initially the autonomy and centrality of both nature and the mind of man, which naturally gives rise to a sharp dualism and polarity, and a continuous (at times comic) oscillation between object and subject; for how can there be two centres of immanence to the same structure?

This dualism produces two diametrically opposed secular outlooks:
1. A man-centred (anthropocentric) outlook: Even though man exists in nature-matter, an organic part of it, he is basically a rational creature, whose mind is vested with certain innate powers of reasoning, abstraction, totalising,... etc. He can use his limitless mind (the *logos* and the centre of immanence) to reach objective and moral truth, without any

reference to any point external to it. In other words, the mind, being autonomous and self-referential, needs no divine inspiration from above, for all knowledge comes from below and from within. The knowledge that man reaches through his objective and detached observation of all phenomena, including himself, is all that he needs to know for a full understanding of himself and nature.

Man, being the organising principle in the universe, is the functional equivalent of God. He is self-sufficient and self-transforming. As Pico Della Mirandola put it: 'God has become man, so man can become God.'[9] God incarnate in Christ becomes God incarnate in man. Nevertheless, this man-centred universe has a measure of duality (or dualism), for on the one hand there is man, on the other there is nature. It is also a hierarchical universe, because of the presence of man in it, and because of his primacy over nature. He gives it meaning and purpose, he acts as its centre, and he is its ultimate point of reference. There is also a measure of freedom, permanence, and if not absoluteness, at least something that approximates it, namely the category of man as an irreducible entity in the midst of natural flux and as a creature capable, through his rising consciousness, of transcending both nature and his natural self. If everything in nature is desanctified and neutralised, man remains a self-sanctified, even self-deified, centre of the universe.

This is the man-centred universe of Renaissance humanism (and of all other non-religious secular humanisms) that assigns centrality to man in the universe, and asserts the primacy of the human over the natural. Despite its initial duality, this man-centred outlook soon becomes a sharp dualism, where man confronts nature with no mediation and therefore enters into conflict with it. The dualism turns into a subjectivist monism, a total solipsism, where the objective world is completely negated, and nothing remains but the Self. This gradually degenerates into an imperialist racist view of the world, where the Self which embodies the *logos*, negates others. We can actually talk here of an 'imperialistic monism'.

2. The nature-centred outlook: It is nature-matter, not man's mind, that manifests the *logos*, man being nothing but an organic part of the world of matter, completely reducible and subservient to it. Nature-matter, through its continuous flux and unceasing evolution, keeps on evolving higher and more complex forms of life and intelligence; in other words. it is the creative and unifying principle in the universe.

The whole world (nature and man) is subject to one and the same natural law. In this nature-centred universe, man is assigned no special status, for nature is neutral and indifferent. Therefore instead of hierarchy, distinctions and dualities, there dominates a complete materialistic monism

---

[9] Pico Della Mirandola was an Italian philosopher and humanist. (1463-94). His works include *Conclusiones* (1486), *De hominis dignitate oratio* (1486), *Heptaplus* (1490) and *De ente et uno* (1492). [Editor's note].

that levels all phenomena to their lowest common denominator, and nothing is left but the object, and abstract, faceless, general laws.

The nature-centred outlook could become more polished and sophisticated, and even more complex (as in the case of dialectical materialism), but in the last analysis, everything is subject to a ruthless monistic causality. In other words, we end up with a sharp dualism, not unlike the dualism of some ancient pagan pantheism. On the one hand, there is the human individual, a complete solipsist and imperialist, who is self-sufficient and self-transforming and self-explanatory, on the other, there is nature-matter which is also self-sufficient, self-transforming and self-explanatory. The autonomous subject is completely divorced from the autonomous object.

It could be argued that even though the monistic nature-centred outlook is indeed dominant, the man-centred outlook, and the humanist hope of transcendence through the sheer power of the mind, is inevitably there, providing a solid and irreducible basis for resisting monism and perhaps overcoming it, and for an endless dialectics without closure, without an end to history. A closer outlook however would demonstrate the fallacy of this hope, for there is neither a duality nor a dialectics, but rather the same pattern of an illusory dualism, dissolving into a total monism. Reality projects itself first as an oscillation between a man-centred and a nature-centred outlook, between extreme individualism and extreme collectivity, between solipsism and reification, between subject and object. Western humanism, which perceived the dualism as a mere duality, tried to resolve the oscillation between man and nature through two strategies, by placing man at the centre of the world, above nature, or by postulating that the categories of matter somehow correspond to the categories of the mind. Eventual reconciliation between mind and matter, subject and object, idea and nature could therefore be somehow achieved, because the general laws of nature are immanent, and to an equal degree, in both nature and man's mind.

Both strategies for reconciling man with nature, and subject with object, fail and end in naturalistic monism, for the Self, placed above nature or made parallel to it, is a natural material Self. In the equation of man and nature, man can deify himself, but he cannot create himself. Only nature is self-existent and self-begotten. It is she who created him in her own image, a natural material man, ruled by laws immanent in her.

The presumed quality of humanness that sets man apart from nature and bestows centrality on him, is also immanent in nature (for within a materialistic frame of reference, and within the context of a metaphysics of immanence, there is nothing outside the world of matter). In other words, the very basis for man's supremacy over nature and centrality within it, or even for his correspondence to it, is very weak, indeed illusory. For how can a natural being place himself above nature or parallel to it? Being natural, he is 'nothing but' a part of nature. When natural man is centred around his Self, he soon discovers that it is a natural Self, not different in any significant way from nature-matter. Man loses what distinguishes him as a separate category and entity, and therefore dissolves into nature, merging with it, eventually reduced in his entirety to nature-matter. Solipsist natural man, in trying to fulfil himself follows the laws of nature, immanent in matter, and, naturally, systematically deconstructs himself. Solipsism gives way to determinism. Complete subjectivity gives way to ruthless objectivity. In lieu of the complex, responsible, free and autonomous individual capable of transcending his material environment and his natural Self, and generating moral and aesthetic norms through his interaction with nature, there appears natural man who is subject to natural laws and to a variety of determinisms, and who is only capable of becoming part of nature, either embodying its laws (and be a superman and a Nietzschean) or slavishly submitting to them (and be a subman and a pragmatist). The noble Prometheus, the mythic hero of secularism, and Faustus, its tragic hero, are gradually replaced first by a mechanistic creation of Frankenstein ('the modern Prometheus', in Mary Shelley's words), then by an organicistic Dracula, who sucks his victims' blood and feeds them on his own.[10]

In ancient paganisms the god of good and light defeated the god of evil and darkness; in this modern dualism, the objective God of nature-matter defeats and eventually dominates a self-deified element that already exists within nature, namely man. The dualism of man and nature is thereby liquidated, and the reconciliation of opposites leads eventually to the primacy of the natural over the human and to the reification of man, and his total absorption in nature. And expectedly so, for to see man otherwise is to attribute to him powers of transcendence that would subvert the very epistemological basis of Western modernity and the metaphysics of immanence that denies transcendence.

The same materialistic monism could be seen in the presumed unity of all sciences. There is no law for man, another for nature; no law for the soul (or the Self), another for the body; no law for man's spiritual longings,

---

[10] Prometheus: In Greek mythology, a Titan, son of Iapetus and brother of Epimetheus; originally a trickster who outwits Zeus; his name means 'the foreseeing'. He made human beings out of clay, and taught them the arts of civilisation. He stole fire from heaven to help mankind, whom Zeus wished to destroy, and was punished by being chained to a rock in the Caucasus; every day an eagle fed on his liver, which grew again in the night. He knew a secret which concerned Zeus' future, and bargained for his release. Heracles, passing through the Caucasus, shot the eagle and set Prometheus free. Faustus, or Faust, is a legendary German scholar of the early 16th century (derived from the historical magician of that name), who sold his soul to the devil in exchange for knowledge, magical power, and prolonged youth. His story inspired Marlowe's *Dr Faustus* (1592), literary works by Lessing (1784), Goethe (1808, 1832) and Thomas Mann (1947), and musical works including Gounod's opera *Faust* (1859). [Editor's note].

another for his biological drives. There is but one method for the observation and study of all phenomena; for the difference between the human
and the natural within this monistic frame of reference is one of degree
not of kind; one of quantity, not of quality. There is one law obtaining for
all creations. This is the implicit assumption in the concept of the unity of
science, *wahdat al-ulum*. Originally the phrase referred to man's complex totality; since he is a unified whole, all the human sciences are one.
But now it refers to the obliteration of boundaries between man and nature and the human sciences and physical sciences, a form of a materialistic
unity of being, *wahdat al-wujud*, where the immanent laws of nature-
matter and value-free science are realised in the realm of man. Man in all
his complexity and rich diversity can be fully accounted for through that
which is non-human, namely, the general laws of nature and matter. He is
thereby deconstructed and reduced to chemical compounds and mathematical equations. The monism of *wahdat al ulum*, just like the monism
of *wahdat al wujud*, has led to the annihilation of man, *fanaa*.

The category of nature-matter could conceal itself under more subtle
categories ('secular absolutes') which duplicate in their very structure
the reductive monism of the category of nature-matter. The most common absolutes are the following: The nation-state, the market economy,
the profit motive, the principle of utility, laws of supply and demand, the
invisible hand, means and modes of production, the territorial imperative, the pleasure principle, the *libido*, *eros*, 'your own thing', the *Volk*,
the Absolute Idea, *élan vital*, the survival of the fittest, will-power, historical inevitability, the dictatorship of the proletariat, the white man's
burden etc. The list can go on almost *ad infinitum*, but the distinguishing
characteristic of all of these absolutes and ultimate points of reference is
that each is a *primum mobile* that has causal primacy and is presumed to
be of comprehensive explanatory power of both man and nature.

If all of these terms and methodologies are but variations on, or manifestations of, the concept of nature-matter, the same could be said of
concepts such as rationalism, progress, growth, planning; they all operate in terms of the causal primacy of one or a combination of material
factors.

The world in this way is caught in the web of materialistic hard causality, of cause inexorably and unambiguously leading to effect, of stimulus
producing response, and of infrastructure secreting a superstructure, just
as matter somehow miraculously produces mind, with 'effect', response', 'superstructure', and 'mind' being but 'a higher form of matter'.

Materialistic (cosmic, naturalistic) monism, the reduction of everything,
including man, to one natural law immanent in matter, is the epistemological basis for a process of neutralisation, depersonalisation, and
desanctification, not only of nature but also of man. Reduced to the level
of undifferentiated matter, everything in this way becomes more

amenable to measurement, quantification, instrumentalisation, utilisation, planning, technocratic engineering, programming, in brief more amenable to value-free rationalisation, that is, rationalisation that takes place within the context of a metaphysics of immanence that denies transcendence.

Deconstruction: solid or liquid

We have argued so far that modernity, *ergo* comprehensive secularism, is a form of immanence, therefore rising levels of secularisation would also mean rising levels of immanentisation. We have also argued that the process of immanentisation leads to the virtual disappearance of God as the transcendental organising force in the universe. God, initially, dwelled in both man and nature, which resulted in the sharp dualism of man versus nature and of subject versus object. The dualism, as argued earlier, resolves itself into a monism.

We can take a step further and point out that the resolution takes place, on the concrete socio-historical level, through the deepening of the process of immanentisation. Different spheres of man's life separate themselves from him and from his grasp to become self-referential, self-activating, self-transforming and self-explanatory. In the Western world, the paradigmatic sequence of immanentisation, *ergo* secularisation, modernisation and naturalisation, began sometimes in the late Middle Ages when some economic enclaves 'freed' themselves from Christian values or concepts such as 'fair price'. The only criteria applied to economic activity and economic success and failure became instead strict economic criteria, unadulterated by any moral or human considerations. In other words, the economic sphere was immanentised, becoming value-free, referring only to itself, its criteria and standards being immanent in it.

The same pattern repeated itself in all other spheres of human activity. The political sphere, for instance, witnessed the birth of the theory of the modern state in the Renaissance. The state, rather than seeking legitimacy on a religious or moral basis, became value-free, justifying itself by the *raison d'état*. The state, in other words, became self-justifying, self-validating and self-referential. The realm of politics freed itself from any values external to it, and was judged by criteria immanent in it.

One sphere of man's life after the other 'freed' themselves from religious, moral or human values and considerations, becoming self-sufficient, self-regulating, self-transforming, and self explanatory, till we finally get to science. It too freed itself from human views and purposes, becoming value-free, and purpose-free. Scientific laws and norms are supposed to be immanent in scientific processes (observation, experimentation, generalisation, etc.) that exclude man's longing and purposes, as something 'external' to them. Emotions and human purposefulness are after all not 'scientific'. They are merely teleological.

The world confronted man as made up of different self-referential spheres of activity, each supposedly having its own laws immanent in it. But the irony is that once a sphere of man's life frees itself from the grip of the human, it becomes subject to the laws of nature, immanent in matter. Different aspects of the human Self (*eros*, emotions, the body, the mind, etc.) were also subjected to the same process of immanentisation (secularisation – modernisation – atomisation), each aspect becoming self-referential, and eventually subjected to the laws of nature, immanent in matter. The human subject is no longer the organising or unifying principle in the universe, it is nothing but a part of the natural material whole.

We can view the whole process of immanentisation/ modernisation/ secularisation in terms of the death of God discourse. God became first incarnate (immanent) not in one man, but in mankind as a whole, and not temporarily but permanently. This led to the rise of humanism, and of the solipsistic subject. This humanism becomes imperialism and racism when God is incarnate in one people; it becomes fascism when He is incarnate in the Leader. But the incarnation is not confined to the sphere of the human, for God becomes incarnate in nature. This gives rise to the sharp dualism referred to earlier and the frantic attempt of German 'idealistic' philosophy to assert the parallelism of man and nature, subject and object. Then God became incarnate in nature-matter only, and this is the point where *hulul* (gradual indwelling) reaches its final point of a materialistic *wahdat al-wujud*, unity of being, with nature-matter at the centre. Spinoza, Kant and Hegel all operate in terms of this stage of immanence, which, despite all its fluctuations and divisions, is logocentric. This gave rise to the Enlightenment, Western rationalism, and what I term 'heroic materialism'.[11]

But the process continued inexorably, and immanentisation (secularisation/ modernisation) got more radical. The centre kept on shifting and the incarnations too many, till we got a multiplicity of centres. Nature itself was fragmented and atomised. It lost its stability, coherence, and self-referentiality. It could no longer serve as a stable centre.

All this means that we have moved from the solid logo-centric stage of modernity to its liquid stage, the stage of materialist irrationalism and anti-heroism, where the world is centre-less. We have left behind us not only Prometheus and Faustus, but also Frankenstein's monster; we now

---

[11] Logocentrism is a term deployed most frequently by Jacques Derrida and the proponents of deconstruction in philosophy and literary theory. In this usage a logocentric discourse is one that subscribes to the traditional order of priorities as regards language, meaning and truth. Thus it is taken for granted first that language (spoken language) is a more or less adequate expression of ideas already in the mind, and second that writing inhabits a realm of derivative, supplementary signs, a realm twice removed from the 'living presence' of the logos whose truth can only be revealed through the medium of authentic (self-present) speech. [Editor's note].

have Madonna and Michael Jackson instead of Dracula, we have now Derrida.

This shift from the solid to the liquid is latent in the nature-matter paradigm. As indicated earlier, nature is made up of either (solid) matter or (fluid) energy. But solid or fluid, the main characteristic of nature-matter, even in its most solid conditions, is the fact that it is in a permanent state of motion. All things change except change itself.

This continuous state of change is called 'flux' (from Latin *fluere* – 'to flow'). This idea of changing, fluctuating nature-matter goes back to the pre-Socratic philosophers. Heraclitus (d. 460 BC) stated that 'nothing remains the same'; 'all things change' (flow, separate, dissolve). This is why 'you cannot step into the same river twice', for reality is a flux, a river that never stops flowing.

But Heraclitus, not daring enough to accept the philosophical implications of a thorough materialism, postulated a *logos*, an immanent cause of pattern and identity that is evident in the constant flux of things. His is a logo-centric universe, characterised by a dualism of permanence and change, of fixity and flux.

But there are those who espoused the flux as the terminal point; the only immanence. They accepted the nature-matter paradigm with all its dark implications. Gorgias, the Sophist, (c.490-385 BC) summarised this philosophical attitude rather dramatically and succinctly when he said that there is nothing. That even if there was something, we could not know it; and that even if we could know it, we could not communicate our knowledge about it. We cannot express any knowledge we may have because no two people can think of the same thing, since the same thing cannot be in two places. Everything escapes man's grasp only to fall in the grip of the flux and absolute relativism; everything is deconstructed.

The modernist secular project takes its point of departure from a similar attitude of radical materialism and absolute relativism; its outcome is the deconstruction of man, then of nature itself, then finally of both. That is what Hobbes discovered from the very beginning. Man, living exclusively within his temporality, is nothing but a wolf to his brother man and the world is nothing but a jungle governed by brute force. Darwin later underscored the fact, and Freud pointed out that the jungle without is also within. The Western philosophical discourse, trying to conceal this dark truth, has evolved the Enlightenment project that proclaimed the rise of a natural man, who has no divine origins, but nevertheless is, somehow, both innately good and perfectible. It also postulated a logo-centric universe with nature-matter and/or Self as centres of organising principle. But the dark enlighteners were there all the time, vigorously denying and deconstructing.

Nietzsche, more than any other thinker, is the philosopher who uncovered, celebrated and clearly articulated this dark truth; man cannot have a world that is both materialistic and logo-centric, temporal and meaning-ful. True temporality means freedom from values and purpose. Even the idea of totality, the very basis of a centred universe, cannot be sustained. This is the true meaning of the death of God; that man will live in the indeterminate and the contingent. To go on talking of causality and total-ity would imply that even though God is dead, His shadow is still there. Nietzsche called for a total erasure of the shadow of God, because only in this way could we attain a truly modern world, a free, centre-less, unive-rse, where there is no essence, no totality, no right or wrong, no cause and effect, no human nature, no purpose or direction, no objective reality, no possibility of rational discourse, no subject or object, and no sacred or profane. Nothing but supermen and sub-men; nothing but autonomous eternal recurrence. Any hankering after transcendence, any talk of 'super-natural naturalism' or 'transcendence through matter' is mere self-delusion, an arrogant self-deification and self-sanctification.

Modernity has been rightly described as the desanctification of the world, both man and nature. One can notice the preponderance of verbs with the prefix 'de' used to describe some aspects of modernity: 'demys-tify', 'debunk', 'demythologise', 'demetaphysicalise', 'detextualise' and 'dehumanise', all of which are the precursors of our omnipresent, om-nivorous 'deconstruct'.

Richard Rorty, using yet another verb with the ominous prefix, spoke of the modernity project as 'the de-divinisation project'; man will not deify anything, will not worship anything, not even himself. He will not deem anything sacred, and will not experience any urge to transcend the spatio-temporal *donnée*, for his origins are not transcendent.[12] And be-cause he is finite and contingent, he will ask no ultimate questions. He will live in a world of innocent signs that have no origin or truth.

Rorty's statement has the virtue of dealing directly with the view of man implicit in the post-modernist deconstructive project. Unfortunately, post modernist discourse is not always that clear. On the contrary, it tends to be too swollen and inflated. Postmodernism was described, for instance, by a postmodernist, as being against 'logo-centric, totalising, transcendental, meta-narratives.' The text was described by another as 'emanating from nowhere, intended by no one, referring to nothing, abominating in the void.' The corruption of language here is an expres-sion of a cultural and philosophical project that has reached a deadlock, that sees reality in terms of post-something or other (post-capitalist, post-industrial, post-ideological, post-historical, etc.) and that looks at the world and sees nothing but void.

Nevertheless, the postmodernist discourse could be deconstructed and reconstructed in more intelligible and general terms. Even void can

---

[12] *Donnée* is the French for datum, given information. It denotes the subject or theme of a story etc. as well as a basic fact or assumption. [Editor's note].

be interpreted. Silence is said to be eloquent. Postmodernism has its metaphysics, despite its frantic attempt to disclaim any metaphysical stance. It denies transcendence, totality, permanence, and duality, and in its very denial it has shown its true philosophical identity, as an expression of the metaphysics of immanence.

In other words, post-modernism is but a higher (or lower) stage in the development of the project of modernity and immanentisation/ secularisation. It could be a mode of reading texts that has produced a lot of verbiage, but there is a paradigm behind the terminological and phraseological labyrinth. There is a definite method, rooted in a paradigm, in the postmodernist indefinite, indeterminate madness.

There are different varieties of monism, depending on the place of immanence and the centre of the universe (the subject or the object, nature-matter, or the Self). But given the fact that neither subject nor object, through the rising levels of immanentisation/ secularisation, could serve as a centre (a *logos*) for the universe, there was no option but liquidity.

All this leads to a new kind of monism, 'atomistic monism', a flat, liquid world of innumerable atoms, with each atom, ensconced in its small narrative, frantically moving without any purpose or direction. There is no *logos* or centre; neither a coherent perceiving subject, nor a coherent perceived object. Flux is all. All reality is dissolved into atoms. All is deconstructed and reduced to a meaningless flux, as the only organising or disorganising principle of the universe.

The whole issue of the relationship between signifier and signified is a manifestation of atomistic monism. If the signifier is separated from the signified by a space, a duality of perceptible and imperceptible, of sensible and intelligible, of speech and writing, and of nature and culture, would result in subverting monism, for it would mean that there is something beyond the mere flux and that there is a meaning, a *telos*.

One face of the duality, the sensible side of the sign, is submerged in flux; but then what about the intelligible? It inevitably turns its face away from the flux to a man capable of interpreting and communicating the meaning he perceives. This means that the human condition is above mere flux and is not entrapped into the limitlessness of the embryonic condition and a meaningless state of nature. But once the intelligible side of the signifier is seen to lie outside the flux of nature, the chain of transcendence would continue till it reaches an ultimate point of fixity outside the flux, namely God. Therefore the demons of deconstruction, dissemination and *la différance* could be exorcised.

As Derrida has averred, the intelligible part of the sign turns its face to God, to a *logos*. In other words, the world turns out to be logo-centric, rooted in a transcendental signified, an ultimate referent, an absolute foundation, outside the play of language, which is adequate 'to centre' (that is to anchor and to organise) the linguistic system in such a way as to fix the particular meaning of a spoken or written utterance within the system. On the other hand, the absence of a transcendental signified liquidates all dualities, extending the domain and play of signification infinitely and exclusively in the world of flux. Therefore, the system of signs has to be freed from its deep rooted metaphysical assumptions, so the whole world would be a game, a true embryonic situation with no boundaries, choice or accountability. This could be achieved if the space separating the signifier and the signified is completely bridged so that they might form a tight organic unity, with no space separating the one from the other, the one actually becoming the other, a veritable unity of being, *wahdat wujud*. The signifier in this way is freed from the signified, from reality, and therefore becomes self-contained and self-explanatory..

But once the signs are emancipated from the transcendental signified, the whole system of signs becomes self-contained. Every sign would then refer to another sign, which would in turn refer to a third. Every interpretation would then refer to another, which in turn would refer to a third, *ad infinitum*. The deconstructive vertigo would then begin. Limitless interpretation, an unrestricted semantic play that is no longer anchored in any signified, is the result. Texts become mere 'black on blank', or like the words in a dictionary, where every word refers to another with no centre to stop the play of the sign, 'the dance of the pen.' Everything is everything else; and everything is a liquid nothing, *fanaa* (annihilation). Or as Derrida put it in his inflated, and unnecessarily convoluted style: 'What deconstruction is not? Everything, of course. What is deconstruction? Nothing, of course.'

Celebrating nothingness, the sixteenth-century Egyptian poet, Ibn Sawdun al-Misri, wrote non-logocentric poems that deconstruct themselves. His poetry is characterised by high organic unity, because it carefully refers only to itself. Signifiers are freed from the signified and the very idea of meaning by making the one identical with the other.

> Earth is earth: and heaven is heaven,
> And hell is said to be infernal.
> We sat amidst running water,
> As if we were people sitting surrounded by water.

The first line in particular sounds better in Arabic, for there is no verb separating subject from predicate. It reads thus: Earth earth, heaven heaven.

Some post-modernists argue that the most iconic and transparent language that approximates, perhaps embodies, the complete freedom of the sign from the transcendental signified, are screams of pain, where there is no space separating the monosyllabic screams of pain and the pain itself. Monosyllabic expressions of sexual *plaisir* are classified likewise. It is all very embryonic and monistic. Derrida found a truly transparent poem written by Antoine Artaud (advocate of the theatre of cruelty). It consists of mere sounds, which refer to nothing outside themselves; they are self-explanatory and self-contained:

afidana/ nakimov/ taudidana/ taukomiv
nasidano/ nakomiv/ trakoniv/ nakomi

These utterances cannot be distinguished from those of lower animals (dolphins have a very sophisticated language of communication). This is a fulfilment of Derrida's dream of finding signs uncontaminated by history or metaphysics, signs used before the eve of creation (presumably when Adam was still mere clay and before God had taught him all the names of plants and animals, creating thereby a space between him and nature and endowing him with his specifically human traits).

But if this is indeed the case, then silence would be the real fulfilment of the paradigm, where man becomes part 'of mute insensate things'. Would not that be the real *fanaa*, annihilation? Wouldn't that be the true realisation of post-modernism and the metaphysics of immanence? Derrida, in his search for an ideal, iconic, self-contained, self-referential text, found the following phrase: 'I left my umbrella'. It was written by Nietzsche on a blank page and found among his papers. We do not know why he wrote this poem, to whom it was intended, if to anyone at all, whether he actually left his umbrella, and whether the umbrella is real or a very private symbol. It is a true signifier without being signified.

The following poem, titled, for no particular reason 'Xfnd-?4g1' should be seen as the ultimate post-modernist text:

It is not black on blank, it is blank on blank. It is the least logo-centric poem ever written (or unwritten). It is so self-explanatory, that it needs no explanation. It is so self-referential, that any one standing outside it, cannot see it. It cannot be reduced to anything more fundamental than itself because it does not exist; it is *nihil*, a nothing. Its language (or non-language) is not in the least contaminated by metaphysics (or physics for that matter). Complete silence is the only language it utters.

But silence, as we know, is eloquent; it signifies and therefore is based on a metaphysics. This alerts us to the fact that our transparent innocent poem is, alas, not that transparent or innocent and is indeed contaminated by metaphysics; it is actually logo-centric, for it refers to void and nothingness, to *fanaa*, the annihilation of the human. In this way, it reveals to us the anti-humanistic *telos* of the post-modernist project and the deconstructive nature of the whole project of modernity (secularism-immanence). So even the silence of the nihilist signifies a *telos*, and *telos* refers to *logos*, to the one God, beyond nature and history.

DESACRALISING SECULARISM

S. Parvez Manzoor

No Muslim endeavour to face the intellectual challenge of the Western tradition can afford to ignore the critical discourse of postmodernism, or fail to recognise the Nietzschean claim about truth's complicity with power. Secularism as truth, as doctrine, therefore, cannot be separated from the theory and practice of secular power. As the *praxis* of statecraft, secularism claims universal sovereignty, and as the *theoria* of history, it subordinates all religious and moral claims to its own version of the truth. The secularist enterprise, furthermore, has been immensely successful in transforming the historical order of our times. But as such, it is a subject proper to the discipline of (political) history and merits the Muslim scholar's fullest attention there. Secularism as a doctrine, as an *-ism*, on the other hand, falls squarely within the province of philosophy and history of ideas. In order to apprehend the secularist gospel and its discontents, one needs to contemplate the ideational visage of secularism. It is this aspect of secularism, the mask of truth worn by the secularist will-to-power, that I intend to uncover. Thus, the secularism that is examined here is not a sociological theory but a philosophical paradigm, not an empirical fact but an ideological axiom.

Secularism: a sacred faith?

Secularism, like any darling child, has many names. In contemporary literature it is presented, either humbly, as a rejection of ecclesiastical authority, a model for pluralism, a theory of society, a doctrine of governance; or augustly, as a philosophy of history, a creed of atheism, an epistemology of humanism; or even more grandiosely, as a metaphysics of immanentism that corresponds to the ultimate scheme of things. Within academic discourse, it is also customary to accord it an almost Socratic definition and distinguish its various manifestations as a process of history (*secularisation*), a state of mind and culture (*secularity*) and a theory of truth (*secularism*). (One may note the close affinity of these terms with *modernity*, *modernisation* and *modernism*!) Needless to say, not everyone championing its cause ascribes to all these claims, nor is every expression of secularist, this-worldly conscience and piety antithetical or inimical to Islam.

81

The first point to note is that the Western attempts to define secularism and its derivatives are not value-neutral and testify to the existence of an intense polemical climate within which these concepts are evoked. For instance, a modern Christian apologist of secularity, Harvey Cox, asserts that 'secularisation is the liberation of man from religious and metaphysical tutelage, the turning of his attention away from other worlds and towards this one'.[1] Previously, however, the Christian church was not as enthusiastic and regarded it as a punitive ideology. For secularisation then simply denoted a judicial measure of confiscating ecclesiastical property for 'worldly' use by individuals or the state.[2] It is only recently that Christian thinkers have started modifying their position regarding secularisation. Dietrich Bonhoffer, for instance, protested against the antithesis of *ecclesia-saeculum* which is axiomatic to the moderns and argued that secularisation 'represents a realisation of crucial motifs of Christianity itself'. Hence, Bonhoffer pleaded further, the term was meaningless and ought to be abandoned.[3]

The whole problem of Christian complicity with the modern world has been the subject of an exhaustive and incisive debate and need not detain us here.[4] Suffice it to say that sociologists, for whom the term 'secularisation' refers to an 'empirically available process of great importance in modern Western history', find no reason either to abandon the term or to agree with Bonhoffer.[5] On the contrary, the insistence is that secularisation, as a *fait social*, can be defined positively as: 'the process by which sectors of society and culture are removed from the domination of religious institutions and symbols'.[6] The typical manifestations of secularisation, then, would be: the separation of Church and state, the expropriation of Church lands, the emancipation of education from ecclesiastical authority etc. Thus, for all its discomforts to the Church, secularisation continues to be the cardinal doctrine of sociology.

Belatedly, however, some sociologists have come to the realisation that, scientifically speaking, secularisation is an inadequate category of societal analysis. According to David Martin, for instance, far from providing an objective description of modern society with scientific validity, the term secularisation acts mainly as 'a tool of counter-religious

---

[1] Harvey Cox, *The Secular City*, New York: Macmillan, 1966, p. 15.

[2] H. Lübbe, *Säkulariserung. Geschichte eines ideenpolitischen Begriffs*, Freiburg: Alberg, 1965.

[3] D. Bonhoffer, *Ethics*, New York: Macmillan, 1959; E. Bethge (ed.), *Die Mundige Welt*, 2 vols, Munich: Kaiser, 1955; Cox, *The Secular City*, pp. 1-2.

[4] H. Blumenberg, *The Legitimacy of the Modern Age*, MIT Press, Cambridge, MA: 1984.

[5] P. Berger, *The Social Reality of Religion*, Harmondsworth: Penguin, 1973 (first published as *The Sacred Canopy*, New York: Doubleday, 1967), p. 112.

[6] *Ibid.*, p. 113.

ideologies'.[7] (We need, however, to question the common assertion that fundamentalism is a revolt against modernity and secularism. Inasmuch as its metaphysical orientations are towards immanentism, it may be regarded as a variant of modernistic secularism. Hence, it is not merely accidental that there is so little love between traditionalists and fundamentalists!) Other, moderate, critics of secularisation theory, who would not go as far as to dismiss it entirely, have also begun questioning its intellectual underpinnings. They readily concede today that 'secularisation, as the integrative idea of social change in the modern world, is seriously flawed.'[8]

A recent critique further contends that the secularisation thesis is basically 'a hodgepodge of loosely employed ideas rather than a theory', and that 'existing data simply do not support the theory'.[9] Similarly, the persistence of religion in the heart of secularised societies, suggesting that 'religion is perhaps truly ubiquitous in human cultures', and the fact that in more countries than ever before, religion has re-emerged as a significant factor in the articulation of socio-political reality, also challenge the assumptions of the secularisation thesis. Even more embarrassing for its supporters is the disclosure that secularisation theory is one 'scientific' theory that traditionally has not turned to empirical facts for its authentication. Indeed, a recent student exclaims, 'before the mid-twentieth century essentially no empirical research and, hence, no foundation for challenging secularisation theory existed'.[10]

The most cogent refutation of the secularisation thesis, few would disagree today, has come from the recalcitrant forces of history. It is history rather than theory which has refused to redeem secularism's claim about the disappearance of religion in the age of science and enlightenment. The death of the sacred remains more of a vain secular hope than a probable historical scenario. And yet, despite its spectacular failure, secularisation theory has not been totally abandoned, not least because it serves a useful purpose in modernity's ideological polemics against its detractors within the West, or against other cultures without. Needless to say, this ideological commitment is also at work behind recent efforts at the restitution and revision of this theory. The persistence of religion in the midst of secular modernity, some secularist theorists point out today, is due to its privatisation. For secularisation implies not the extinction but the privatisation of religion. However, according to another revisionist, 'the assignment of religion to the private spheres is like

---

[7] David A. Martin, *The Religious and the Secular*, London: Routledge & Kegan Paul. 1969, p. 9.

[8] J. Hadden, and A. Shupe (eds), *Secularisation and Fundamentalism Reconsidered (Religion and Political Order*, vol. III), New York: Paragon, 1989, p. xv.

[9] *Ibid.*, p. 13.

[10] *Ibid.*, p. 4.

having one's cake and eating it too. One can hold steadfastly to the Enlightenment image of the demise of religion and still account for its embarrassing persistence. It is not necessary to establish a timetable for the disappearance of religion'.[11]

Clearly, the modern advocacy of the secularisation thesis stems from an ideological commitment rather than from any fidelity to the scientific method. And even the sociologist has to concede that secularisation is more than a socio-structural process, for it affects the heart and soul of the symbolic and cultural world of a society. It manifests itself in 'the decline of religious contents in the arts, in philosophy, in literature and, most important of all, in the rise of science as an autonomous, thoroughly secular perspective on the world'.[12] Secularisation of societal institutions, then, leads to the secularisation of consciousness and bestows upon the modern man his peculiarly anti-religious prejudices and passions.

Today, the term does not merely describe what happens in history but expresses a *value*, perhaps the most sacrosanct value of our age. Secularisation represents more than a Promethean bid for the banishment of God from the governance of the human *polis*. The idea of secularisation itself has become sacralised and secularism as doctrine has now replaced secularisation as process. It has turned itself into a faith: a faith in man and a faith in progress, both a secularised faith and a faith in secularisation.[13]

Authority without transcendence

Whatever the cogency and validity of the secularist argument, it is contingent upon a conception and understanding of 'religion' that is idiosyncratically Western. The modern definition of religion as 'the exclusive zone of human reality for the experience of the "holy"' bears the distinctive insignia of the secular man and applies only to his world. The intellectual cosmos and life-world of the pre-modern man of faith is a unity: it knows of no religious and non-religious dominions. No faith regards itself as anything but a total system of morality and knowledge that can cope with any human situation in terms of meaningful answers. None is willing to disenfranchise itself to the extent of positing that there could be spheres of human experience outside of its arbitration.[14] For the devotee, there is no optional metaphysics of *belief*, only the integrative life-world of *faith*.[15] Indeed, even anthropologists argue that there

---

[11] *Ibid.*, p. 20. See also, Jorge Casanova, *Public Religions in the Modern World*, University of Chicago Press, 1994 for an intellectually sophisticated update and an empirically valid refutation of this position.

[12] Berger, *Social Reality of Religion*, p. 113.

[13] Gianni Vattimo, *The End of Modernity*, Oxford: Polity Press, 1988, p. 100.

[14] Willfred Cantwell Smith, *The Meaning and End of Religion*, New York, 1962.

[15] Willfred Cantwell Smith, *Faith and Belief*, Princeton University Press, 1979 (new edn Oxford: Oneworld Publications, 1998).

can be no generic definition of 'religion', a universal genus of which all particular religious traditions are mere historical variations, 'not only because its constituent elements and relationships are historically specific, but because that definition is itself the historical product of discursive forces'.[16] Religion, in plain words, is the foundational myth of secularism!

Paradoxically, if the peculiarly modern notion of 'religion' is the creation of secular man, it was the sacred that gave birth to the secular in the first place and legitimated it as an autonomous domain of human reality! (The sacred and the secular here refer to institutional divisions within Western society and do not allude to any putative schism in the human soul.) This fateful dichotomy, upon which most of modernity's self-authentication hinges, owes its genesis to one of the bitter-sweet ironies of history. Its roots lay in the sacred nature of Roman politics where religious and political activity could be considered as almost identical. It is within that context that the concept of authority (*auctoritas*) originally appeared and came to be distinguished from power (*potestas*). The most conspicuous characteristic of those in authority, notes Hannah Arendt in a particularly suggestive and seminal study, is 'that they do not have power. *Cum potestas in populo auctoritas in senatu sit*, "while power resides in the people, authority rests with the Senate".'[17]

For Romans, the binding force of this authority, 'more than advice and less than command', is closely connected with the religious force of *auspices*. Further, this conception of authority is similar to that of the Sunna in the Islamic tradition: precedents, deeds of the ancestors and the customs that grew out of them are deemed paradigmatic and binding. Indeed, the expression *auctoritas maiorum*, which may uninhibitedly be translated as *sunnat al-awwalin*, became for the Romans identical with normative models for actual behaviour, with tradition. However, when the Church after Constantine succeeded in overcoming 'the anti-political and anti-institutional tendencies of the Christian faith' and embarked upon its political career in the fifth century, it adopted the Roman distinction between authority and power. But, most significantly, she claimed for itself the old authority of the Senate and left the power of the state to the princes of the world. Thus were sown the seeds of the strife between *regnum* and *sacerdotium*, but also of the 'sovereignty' of the state within its own, secular, realm!

This continuity of the Roman tradition, according to Arendt, had two consequences for the history of the West: one, the permanence of the clerical institutions, the other, the degradation of the political ones:

[16] Talal Asad, *Genealogies of Religion: Discipline and Reasons of Power in Christianity and Islam*, Baltimore, MA: Johns Hopkins University Press, 1993, p. 29.
[17] Hannah Arendt, 'What is Authority?' in *Between Past and Future*, New York: Viking, 1961. (Re-print: New York, Penguin Books, 1977) p. 122.

On one hand, the miracle of permanence repeated itself once more; for within the framework of our history the durability and continuity of the Church as a public institution can be compared only with the thousand years of Roman history in antiquity. The separation of church and state, on the other hand, far from signifying unequivocally a secularisation of the political realm and, hence, its rise to the dignity of the classical period, actually implied that the political had now, for the first time since the Romans, lost its authority and with it that element which, at least in Western history, had endowed political structures with durability, continuity, and permanence.[18]

The Christian identification with *auctoritas*, which insinuated that the Church represented a truth higher than the mundane concerns of earthly empires had, however, the unintended consequence of removing God from the realm of the political, indeed of dispensing with God as the organising principle of Western civilisation altogether. It also meant rupturing the Roman unity of religion, authority and tradition which had conferred upon the political realm its foundational pathos and its imperial grandeur. Hence, having acquired this insight, Hannah Arendt can justly claim that:

whenever one of the elements of Roman trinity, religion or authority or tradition, was doubted or eliminated, the remaining two were no longer secure. Thus, it was Luther's error to think that his challenge of the temporal authority of the Church and his appeal to unguided individual judgement would leave tradition and religion intact. So it was the error of Hobbes and the political theorists of the seventeenth century to hope that authority and religion could be saved without tradition. So, too, was it finally the error of the humanists to think that it would be possible to remain within an unbroken tradition of Western civilisation without religion and without authority.[19]

In fact, for Arendt, 'the decline of the West' consists primarily of 'the decline of the Roman trinity of religion, tradition and authority'.[20]

Similar concerns have been expressed by an uncompromisingly secularist thinker, Michael Harrington, who in a recent work mourned the death of the 'political God of the West' with great eloquence, anguish and sorrow.[21] For him, the eclipse of religion entails pre-eminently a crisis of political theory and a loss of authority. The fact that the West, for the past two centuries at least, has been a civilisation without any avowed faith in the transcendent is therefore for him a cause of acute metaphysical pathos and spiritual disquietude. Prior to his 'demise', notes Harrington, the *societal* God of Judaeo-Christianity possessed certain *political attributes* that included:

[18] *Ibid.*, p. 127.
[19] *Ibid.*, p. 128.
[20] *Ibid.*, p. 140.
[21] Michael Harrington, *The Politics at God's Funeral*, New York: Holt, Reinhart & Winston, 1983.

- *the legitimisation of established power* and sometimes a revolt against it;
- the transcendent symbol of common consciousness of an existing community;
- the foundation of all other values;
- *the organising principle of a system of the authoritative allocation of social rules* (God of feudalism) or *the motivating and ethical principle of individual mobility* (God of capitalism);
- the guarantor of personal, ethnic and national identity;
- a philosopher for the non-philosophers, including the illiterate.[22]

God, claims Harrington, was 'the most important *political* figure in the West' and, hence, his banishment from public consciousness has had calamitous social and political consequences for the Western body-politic. Some of the most noticeable among them are:
- a crisis of legitimacy in late capitalist society as one of the prime motives for non-coerced obedience and acquiescence in the social order begins to disappear;
- the shift from 'Protestant ethic' to a compulsory hedonism of unplan-ned and irresponsible growth;
- the appeal of totalitarian movements as substitutes for religious solidarity;
- the loss of philosophic "common sense" basis of responsibility before the law;
- the dangers of a purely technological and instrumental attitude towards nature;
- the decline in the sense of duty toward unborn generations;
- the loss of one of the most important constituent elements in both group and personal identity;
- the relativisation of all values and a resultant crisis of individual conscience;
- the weakness of the 'superego', and the cult of the self.
- the thinness and superficiality of the substitutes of religion by sex and drugs and so forth.[23]

Harrington's search for legitimacy within modern socio-political structures also entails the coming together of the men of 'atheistic hu-manism' and 'religious faith' in the West – because capitalism, the chief source of mindless *de facto* atheism, is the enemy of both. Against the tyranny of thoughtless, norm-less, selfish, hedonistic individualism, which is the gift of capitalism so to speak, he hopes, there could emerge a consensus based not on the affirmation of the same conception of the world, man and knowledge, but on a common will to action. Further,

[22] *Ibid.*, p. 7-8. Emphasis has been added.
[23] *Ibid.*, p. 8.

this consensus has to be, even if Harrington imagines it arising in the West, universal.

No one need deny the moral urgency and persuasive force of Harrington's sentiments; yet the tyranny is that his 'social democratic' vision cannot free itself from the compulsion to compromise. At the end of his superbly conducted tour of the Western intellectual landscape, his gaze refocuses itself on the familiar mileposts of his own ideological pastures. Like a mole, Harrington would have us burrow our way through the mountain of spiritual crisis in a spirit of political compromise. Little wonder that the rocky impediments of unbelief allow him only the comforts of the tunnel vision of a mole. He lacks the power of faith that moves mountains. The Grand Coalition of 'atheistic humanism' and 'religious faith' which is offered as a path to planetary conscience is a half-measure, begotten of half-truths, that is unlikely to end the apartheid of 'faith' and 'reason' that is the legacy of Western man and his civilisation to our age.

Despite Harrington's justified strictures, however, modern thought neither denies the 'political necessity of religion' nor dismisses the indispensability of 'civil theology' for political order. Nor, in fact, is there any real dispute about the need for 'transcendentals'. Rather, the principal cause of the legitimacy-crisis is the realisation that the basic religious tradition of the West can no longer, as a *religious* tradition, provide the core values of Western society. A revival of Judaeo-Christianity, a return to the theocratic past, is, in other words, both impossible and undesirable. The roots of the present political crisis are cognitive, epistemological and metaphysical and no 'pragmatic' acceptance of the Christian solution could appease the secularist conscience. Nothing that does not remove the seeds of cognitive doubt is worthy of the secularist's voluntary societal assent.

In any genuine dialogue with the atheistic humanist, then, the Muslim would be justified in insisting that the Western experience of the 'death of God' is quite provincial and parochial; that religiously and politically it does not represent humanity's ultimate longing for a vacuous emancipation and enlightenment but that both the malaise and the remedy are appropriate only to the Western patient. It would be equally appropriate to point out that Western man's loss of faith represents the logical fulfilment of the 'secularistic' dogmas of his own creed. One could also take comfort that Islam as a *civilisation* that has never renounced God. In fact, dismissing all the oracles of doom would not be an unreasonable Muslim reaction, nor would be the search for epistemologically and experientially cogent Islamic answers. However, as a man of faith, the Muslim should tell the secularist that humanism, whether Christian or atheistic, Marxist or liberal, cannot end the present crisis of values. For, so long as man has himself as the locus of his values and concerns, he is unable to judge his own conduct. Only by defining himself from an external point of reference, can man hope to acquire the trappings of a cognitive and moral arbitration. The religious man has always measured the cardinal point of his personality and his civilisation against God – the external (transcendent) source of all values. Before he can make a common cause with the atheistic humanist, he has a right to ask, whom does the latter accept as the referee?

What is true of Harrington is true of secular man in general. His epistemology of questions, his loss of meaning, indeed the uncertainty of his being, is the natural cry of the self-reproaching, tormented soul, *nafs al-lawwamah* as we know it through the parlance of the Qur'an. By renouncing God, secular man has been rendered impotent in the face of the problems of knowledge and power. Theology and political philosophy, it has always been a matter of common knowledge, are indispensable to each other. The modern debate on the legitimation of knowledge also shows that even epistemology without theology is not a viable option; for, with the 'death of God' comes not only the darkness of the human soul but the blankness of the human mind as well. Without a transcendent referent, there can be no science of morals, only the cognitive uncertainty of relativism. Without a beyond, there is no categorical imperative, only the whim of subjectivity.

The clerical paradox

Secularisation, we have seen earlier, is more than a process in the mind, a loss of religious belief and an acceptance of the scientific view of the world. It is an institutional arrangement, a structural differentiation and an ideational division of labour whereby the sacred is separated from the realm of power. It is the sacred that gives birth to the secular by hiding behind a veil as it were. Where the sacred is not self-conscious, or narcissistic, enough to conceal itself in a sanctuary, to confine itself within an inviolate haven, the secular also remains unnoticeable. Such was the case in traditional Islamic societies where the sacred had no special retreats and the secular had no boundless freedom outside them. With Christianity, and Buddhism, however, it is a different matter. The Church – or Sangha – represents an institution specifically concerned with 'religion' in counterposition to all other institutions of society. The confinement of religious activities and symbols to one institutional sphere *ipso facto* defines the rest of society as 'profane', outside the jurisdiction of the sacred. It is then that the world outside becomes the *saeculum*, the profane domain with which the sacred has neither any concern nor any quarrel. The logical development of this, notes a modern scholar, may be seen in the Lutheran doctrine of two kingdoms, 'in which the autonomy of the secular world is actually given a *theological* legitimation'.[24]

---

[24] Berger, *Social Reality of Religion*, p. 128.

Secularity, it would appear, is from the very start a Christian ambition and a Protestant necessity!

Muslim societies, as both indigenous and foreign lore relate, did not have any sacerdotal institutions, any churches, and hence were spared the sacred-secular dichotomy of the West. Whatever the validity of this thesis, early Islam did witness some attempts at the establishment of a theocracy, and in the event of its failure, at the creation of a surrogate *imama* which was more like a papacy than a political government. Nonetheless, in practice not even Shi'ism, which championed the cause of an infallible *imama*, completely severed its bonds with history and it too remained loyal to the common Islamic ideal of the unity of the religious and the political. Like Sunnism, it simply responded to all the challenges of history and to the perennial tension between state and religion in Muslim societies with the intellectual and moral resources of a single, unified vision.

Notwithstanding the received wisdom, Muslim civilisation is heir to a peculiar set of tensions that have been as detrimental to its body-politic as the most nefarious conflict between church and state in the West. Though as an *institution*, the Muslim state was all-pervasive and never had to contend with any challenge from a non-existent church, in terms of *ideology*, it was a different matter altogether. For the state, despite all its absolute power, never succeeded in establishing its autonomy and legitimacy: it remained merely the coercive forearm of political society which could have no pretence to any redemptive functions. The body-politic of Islam, the Muslim *ummah*, expressed its ultimate aspirations through the sacred law whose legitimate guardians were the *ulama* and not the Sultan. Civil society in other words was sovereign over the state and the ruler did not represent the body-politic. He merely embodied his personal rule or misrule. Or, seen differently, the state as the locus and seat of sovereignty did not exist.

Despite the absence of the church, and of the concomitant rivalry between church and state, the civilisation of Islam generated its own sources of tension between the sacred and the secular. It too was forced to choose, as it were, between two contending texts: the one of the sacral kingship of the *khalifah* and the other of the clerical authority of the *ulama*. What triumphed in Muslim history can only be characterised as a duality: the State as the body, *phenomenon*, of Islam and the Law its spirit, *noumen*. The state shared power with no rival association, but was not the ultimate focus of Muslim loyalty; the *ulama* possessed no institution of their own, but acted as the expounders of Islamic dogma! Institutional power without a legitimating text and textual authority without any institutional power: a this-worldly state in the service of the other-worldly norm! Indeed, the mutual dependency of the one upon the other has produced a highly immanentist reading of the supremely transcendental text of the revelation. Little wonder that in the discourse of the jurists *raison d'islam* becomes indistinguishable from *raison d'état*!

The triumph of secularism, or the encroachment of Muslim order by Western powers, has seriously disturbed the traditional equilibrium between state and clergy. The modern state which had become too secular and had emancipated itself from the *ulama*'s influence is under siege today. The clergy is not only very much part of contemporary Shi'ism, especially in Iran, but is gaining strength in other parts of the Muslim world as well. Today, it aspires to assuming special sacerdotal functions within Muslim societies and has even adopted the non-traditional term, clergy, with alacrity. Contrary to the populist rhetoric, secularisation of Muslim societies, it would appear, is in full swing. In fact, according to a modern observer, the most powerful factor against the realisation of the professed and sought after unity of the sacred and the secular in Islam is the emergence of the clergy in recent times.[25]

Institutionally and sociologically, then, the clergy is the progenitor of secularism – albeit by default. Little wonder that the secularist ideal expresses itself in terms of a revolt, institutional as well as intellectual, against clerical hegemony. The secularist passion for purging Western societies of all vestiges of ecclesiastical influence, then, is grounded in a specific experience which makes sense only within the historical context of church-state strife. Only the church's attempt to subordinate supreme political power to its own authority, its scrambling for the riches of this world as it were, can be held responsible for the virulence of the anti-religious sentiment in the Enlightenment. However, this specifically, if not uniquely, bitter Western experience renders the secularist solution to the alleviation of sacred-secular tension within modern society much less of a universal cure.

For all the benefits of the secularisation process, it cannot be mechanically transferred to other cultures simply because they do not share with the West the 'medieval' experience of ecclesiastical tyranny and obscurantism. Hence, the odd Muslim thinker who proposes a conscious policy of secularisation for the modernisation of Muslim societies may justifiably be criticised for not understanding the dialectics of either Islamic or Western history.[26] Further, as to the mechanics of this process, Muslim secularists are frustratingly reticent. They never spell out, in the absence of the church-state dichotomy, how and by which institutional mechanism, may the churchless Islamic societies trigger this process (as compared, for instance, to the legal and political appropriation of ecclesiastical property for 'worldly' uses, which is the Western

---

[25] Olivier Roy, *The Failure of Political Islam*, Cambridge, MA: Harvard University. Press, 1994, p. 45.

[26] Bassam Tibi, *Islam and the Cultural Accommodation of Social Change*, Boulder, CO: Westview Press, 1990, p. 39.

precedent?) The secularist solution, then, does not move beyond the stating of the problem and provides no indication that a superficial reading of Islam as a *fait social* can sensitively comprehend its historical crisis and prescribe any cure for its cultural malaise.

No moral restraints to power!

The most respectable theory with regard to secularism is the one which portrays it not only as the breakdown of ecclesiastical authority but also as the collapse of the theocentric model of the universe. It construes the development of secularism in terms of a devolution of human consciousness 'from Divine Cosmos to Sovereign State'.[27] Within secular political order, it is argued, concerns with temporality and mortality replace the search for immortality and a trans-temporal salvation. Secularisation entails journeying into modernity and partaking of its sacrament of rationality and progress.[28] In modernity, man creates not only the self, which is the historical and cultural medium for redemption, but also the representative secular sovereign state which renders his reliance on any benign cosmic and theocratic order superfluous. Secularity, quite simply, is man's coming of age.

Obviously, the modern march away from theocracy to secularism signals a new conception of 'reality' in political philosophy. Secularism self-consciously repudiates the Christian solution to the human condition according to which the true end of man lies beyond the world of politics and history.[29] It posits, in the name of realism, a new conception not only of the polis but of the cosmos as well. Indeed, there is a general turn away from transcendentalism to immanentism, from theology to positivism and historicism, which renders politics more of an art of the possible than a quest for virtue, justice or redemption.[30] The architect of modern political realism and the first theorist of the modern secular state is no other than Machiavelli.[31] Religion, declared Machiavelli, has to be banished from politics not because it teaches morality but because it teaches a wrong kind of morality, the kind that does not enhance the

[27] Stephen L. Collin, *From Divine Cosmos to Sovereign State*, Oxford University Press, 1989.

[28] S. Whimster & S. Lash (eds), *Max Weber, Rationality and Modernity*, London, 1987.

[29] James, V. Schall, *Reason, Revelation, and the Foundation of Political Philosophy* Baton Rouge: Louisiana University Press, 1987.

[30] *Cf.* I. Peter, *Redeeming Politics*, Princeton University Press, 1990 for a historical account and Leo Strauss, *Natural Rights and History*, Chicago, 1950, for a theoretical background to this problem.

[31] See Friedrich Meinecke, *Machiavellism: The Doctrine of Raison d'état and its Place in Modern History*, Yale University Press, 1957 (re-print, Transaction Publishers, London, 1998) for a masterful account of the moral problem in politics that has become associated with Machiavelli's name.

power of the state. For him, the religious claim to rule over the secular realm, the dilemma posed by the problem of church and state as it were, produces only two alternatives: either the public realm becomes corrupt, in which case religion itself gets abused, or the religious body remains uncorrupt and hence destroys the public realm altogether. Either a corrupt state and the doom of religion, or an uncorrupt religion and the ruination of the state!

The dialectic of church and state, it has been long recognised, poses an almost insoluble problem for Christian conscience. Or, expressed more cautiously, 'There are no absolute relationships of church and state, of religion and politics, and perhaps no ideal ones either.'[32] The state being the outcome of original sin is at best a necessary evil, and politics, to the extent that it incarnates the sheer struggle for power, 'is bound, in Christian terms, to be the realm of the devil by definition'.[33] The church, in other words, may neither forsake the state nor claim it as its own! Paradoxically, the Machiavellian and the Christian concepts of politics, despite their radically diametric moral foundations, are identical insofar as they both result in a devaluation of politics. Politics is not a quest for virtue or justice, but it is, at best, an activity proper either to the fallen man (Christianity), or to the half-human, half-beastly statesman (Machiavellianism).

The traditional vision of Christianity as 'Christendom' was at best an uneasy balancing act, for it was under obligation neither to dismiss instrumental goods nor to encourage a theocratic temptation. However, even this Christian compromise crumbled in history and was replaced by a modernity in which politics, arts, science and philosophy asserted their autonomy from divine supervision. Modernity, however, created its own impasse, namely, that if each of these domains of human spirit had to look for its own criteria of validity, beyond and outside the biblical tradition and the church, where was this normative foundation to be and how could it produce *ex nihilo* its own principles without making them a matter of arbitrary choice. The crisis of authority lay already in the secularist's quest for autonomy. For while art, perhaps also philosophy and science, could live with this nihilistic liberation, it cannot be made an unrestrained principle of politics. Politics, in order to remain politics, needs to distinguish itself from anarchy.

And this brings us to the poverty of secular polemics against religious faith. For, they misconstrue theocracy, either by incapacity or by design, as a theory of politics and a model for governance. Theocracy, however is pre-eminently a *moral* doctrine which proclaims the futility of 'political

---

[32] Edward Norman, 'Christian Politics in a Society of Plural Values' in D. Cohn-Sherbok, & D. McLellan (eds), *Religion in Public Life*, London: Macmillan, 1992, p. 17.

[33] Leszek Kolakowski, *Modernity on Endless Trial*, University of Chicago Press, 1990, p. 175.

solutions' or the illegitimacy of secular rule.[34] It represents a utopia which, as observed acutely by a modern philosopher, 'is a form of suggestiveness from afar. It is not primarily a project of action but a critique of the present.'[35] Theocracy, accordingly, cannot be institutionalised and must be distinguished from hierocracy, or clerocracy, which simply stand for 'priestly government'. In terms of moral orientations and relationship to power and truth, then, theocratic perception is the exact opposite of that of secularism. For, secularism proclaims not only a doctrine of power but also that of its supremacy over truth. Truth is merely a mask which will-to-power wears in order to realise itself. Indeed, in its Nietzschean form, secularism takes an aim right at the heart of religious faith by claiming that power is, essentially and ultimately, amoral. Of course, it is a stupendous claim which can only be sustained within the consciousness of nihilism, a consciousness which is convinced of the 'death of God'.

Given the amoral nature of the secularist truth, it is not accidental that the highest secularist power, the modern, anti-theocratic state, proclaims for itself the morally indefensible attribute of 'sovereignty'. The distinguishing characteristics for a power which is sovereign, according to a modern theorist, are: 'its possession of a legislative authority; its capacity to alter as it pleases its subjects' rules of behaviour, while recasting at its own convenience the rules which undermine its own; and, while it legislates for others, to be itself above the laws, *legibus solutus*, absolute'.[36] Similar misgivings have been expressed from a radically different vantage-point by political scientists. The concept of sovereignty refers to some idea of moral goodness, to something intrinsically valid and commanding that lies outside the realm of procedures and juridicality. The state as a formal *legal* entity cannot incorporate it and by claiming it produce its own legitimacy.[37]

From the point of view of political philosophy, and not merely that of jurisprudence, pleads a modern Catholic thinker, 'the concept of

---

[34] This is the conclusion of the respected Jewish scholar Martin Buber (*Kingship of God*, New Jersey & London: Humanities Press International, 1967) whose insight is based mainly on Julius Wellhausen's account of the early history of Islam (J. Wellhausen, *Die religiös-politischen Oppositionsparteien im alten Islam*. Göttingen, 1901. (Eng. tr. by R.C. Ostle & S.M. Walzer, *The Religio-Political Factions in Early Islam*, Amsterdam, 1975.)

[35] H. Gadamer, *Reason in the Age of Science*, Cambridge, MA: MIT Press, 1981. Cf. Paul Tillich, 'The Political Meaning of Utopia' in his *Political Expectation*, New York: Harper & Row, 1971 (re-print: Mercer University Press, 1981) for a suggestive reflection on this theme.

[36] Bertrand De Jouvenel, *On Power: The Natural History of its Growth*, Indianapolis, Liberty Fund, 1993 (original French edn: Geneva, 1945), p. 31.

[37] This thesis was formulated by Carl Schmitt in his celebrated, albeit controversial, work: *Political Theology: Four Chapters on the Concept of Sovereignty*, Cambridge, MA: MIT Press, 1988 (orig. German edn: Berlin, 1922/34)

sovereignty is intrinsically wrong'.[38] The source of the logical, not to speak of the moral, error lay in the original concept advanced by Jean Bodin which separated the sovereign from the body-politic. Likewise, sovereignty of the people is untenable as 'it is nonsensical to conceive of the people as governing themselves *separately from themselves and from above themselves*'.[39] Rousseau compounded the problem by endowing the concept with another mystical notion, the General Will. Rousseau's mythical, and totalitarian, entity stipulated the sovereignty of the people as a whole but excluded the possibility of any particular bodies of citizens or associations enjoying in the state any kind of autonomy! Finally, the doctrine of sovereignty required that no decision made by the sovereign, whether conceived as the Moral God or the General Will, could possibly be resisted by the individual conscience in the name of justice. Sovereignty thus came to possess a status above that of the moral law itself.

The concept of sovereignty, being one with that of Absolutism, must be done away with, as must the claim of the non-accountability of the state. For, what has transpired in modern political theory is that the power without accountability of the personal sovereign of the age of Absolutism has been transferred to the so-called legal personality of the state. However, the concept of sovereignty, even if improper to political philosophy is proper to theology, for 'it loses its poison when it is transplanted from politics to metaphysics. In the spiritual sphere there is a valid concept of Sovereignty. God, the separate Whole, is sovereign over the created world.'[40] In any case, state-sovereignty is no guarantee for justice and righteousness. For, construed strictly legally within its formal framework, even a Nazi state is sovereign and legitimate! Little wonder that the most disquieting consequences of the Nietzschean concept of amoral power is that genocide has become the measure of civilisation itself.[41]

Secularism does not present a unified theory or a systematic doctrine and the Muslim critic is obliged to resist the temptation of imparting on it a theoretical and epistemological unity which it manifestly lacks. Secularism, in short, must not be sanctified as a 'Grand Theory', or the 'Master Paradigm' of the West. Like any other human reality, Western civilisation is beset by its own inner contradictions which do not lend themselves to the postulation of any absolute theoretical unity. Indeed, the only lesson worth learning out of this exercise is about the complexity and richness of human experience and the inadequacy and poverty of theory. Or as Goethe has expressed so eloquently:

[38] Jacques Maritain, *Man and the State*, University of Chicago Press, 1951, p. 29.

[39] *Ibid.*, p. 44.

[40] *Ibid.*, p. 49.

[41] Z. Bauman, *Modernity and the Holocaust*, Oxford: Polity Press, 1991.

Grau, teurer Freund, is alle Theorie.
Und grhn des Lebens goldner Baum.
(Grey, my dear friend, is every theory,
And green alone life's golden tree.)

We must also avoid looking at the ideational landscape of our times as a battlefield between Islamic theocracy and Western secularism. The contest is not between Islam and modernity, neither is it between Islamic faith and secular rationality; indeed, not even between Muslim will-to-power and the secular world-order (whose rhetoric solicits a cultural and political pluralism but whose institutions dictate monism), but between faith in a transcendent being and the totalitarian project for an immanent social utopia conceived as the ultimate end (*al-akhira*). So long as the western man has taken upon himself to act as the advocate of secularism, so long as modern man, whatever his descent and persuasion, is adamant upon renouncing transcendence, *Homo islamicus* has no other option but to stand firm in his faith in an ultimately trans-secular order of reality.

SECULARISM IN THE ARAB MAGHREB

Rachid Al-Ghannouchi

The model of secularism that emerged in the Arab Maghreb is one of its most radical forms. It has given rise to autocratic regimes such as the Tunisian regime, which is known for espousing a form of secularism more radical than Kemalism itself. Ruling elites in both Algeria and Morocco have espoused the same model of secularism since independence. What is common to the secularist elites of the Arab Maghreb is that they are all graduates of the French school of thought which declared war against the church and had absolute confidence in reason, in the human being as the centre of the universe and in science as the ultimate solution to human problems. Notwithstanding this clear cultural background, North African secular elites did not pursue the model of their Western inspirers or even a model similar to that of Turkey, where a relative separation was established between religion and the state, and whereby the state withdrew from the spiritual sphere, leaving it in the hands of the religious establishment.

The constitutions of the Arab Maghreb countries state clearly that 'Islam is the religion of the state'. One would, thus, expect these states not to be strictly secularist, that is in the sense of the separation of state and religion. But this is not the case. Whereas in classical theocracies the religious establishment is controlled by the state, in the Arab Maghreb it is the state, which is run by a secularist elite in every case, that controls religion and runs its institutions. *Imams* (prayer leaders) in mosques are appointed by the state, which administers their affairs and may even dictate the content of the Friday sermon. A dual role is played by the head of state: on the one hand he is *amir al-mu'minin* (leader of the faithful) and *hami hima al-din* (protector of the sanctuary of religion), who orders the establishment of a special department for issuing *fatwas*, or religious judgements, and the formation of special councils for Islamic *da'wah* (preaching); and on the other he is the apostle of 'modernisation'. Former Tunisian President Bourguiba is known to have said that the mission of the state was to raise Tunisian society to the standard of civilised nations. The state here is a superior and capable power, all-wise, far-sighted and having thorough knowledge of what is best for the public interest. It is above society and above class conflict; a patriarchal state that guides groups and individuals enlightening them of their interests. But it does not hesitate when necessary to punish the pigheaded, those whom it regards a threat to its interests.

Nationalising religion

'Pseudo-secularism' is what this model of secularism should be called; it is a counterfeit that takes from Western secularism its most negative aspects and discards the positive ones. The proponents of pseudo-secularism believe that modernising society should not be restricted to propagating knowledge and science, but should also include reshaping society according to how they envisage the French model, a model that advocates a break with the past. Instead of establishing a separation between what is mundane and what is religious, or merely marginalising the role of religion in society, pseudo-secularists seek to impose full control over the institutions and symbols of religion, and not only to claim, but even monopolise the right to reinterpret religion. In other words, the Arab Maghreb version of secularism has been turned by its advocates into some form of a 'church', which one may compare to the church in medieval Europe.

The Tunisian head of state, for instance, acts as if he were a *mujtahid* (leading scholar) and in doing so he sees no need for the testimony of experts. Former President Bourguiba went so far as to call upon his people to follow his example by not observing the fast during the month of Ramadan. In fact he ordered state employees to break the fast. In one of his speeches he ridiculed belief in the existence of Paradise and Hell; he also ridiculed the Qur'an and denied the miracles of the prophets. He closed down the well-known Islamic university of Al-Zaytouna and decreed the prohibition of the *hijab* (women's Islamic code of dress). Both he and his wife made a point of appearing in public wearing swimsuits and he openly boasted that he had extra-marital relationships. Furthermore, he imposed restrictions on the number of citizens allowed to perform pilgrimage every year. Worst of all, he nationalised the endowments of religious institutions.

The Tunisian regime is undoubtedly the most radically secularist in the region. Nevertheless, other regimes in the area that might not have reached the same level of defiance are in essence no different in their policy of nationalising religion and its institutions, in employing religion as a source of legitimacy, in granting themselves the right to dispose with it as if it were their own private property, and in monopolising the right to speak in its name and interpret in it the way they deem fit in order to fulfil the mission of 'modernising' the state. Hence, not a single state in the Arab has permitted the establishment of any religious institution that is independent of the state. None of them has ever hesitated to describe as obscurantism any interpretation of religion that is different from their own, so as to justify repressing it and excluding those who subscribe to it.

Claiming to undertake a modernising mission, the state in the Arab Maghreb justifies the pursuit of an authoritarian policy and the exercise of oppression in order to fulfil its mission. Society is, therefore, not the source of authority but its field of action. Two methods have been used in this regard. The first is the invention, in imitation of the Western experience, of a national identity that is considered to be superior to any other identity such as Arabism or Islam. The second is to reform, in Stalinist fashion, the people's 'mental framework' so that it become sound and compatible with modern life, and to uproot obscurantism.

The 'modernity-modernisation package' brought by the colonialists to the Arab region, and then adopted by the national governments that succeeded them, was carefully designed to impose foreign hegemony on Arab and Islamic societies, especially in the Maghreb, denying them the beneficial aspects of modernity that brought about political and economic successes in the West. Secular elites in these societies, who claim to be the missionaries of modernity, have inherited the role of the colonialists and have inherited their thoughts as well as their means and methods of dealing with the masses which they view as primitive and backward. In the absence of democratic institutions and intoxicated with power, Westernised elites have become so corrupt that they have ended up having a relationship with the masses very similar to the one that existed between the ruling white minority and the black majority in South Africa, except that in the South African case the white minority was more independent of Western influence. As the lust for power vanquished the desire for genuine modernisation, the state was transformed into a machine of total repression, especially as the people increasingly moved toward Islam to reassert their identity and shield themselves from the state, the state of pseudo-modernity.

The state of pseudo-modernity has taken over the remaining institutions of civil society. Mosques, endowments, courts, religious institutes, trade unions, parties, charities and the press have all been seized. In Tunisia, as part of the war against backwardness as Bourguiba called it, the state took control of the economy too. The remarks made by Bourguiba in this regard stand witness to the nature of this pseudo-modern state:

The era of the independence of national organisations is over. There is no more room for the party to stand as an independent unit, or for the General Labourers Union to stand as an independent unit, or for the National Union of Farmers to stand as an independent unit, or for the Union of Industry and Commerce to stand as an independent unit, or for the General Union of Students to stand as an independent unit. Tunisians, whether they are in the General Labourers Union, or in the National Union of Farmers, or in the Union of Industry and Commerce, or in the General Union of Students, are before anything else members of the National Constitutional Party.[1]

Throughout much of the Arab world, to varying degrees, modernisation as pursued by the ruling elites was based on nationalising society and containing it within the elitist state, the state within the party and the party within the person of the leader. The primary concern of the modern Arab state has been to maintain its hegemony over society and its educational, judicial, cultural, economic and vocational institutions. An important target of state hegemony has understandably been the army and the police. These were the first state institutions to be 'modernised', or in other words transformed into repressive apparatuses. The emerging oligarchies needed to shield themselves and protect their interests from the general public. They also needed to legitimise their monopoly of power. The powers granted to both departments increased as the first signs of social rebellion surfaced. Today prisons of the 'pseudo-modern' state have become the abode, not of criminals, but of writers, artists, intellectuals, athletes and all sorts of talented people, whether Islamists, nationalists, leftists or otherwise. Their crime is that they dream of democracy. Some of them may have objected to the deteriorating situation and some may have only thought of protesting. Most of society lives on the peripheries of the state, terrorised and crushed by its apparatus.

The West bears moral responsibility for creating and maintaining undemocratic secularist regimes in Northern Africa in the name of promoting modernity. One wonders whether the West would pride itself on having accomplished a modernity that has ended in police states whose regimes legitimise repression in the name of democracy and human rights and in the name of defending civil society against an alleged 'obscurant fundamentalist onslaught'. It is regrettable that some in the West have been deluded into believing that the conflict between the Islamists and the regime in Tunisia is between fundamentalism and modernity, between democracy and religious extremism. We wish it were! For had it been at heart a civilisational conflict, it would have been possible to search for common denominators.

Instead of pseudo-modernity, Islamists today seek genuine modernity, one that emanates from within, one that is in response to local needs and that is in conformity with the local culture and value system. No Muslim would reject modernisation in as far as it means employing modern tools, procedures or mechanisms in managing politics or in running the economy. We, the Tunisian Islamists, value human dignity and civil liberties, accept that the popular will is the source of political legitimacy and believe in pluralism and in the alternation of power through free elections.

[1] From a speech given by the former President of Tunisia on 2 April 1963.

We recognise, however, that conflict between Islamic culture and aspects of the incoming Western culture does exist, whether in Tunisia or in other parts of the Arab or Muslim world. Perhaps it is these points of conflict that provide existing regimes with the opportunity to claim in their pursuit of Western support and protection that they represent the forces of modernity that are engaged in conflict with the forces of reaction and obscurantism. But are they really the representatives of true modernity? Consider the example of the most infamous pretender to modernity in modern Arab history, former Tunisian President Bourguiba. He was not a moderniser except in as much as he was anti-religion and in as much as he was infatuated with the French or American model of industrial and scientific progress. But as far as governance was concerned, he resembled more the kings of medieval Europe or the defunct rulers of Eastern Europe than the liberal democratic systems of the West.

The point here is that contrary to what the official media in Tunisia, as well as in its neighbouring Arab states, propagate, the conflict between governments and Islamic movements has no relevance whatsoever to those points of disagreement which may exist between Islam and modernity. The conflict is not a religious conflict. Nor is it even a conflict between religion and the Western concept of secularism. It is a political conflict between the oppressor and the oppressed, between a people that has been struggling for its freedom and dignity, for power-sharing as well as resource-sharing, and against an absolute corrupt ruler who has turned the state into a tool for repression. Like snakes, despotic rulers keep changing their skins. In the past Bourguiba practised repression in the name of national unity, while Nasser did it in the name of liberating Palestine and uniting the Arabs. Today, it is practised in the name of democracy, human rights, defending civil society and making peace with Israel. But slogans do not alter the fact that the nature of the conflict is straightforwardly political. It is about legitimacy and to whom it belongs. It is about the nature of government, about the choice between autocracy and democracy.

More than a century of modernisation has produced disastrous results: the most terrible of all has been undermining the cultural identity of the people. For instance, modernisation undertaken in the Arab Maghreb countries was accompanied by a persistent campaign to replace the Arabic language, the symbol of identity and the official language of Islam, by French. So far, all the Arabisation projects executed in the three countries of the Arab Maghreb to repair the damage done over the years have failed. The new generation is torn between two languages, neither of which is commanded well. At the institutional level, Islam has been emptied of its legislative and juridical components. Its institutions have been stripped of their traditional independence and the ruling elite monopolises the right to speak in its name. In the wake of the coup against

democracy in Algeria, the law on Arabisation was repealed and plans to
revoke customary family law were set in motion. Parties or organisations
suspected of having an Islamic orientation have been outlawed. The institutions of civil society, such as trade unions, private organisations and
political parties, have become dominated and controlled by the state.
The role of the police and the army has been enhanced, and they have
been awarded excessive powers. Economic institutions have been
taken over by the ruling elite, and the state has been transformed into a
Mafia-like family of interests. The gap between the ruling elite and the
rest of society has increased, and less and less people are involved in
decision-making or in benefiting from the policies of the government.
Democracy, as a set of mechanisms for the proper administration of
society and a formula for power-sharing, has been rejected and only a
decorative form of 'democracy' has been installed, mostly in response to
pressure from an embarrassed West. The circle of repression has been
on the increase and the number of political prisoners has been on the
rise. In response to state repression, at least two of the three countries
have witnessed the eruption of extreme forms of violence that are only
likely to persist and escalate so long as the root of the problem is not dealt
with.

   Such are the outcomes of a century-long modernisation at the hands of
a corrupt elite that has led the region to the threshold of civil war, economic bankruptcy, social disintegration, moral dissolution and greater
subordination to Western powers. In this tortured century the modern
Arab state has developed into a machine of repression whose mission is
to strip society of its identity and uproot it from its history and civilisational
links. Violence, both overt and covert, has been the means; and the extent
to which the state relies on violence is inversely proportional the degree
of its legitimacy. Nowhere in the Arab world, let alone in the Arab
Maghreb, has a state been founded on democratic legitimacy. The National Liberation Front (FLN) in Algeria and the Constitutional Party in
Tunisia ruled alone for nearly a quarter of a century deriving legitimacy
from the struggle during the war of liberation. In Morocco, however, a
cocktail of the legacy of liberation, religion and a small dose of democracy has constituted the source of legitimacy. In all three, over the years,
the legacy of the war of liberation diminished as a source of legitimacy
due to the 'bankruptcy' of the Westernisation project. The failure of the
modernisation process in fulfilling the basic needs of the masses prompted a rise in public protests and in demands for justice and democracy.
The state's response has been a mixture of violence, manoeuvring and
containment. In every case some kind of a strictly controlled form of
pluralism has been permitted.

   In Algeria, under mounting pressure in the wake of the popular uprising in 1988, the state had no option but to concede to the will of the

people and opt for pluralisation. The objective was to give the state a chance to regain control and then withdraw its concessions. The popular impact was much greater than expected, and the containment plan ended in failure. The elitist, oppressive, Westernised and corrupt state reacted, only to expose its true nature as an imperial legacy and remnant of colonialism in the land of Islam. A comparison between the methods used in the Algeria of 1992 to suppress the people, who have been marginalised by a fake and backward version of modernity, with the methods pursued by the French occupation authorities in pre-independence Algeria would show clearly the resemblance and the linkage between the colonial state and the subordinate post-independence state and between the old and the new liberation revolutions. The resemblance in attitude and the connection between the Algerian secularists and their French counterparts is evident in a *Le Monde* editor's remark expressing bafflement at the success of the Islamists in the Algerian elections, asking 'Will the army save democracy in Algeria?'[2] In a statement aimed at calming the fears of the dismayed French people and dissipating their anxieties in the wake of the Algerian 'volcanic eruption', French politician Michael Jobar proclaimed with confidence: 'The Algerian army has not spoken yet.' The army in Algeria eventually did speak. Just a few days before the second round of elections was due to be held, the military took over, suspended the democratic process, cancelled the first round of elections, sent the victors and their supporters to desert concentration camps and set fire to the entire country.

The Western response to the cancellation of elections in Algeria has been a source of great dismay and disappointment for many Muslims around the world. Muslims have discovered that only the ends matters in Western political rationale. Ethics and human rights are subservient to interests; values are only necessary if they will bring to power 'liberals' (as in Eastern Europe), but they are dispensable if the result is power for the genuine and sincere children of the land, and an end to minority regimes that are the legacy of the colonial era. To prevent the latter situation from occurring, prisons may be packed with political opponents and the state may resort to torture, economic deprivation and even rape, as has become official policy as evident in Amnesty International's reports on Tunisia and Algeria.

Islamists today are the victims, repressed under the pretext – witness Algeria – of saving democracy from themselves. Alleging that if the Islamists were permitted to gain power through the ballot box they would put an end to democracy, the purported supporters of secularism justify for themselves the undermining of what they set forth to protect, and so justify the violation of every single human right. All the while,

---

[2] *Le Monde diplomatique,* 1 Jan. 1992.

their Western friends are expected to remain silent. We find ourselves
asking a question also posed by some of our friends in the West: 'Is it fair
to turn a blind eye when the secularists break the law in the present and
condemn the Islamists for the mere supposition that they might break
the law in the future?'[3]

The plights of Algeria and Tunisia are not dissimilar. For in both cases
when the democratic choice of the people is not in favour of the secularist elite, undemocratic measures become acceptable. These may include:
emergency laws, government-appointed parliamentarians and forged
elections in which the ruling party can gain up to ninety-eight per cent
and the only presidential candidate wins no less than 99.99 per cent of
the vote, of course after sending his competitors, who may not necessarily be 'fundamentalists', as in the Tunisian case, to prison.[4]

One may suppose that North African secularist regimes are in a real
dilemma: while their programmes of development and modernisation
have proven to be a total failure and their records of human rights are so
'shameful' that they have been condemned by every single human rights
organisation in the Western hemisphere, they are seriously challenged
by the Islamic movements which have adopted the people's demands for
justice, democracy, dignity and independence. What makes things worse
is that the repression resorted to by these regimes – whose legitimacy has
been eroded by corruption and bankruptcy – is not restricted to the Islamists. The Islamists have not been targeted just because of their ideology,
although admittedly repressing them causes fewer problems at the international level, and may even be profitable.[5] Repression is practised against
the entire society and is necessitated by the nature of the ruling elite and
by its interests and associations.

Linguistic illusions

Nevertheless, one must distinguish between the Western and the Arab
experience of secularism. The ruling political mode in Tunisia and other
similar places in the Arab world since independence does not resemble
the Western liberal form of government except in its rebellion against

---

[3] *Promise Unfulfilled: Human Rights in Tunisia Since 1987*, Lawyers Committee for
Human Rights, October 1993, p. 62.

[4] During the March 1994 presidential elections in Tunisia Dr Moncef Marzouki, former
president of the Tunisian League of Human Rights, and Mr Abderrahman Hani, a minor
politician, were both arrested for nominating themselves for the post of President of the
Republic. Even though a constitutional obstacle prevented either from making it on to
the ballot, the regime was furious. See Francis Ghiles' article in *The Financial Times* of
18 March 1994, and *Ennahda*'s 22 March 1994 statement on the elections.

[5] In a symposium on German policy in Africa organised by the German Corporation for
Africa on 27 April 1994, a German expert by the name of Dr Koon noted that the
dominant impression in some African states, such as Tunisia, is that if the state combats

religion and its inclination toward libertinism. In all other aspects, the similarity is with fascist and communist regimes. Unlike Western secularism, which led to the emancipation of the mind from the authority of religion, and emancipated both religion and society from the authority of the church, secularism in the modern Arab experience resulted in pledging religion, society and the mind to the hegemony of a new church, the state of the secular elite, or what one may call the state of 'secular theocracy'. An example of 'secular theocracy' in Tunisia is the indictment made by the state's attorney general demanding the execution of Sheikh Rahmouni in 1962. The indictment read: 'The defendant has permitted himself to have an understanding of the Qur'an contrary to the understanding of his excellency the president.' A more recent example is that of a meeting of the *imams* (mosque prayer leaders) on the 29th day of the fasting month of Ramadan in March 1992, during which Tunisian President Ben Ali addressed the congregation saying: 'The State has sole responsibility for religion.' In another incident, the Tunisian minister of religious affairs took it upon himself to issue a *fatwa* declaring one of the main Tunisian political parties, Ennahda (Renaissance), godless. It is in the shade of this secular theocracy that mosques are considered to be the property of the state, and their *imams* held fully accountable to its authority. They are appointed by the state, and punished or sacked if they violate the directives of the prime minister.

In contrast to the Western experience, where secularism is associated with scientific progress, industrial revolution and democratic government, pseudo-secularism in the Arab experience has destroyed society and rendered it easy prey to a corrupt elite that very much resembles the Mafia in Italy or the white minority in the defunct apartheid regime of South Africa. Secularism in North Africa is a church of the same type against which the West rebelled.

Sometimes, language overwhelms us with a world of illusions, and causes the West to sympathise with its secular 'children' who are now claiming to lead the Muslim world toward modernity. These are linguistic illusions and not the realities of the Muslim world. The Muslim world is governed by pre-modern European-style regimes from the age of theocracy and absolutism. Such regimes certainly do not belong to the age of democracy, freedom, people's sovereignty and the right to self-determination.

Nevertheless, not all models of secularisation in the Muslim world are the same. In spite of the fact that some ultra-secularist Arab Maghreb governments claim to emulate the Turkish model of Kemalism, in many respects, the latter could be deemed mild in comparison. In the Turkish

---

fundamentalism it is more likely to get what it wants from the West and that it will not be accused of violating democracy.

experience, some room has been left for religious freedom, and society has retained many of its religious institutions which remain relatively independent. In Tunisia, in contrast, the 'Pope' is represented in the person of the president, whether Ben Ali or Bourguiba, who proclaims: 'I am the representative of Islam and no one has the right to speak in the name of Islam but me.'

While secularism is incompatible with Islamic values, Muslims require 'genuine' modernity no less than anyone else. Genuine modernity entails human emancipation and establishing the right to freedom of choice; the propagation of scientific and technological progress; and the establishment of a democratic system and reassertion of the sovereignty of the people. However, we need to enter modernity in our own way, and not necessarily that of France, the US or Russia. This is the difference between the Islamic approach to modernity and that of the Westernised elite in the Muslim countries. The minority Westernised elite seeks to impose on the majority a false modernity that entails the destruction of the institutions of traditional society, a process that was started by the colonial invaders who came to the Muslims promising them industrial progress and deliverance from backwardness if they rebelled against Islam in its totality, both *Shari'ah* (law) and *'aqidah* (creed).

False modernity has manifested itself in the demolition of Islamic society and its rebuilding on non-religious foundations, not by means of a separation between religion and state, but by totally excluding religion from all aspects of public life. In other words, modernity in the Arab case has not implied the adoption of scientific methods and industrialisation, but a process of radical secularisation whose main concern is to struggle against Islam and its heritage, although modernity and secularism, as far as we understand them, are not inevitably linked except perhaps in the French and Marxist models.

Depending on definition, many Muslims may, justifiably, see that some congruence exists between Islam and secularism. I once had a discussion with Muhammad Arkoun on the relationship between Islam and secularism and asked him to define secularism. He said it meant giving the mind the right to search with no restrictions, or in other words granting reason absolute authority to search without obstruction. I said to him that this particular concept is perfectly compatible with Islam. Islam places no restrictions on the mind, and the Qur'an clearly encourages believers to explore, think and search. Faith itself must be grounded in conviction based on reason; there is no compulsion in religion. Islamic doctrine places no limits on thought, reason or exploration. But, as I explained to him, none of this was characteristic of the secularism of its proponents in the Arab world. The model of secularism preached there has only been conducive to despotism, to the absolute control by a tiny elite of the resources, religion and conscience of the nation in the name of democracy, modernity and secularism, and sometimes even in the name of Islam itself.

As for the values of true modernity, many of them are perfectly compatible with Islam. Once the Muslims are given the chance to comprehend the values of Western modernity, such as democracy and human rights, they will search within Islam for a place for these values where they will implant them, nurse them and cherish them just as Westerners did before implanting them in much less fertile soil.

Pseudo-secularism and Tunisian civil society

Today, the concept of civil society is associated with non-governmental organisations which seek – as mediators between the state and the individual members of society – to improve and bolster the intellectual, spiritual and moral standards of these members and of the community as a whole. The purpose of these organisations is to achieve as much self-sufficiency and independence from the state as possible, curbing its power of intervention and, when necessary, to mature into a force to influence the state and supervise its performance. This conception concurs with the role of the *ummah*, the society Muslims established more than fourteen centuries ago. As a society founded to a large extent on freedom and voluntary cooperation, where authority is not repressive, and having regard to relations among its individual members, traditional Muslim society is a model of civil society. Many characteristic features of Islamic society can be seen as common to the modern conception of civil society: power is not monopolised by the state, but rather shared between government – the political authority – and society, with the balance in favour of the latter; the state has no monopoly over the people's sustenance, so that private ownership is guaranteed; initiatives, whether individual or collective, are free; and the state monopolises neither education nor the rendering of social or cultural services. It is by virtue of their independence that these institutions fulfil many of the people's needs; and by doing so they secure society against paralysis and protect it from total dependence on the state.

Tunisian civil society remained invariably lively and intact from the Islamic conquest in the late seventh century until independence in 1956, notwithstanding the threat that started creeping in with the advent of French colonialism in 1881. Throughout the ages and until the French took over, all property in the pre-colonial era was privately owned, belonging to tribes, families or *awqaf* (endowment trust). Education, at all levels, was available free of charge and was independent of the government having been paid for by the *awqaf*. An individual citizen sought protection in his tribe, his family, his Sufi denomination or his professional association. One third of all agricultural properties were owned by endowments. The colonisers embarked on a 'modernisation' campaign aimed primarily at undermining traditional values and institutions. The colonialists' onslaught on the country's cultural edifice strangled the values of compassion, cooperation and fraternity in favour of materialistic and individualistic incentives. A considerable proportion of public properties was seized, and the local market – which was based on the principle of self-sufficiency – was linked to the French and European markets. Formal cultural, judicial, political and social institutions were set up to compete with and undermine local, or *ahli*, institutions. Despite all these measures part of civil society remained intact, though weakened. Schools and mosques remained independent. The profound roots of traditional civil society, with its values and civil structure, managed to generate a resistance movement that struggled against the occupier and confronted its plan to destroy civil society. However, the secular trend, which was created and sustained within the parallel educational institutions that were founded by the coloniser, succeeded in infiltrating the resistance movement and in controlling it.

Thus, the independence achieved from the French in 1956 was not a real victory. In fact it turned out to be a continuation of the process of destruction in the form of an intensive campaign to culturally annex Tunisia to France as fast as possible. Whereas the French failed in their bid to undermine Tunisia's Islamic heritage, their successors, the Tunisian nationalists, in the name of modernity, succeeded. Westernisation, the process of stripping society of its cultural identity, continued ever more vigorously through the propagation of self-debasing values and institutionalising admiration for the coloniser, which meant blindly imitating them, considering them to be the model for civilisational progress. But while doing so, the modern post-independence state made every effort to avoid imitating the Western values of freedom, rule of law and democracy. The government of independence had become an oppressive autocracy. For in order for the process of subordination and destruction to be complete, it was necessary to destroy the Islamic cultural foundation and the civil institutions of society. Tribal and public endowment properties were completely seized. To complete the destruction of the tribal sector, Bedouins were forced to urbanise. The system of education was Westernised and, under the pretext of the emancipation of women, a campaign was launched to encourage relinquishing family values. Women were told their freedom lay in adopting a Western lifestyle and their true value in their economic contribution. Through the control of educational and economic institutions, the post-colonial government succeeded in undermining society in favour of state power.

It did not take long for the people to realise the failure of the modern state model. Society felt the danger such a state model posed to its integrity and viability. A popular uprising against dictatorship and pseudo-modernisation ensued. It was initially leftist, in pursuit of justice; then became liberal, in pursuit of democracy; and in the final stage it became Islamic, in pursuit of an Islamic cultural identity, a common ground on which all those who struggle for justice, democracy and development in Tunisia can stand. This has been the declared mission of the Tunisian Islamic Movement, an endeavour that is aimed at reviving the Islamic spirit so as to constitute a foundation for the reconstruction of civil society. In pursuit of this goal, the movement supported and joined the workers and students and sought to restore the role of the mosque as a centre of cultural and educational activities. Realising that the conflict in Tunisia is in reality between freedom-lovers and tyrannical rulers, between those who defend society and those who defend hegemony, the Islamic movement has marched along the painful path of reconstructing civil society. The Islamic movement's success in breathing new life into civil society by tilting the balance in favour of the people's state rather than the state's people, and its potential threat as seen by the ruling autocracy, prompted the police-state to intervene with all forms of repression and persecution, and with the staging of an election in which the president and his party won 99.99 per cent of the votes.

French versus Anglo-Saxon

In liberal thought civil society is supposed to be founded on 'civil sentiment', on an upbringing that encourages law-abiding. It is a society in which moral obligation and the need to coexist with others is an overwhelming sentiment. Civil society stands in contrast to natural society, and 'civility' is the transition from a natural condition to political condition, where an individual concedes some of his or her freedom for the sake of coexisting with others and attaining certain social benefits that bring peace, security and development. In the natural condition an individual enjoys unlimited freedom, but cannot fully develop his or her moral, intellectual, and creative abilities because such a development essentially requires coexisting under an umbrella of law and authority. Hence, the social contract assumed that in the transition from the natural to the civil condition – that is the political condition – man conceded or lost, some of his freedom in exchange for the benefits of a social existence.

As a result of extreme secularisation, the concept of civil society has been used to counter religious practice. This has been more so in Francophone cultures under the influence of the French experience of violent conflict between Church and Revolution. This radical secularist culture has tended to exclude religion, barring it from having any influence on the social process. Some of the foes of religion in the Arab world, who are strongly opposed to the Islamic project, among them the 'Bolshevists' who are enemies of liberalism and contractual society, have adopted the French tradition and donned the robes of civil society so as to undermine their Islamic foes. Stressing that the concept of civil society has been used in Tunisia as a weapon against the Islamists, sociologist Abdelqadir Zghal points out that Tunisian communists, both Marxists and Leninists, have made use of the concept to counter the Islamists, though after some hesitation.[6]

The influence of the French Revolution's thought upon North African secularists, which had in the past driven many of them to an extreme form of Marxism, is a major obstacle to dialogue between them and the Islamists. These secularists have been less influenced by Anglo-Saxon thought, which is much more tolerant in its view of the relationship between the religious and the political. They have sought in recent years to use the concept of civil society not as a tool of struggle against dictatorship but as a weapon in the war against the phenomenon of Islamic resurgence. In so doing, they have endeavoured to impart on civil society an anti-religious, anti-Islamic, dimension. Portraying the civil to be a function of the secularist, and secularism to be a condition for democracy, Islam has been portrayed as an associate of obscurantism and despotism. Arab societies are then told to choose between a combination of religion, dictatorship and totalitarianism on the one hand, and a combination of civility, democracy, freedom and secularism on the other.

This is an 'arbitrary dogmatisation' of a process; a dogmatisation of a Marxist or French heritage imported and removed from its original habitat and stripped of its sociological and historical significance. It is arbitrary because the European tradition is not, and should not be thought of as, based exclusively on the French experience of conflict between religion and modernity. In Anglo-Saxon societies, no such sharp conflicts between the religious and the civil, or the religious and the political have been experienced. In this tradition, the church was a central station along the path to modernity; religious reform was a principal contributor to the Enlightenment. From the Reformation onwards, religion gradually ceased to be an obstacle; it acted, with varying degrees, as a catalyst in the process that reinstated the value of mundane action whereas prior to that mundane activity was portrayed as antithetical to religion.

Today the religious establishment in the West is not just one of the main institutions of civil society but its largest institution ever. Represented by the church (though increasingly pluralistic – mosques, synagogues, Hindu temples etc.), the religious establishment is well organised

---

[6] Abdelqadir Zghal, 'Al-Mujtama' al-Madani wal-Sira' min Ajl al-Haymana al-Aydilujiyah fil-Maghrib al- 'Arabi' in *Al-Mujtama' al-Madani fil-Watan al-'Arabi*, Arab Unity Studies Centre, Beirut 1992, p. 431.

and enjoys an independent status which qualifies it to contribute substanti-
ally to checking and balancing the power of the state in favour of society.
The church has a significant moral and spiritual influence on the public;
it possesses a large network of educational, social and relief organisations
and is financially independent of the state thanks to the collections it
makes and to the revenues obtained from its huge investments, which
make it one of the richest institutions of civil society. The church provides the members of the community with spiritual warmth and a kind
of moral protection against the atheistic culture that is propagated by the
institutions of the secular state in the West. While contributing to the
initiation and maintaining of dialogue, the church provides, through the
various charities that belong to it, financial aid to the destitute and the
needy. The church in the West is not, therefore, considered antithetical to
civil society.

Those who insist on perceiving civility as a rebellion against religion
fail to see a distinction between the modern, civil and benevolent role
played by the church today and the historical inhumane and anti-social
role played by the religious establishment in the Middle Ages when wars
of extermination, colonial ambitions and horrible repression were carried out in the name of religion; when in the name of heaven intellectual
and scientific progress was suppressed and innovation prohibited; and
when legitimacy was bestowed upon despotic governments that exploited
the weak and prospered on the spread of myths and illusions. The role
and image of the church in the West have changed. It is true that some
churches have not yet been completely cured from the addiction to justifying the exploitation of the weak and the legitimation of genocide, as
has been the attitude of the Orthodox Church in Serbia with regard to the
ethnic cleansing carried out against the Muslims of Bosnia. But this is to
be contrasted with the humane conduct and noble stand of the Catholic
Church which stood against fascism in Croatia.

Civility versus barbarity

Civility is the transition from the legitimacy of power and necessity in the
natural state to the legitimacy of law, or to what may be called the people's
legitimacy, the legitimacy of choice. This process represents a transition
from the condition of natural association with the clan. Natural association here is analogous to the type of association that exists in beehives
or ants' nests. Such communities are unlike civil society: although they
do exist as a community, theirs is a natural community, membership
is involuntary and their administration is instinctive. In contrast, a civil
society is a community whose members associate together voluntarily,
and in which relations are governed by law, which in itself is an expression of their free will. Whereas law in civil society is chosen by the

community, which has the potential and the power to develop it further, this is not the case with bees and ants, whose system of operation is instinctive and whose law is not only unchangeable but is adhered to by the members involuntarily.

Similarly, a tribal society cannot be called a civil society, simply because belonging to it and administering its affairs has very little to do with reason, free will or free choice. Individuals belong to the tribe because they happen to be born in it. They cannot choose to belong to another tribe, and they are compelled to carry the legacy of their forefathers irrespective of its burden. An Arab poet from the tribe of Ghuzayyah had described this condition of barbarity saying: 'I am only a Ghuzayyan; if Ghuzayyah strays, I follow suit, and if it heeds guidance, this is my route.' What Islam did was to transfer, or elevate, the people from the stage of instinctive, or natural, belonging – as seen in the tribal condition – to the level of belonging to the community of faith. The transfer was from inherited modes of involuntary belonging to the tribe to a voluntary belonging to an Islamic society. The first Islamic society was therefore a civil society to which individuals progressed from the primitive society of the tribe. This resembles what is known today as the modern state or modern political association, although the latter carries some residues from the tribal society because its association is founded on race, or colour or language or history, whereas an Islamic association is founded solely on faith which individuals embrace freely. Hence, true civility is found in Islamic society, because belonging to it is not founded on instinct or fear. Furthermore, an Islamic society is administered by a state whose relationship with its citizens is based on *bay'ah*, a contract from which the ruler derives the authority to order or forbid, which in turn is an authority that is bound by law or *shari'ah*.

Civility and faith

What distinguishes an Islamic civil society from any other kind is the Islamic faith, which has a profound civilising influence on believers, and so consolidates civil society. To begin with it declares all humans to be equal as the descendants of Adam and as the creation of the one and only Lord. Before their creator, humans, irrespective of their colour, race or gender, are judged according to their deeds. Divine honour is bestowed upon all, and no human is held responsible unless in possession of intellect and the freedom to choose. The entire universe with all its resources and laws has been made subject to humans. They are encouraged to use their intellect and physical power to search for the best means of making use of this universe, which is God's bounty from which no human is to be excluded.

Those who choose to embrace the Islamic faith are told that working hard to earn their living is the only honourable way to fulfil their material needs and preserve their dignity. This is not only encouraged but is considered a religious duty, an act of worship. A person who exerts his physical energy and spends his time seeking to provide for himself and his dependants is more honourable in the eyes of God than he who dedicates himself exclusively to worship expecting others to provide for his needs, or as the Prophet put it: 'An upper [giving] hand is better and more beloved to God than the lower [receiving] one'. Furthermore, by attributing wealth to God, Islam encourages people to seek wealth through hard work. On the other hand, poverty is condemned for being a burden and a companion to infidelity. While the right to private ownership is sanctified, exploitation, monopoly and the acquisition of wealth other than through lawful means are forbidden. Wealth is assigned a social mission that is fulfilled through the concepts of *zakat* and *sadaqah* that constitute the foundation of the Islamic welfare system.[7] If poverty strikes and the wealth collected from *zakat* and other forms of *sadaqah* is insufficient to alleviate the suffering and meet the requirements of the population, the state has the right to levy additional taxes until the crisis is surmounted. This opinion is derived from the principle that preserving life, and saving the community as a whole, have priority over preserving the wealth of individuals.

The third feature of the Islamic faith is that the authority of religion in Islamic society is founded on the freedom of *ijtihad*, which provides a large space for innovation and creativity. A ruler in an Islamic state has no right to monopolise the interpreting of religious texts, nor has he the authority to impose on the public any particular interpretation. Such authority lies in the hands of the *'ulama* (scholars). However, the authority of the *'ulama* cannot be compared to that of the church in Christianity. No such religion-monopolising, paradise-selling establishment exists in Islam. While respecting its *'ulama*, an Islamic society does not lose its freedom of choice. The *'ulama* interpret religion in their capacity as

---

[7] *Zakat* is one of the five pillars of Islam, the others being the *Shahadah* (declaration of faith), *Salat* (prayer), *Siyam* (fasting) and *Hajj* (pilgrimage). Muslims with the financial means (*nisab*) to do so are obliged to give a certain percentage of their wealth (2.5% of net worth, deducted annually) as *zakat*. Other forms of wealth such as cattle, crops, etc. are *zakat*able in their own way. Although it has commonly been defined as a form of charity, almsgiving, donation or contribution, *zakat* differs from these activities primarily in that they are arbitrary actions. *Zakat*, by contrast, is a formal duty not subject to choice. It compels believers to disburse a specific amount of their wealth; and it conditions their identity as Muslims on their willingness to adhere to this fundamental precept of Islam. *Sadaqah* comprises *zakat* as well as all other voluntary charitable contributions. Whereas *zakat* is a compulsory small percentage paid annually by the rich, many other forms of *sadaqah* (charitable contributions) are encouraged; they are optional and neither a minimum nor a maximum is specified. [Editor's note]

mujtahidin[8] not as representatives of some kind of an official establishment that monopolises speaking in the name of God or interpreting his
revelation. What the *'ulama* suggest is no more than their understanding,
or their *ijtihad*, a proposal submitted to the community, which has the
final word in accepting or rejecting. This is an excellent example of the
compatibility of democracy – which may be summed up as the right of
the public to free choice – with Islam. An *ijtihad* that is accepted by the
majority is usually adopted, though on most matters there could be more
than one *ijtihad*. In this case people subscribe to the *ijtihad* they feel
more comfortable with. This shows that an Islamic society is a pluralistic
society in which religion neither suppresses the mind nor confiscates the
right of individuals and communities to free choice.

Islam as a religion has neither been turned into an establishment, nor is
it monopolised by any particular institution, whether private or public.
It remains a source of inspiration and guidance, and is available to all
members of the community.

In traditional Muslim societies, scholars proposed their *ijtihad* to the
people who made the final choice. This explains why Islam has known
four main schools of *ijtihad*: the Maliki, the Hanafi, the Hanbali and the
Shafi'I, to which the Muslim chooses to adhere. Other schools have not
been publicly adopted and remain restricted to the shelved writings
of their founders. This was not due to the actions of any particular political authority nor due to a policy adopted by this state or that, but out of
the free choice of the public. In other words, the schools of *ijtihad* are
societal projects that materialise out of the interaction of Islam with specific social and cultural conditions. Once these conditions change, the
school would have to accommodate them. A failure to do so would inevitably cost an intractable school of jurisprudence its hold on the public,
who might opt for another, and are free to do so.

In a modern Muslim society, the process through which the community may choose from among various *ijtihadat* (pl. of *ijtihad*), or through
which a chosen *ijtihad* becomes law, can be undertaken by an elected
parliament in coordination with a council of legal experts, appointed to
the council on the basis of their qualifications. In a modern Muslim civil
society, one would expect scholars to organise themselves and their
activities in associations or syndicates that would cooperate in one way
or another with the council of experts as well as with the parliament.

The fourth feature of Islam is that faith generates within the believer
a passion for freedom. According to the Algerian thinker Malik Bennabi
the Islamic faith accomplishes two objectives: first, it liberates man from

---

[8] *Mujtahidun* (or *mujtahidin*) is the plural of *mujtahid*: a jurist formulating independent
decisions in legal or theological matters, based on the interpretation and application of
the four *usul*, that is the four foundations of Islamic jurisprudence: Qur'an, Sunna,
qiyas (analogy) and *ijma'* (consensus). [Editor's note]

servitude and renders him un-enslaveable; and second, it prohibits him from enslaving others. This is where the concept of *jihad* lies. *Jihad* is the constant endeavour to struggle against all forms of political or economic tyranny because life has no value in the shade of despotism. Islam wages war against despotism using the weapon of *al-amr bil-ma'ruf wal-nahy 'an al-munkar* (enjoining good and forbidding evil) through a series of actions starting from the heart, that is shunning of evil. This may then progress, depending on ability and resources, to its condemnation through non-violent means of expression, such as speaking up, writing or demonstrating, and, if necessary, to the use of force. What matters here is that oppression should never be given a chance to establish itself in Islamic society. The Muslim is supposed to be a conscientious individual responding with appropriate action to whatever injustice may be perpetrated in society. He is thus a force for positive change, a citizen whose faith reinforces within him the sense of responsibility. This is undoubtedly one of the fundamental concepts of a civil society that is based on voluntary belonging.

This leads to the fifth feature of the role played by the Islamic faith in promoting civility and bolstering civil society. Not only does the Islamic faith permit a Muslim to resist despotism and rebel against it, but it makes it incumbent upon him to do so with whatever means available to him. It is understandable that a Muslim may lose his life struggling against oppression, and for this faith promises a great reward in the life after death. In other words the effort made is not wasted and the sacrifice is not in vain. A magnificent reward awaits a Muslim who loses his life in the cause of fighting oppression. *Iman* (believing) plays an essential role in sustaining the determination of individuals and communities to rise against injustice. *Iman* disarms the pragmatists, who like to use the pretext of an unfavourable balance of power to justify inaction. The Prophet is reported to have said: 'The noblest of *jihad* is speaking out in the presence of an unjust ruler;' and 'Hamza is the master of martyrs, and so is a man who stands up to an unjust ruler by enjoining him and forbidding him, and gets killed for it.' Martyrdom in the Islamic standard is not failure, and a martyr is an aspirant who offers his life for what is much more valuable and, at the same time, eternal.

Tawahush

In spite of the attribution of civility and civil society to the Western liberal tradition, one may find signs of profound potential for *tawahush*[9] in modern Western societies.

---

[9] *Tawahush* is derived from the Arabic word *wahasha* (to be unable to warm or reconcile, or to be alienated or become estranged). *Tawahush* is the return to a wild or savage state, to barbarity. *Wahsh* is Arabic for a wild beast. [Editor's note]

One may cite as signs of this *tawahush* the murder of a young Moroccan man who was thrown into the waters of the river Seine in the heart
of the French capital, by supporters of a right wing political party. One
may also cite the example of the recurrent arson attacks by extreme
right wing German youth on houses belonging to members of the Turkish community, with the savage burning alive of many blameless women
and children. Such things indicate a serious reversal of civility, and a
trend in the direction of the 'jungle'; a return to a barbaric condition
which has seemingly only been abated by economic growth, the source
of much of which has not been local resources, but the colonial pillage
of other nations' resources.

Humans, by nature, have the readiness to become brute. Such readiness is inherent in the human personality which is an arena of constant
struggle between the factors of 'ascent' and 'descent'. The Western
solution to this problem, apart from inventing the concept of the monopolisation of physical violence by the state, has been colonialism. Not
only were the natural resources of other nations pillaged and brought
home to improve the living conditions of citizens, but criminals and
rebels of all sorts were banished to remote colonies. In other words, in
addition to reaping economic benefits, European powers found in colonialism a means of resolving some of their social problems.

Colonialism is also to blame for the present signs of *tawahush* in
various parts of the Muslim world. The phenomenon of violence is a
reaction to Westernisation, the colonial process undertaken by the
Western invaders to divide the Muslims, nurture hostilities among
them and perpetuate their weakness and backwardness through the in-
stallation of puppet Western-supported governments in territorial states
they themselves created. Violence in Algeria, for instance, could not have
erupted, or at least lasted this long, had the French not supported the
ruling military junta in spite of its coup against the democratic process.
In Algeria, as in other Muslim countries where violence is prevalent,
tawahush has been instigated by state security agencies to undermine
the efforts by moderate Islamic movements to promote civility and
peaceful reform. Prior to the coup against democracy in Algeria, the
Islamic Salvation Front (FIS) succeeded in defusing many potentially
explosive human bombs made of the clusters of thousands of deprived
and trivialised young men who were driven to desperation by the system.
Within the ranks of the Front, these, mostly unemployed and frustrated,
individuals not only found something useful to do in the present and
were made to see hope in a better future, but were also persuaded into
accepting, and engaging in, a peaceful process of change through the
ballot box. When FIS leaders were sent to prison, their party outlawed,
the ballot boxes crushed by tanks and thousands of their colleagues banished to desert concentration camps, the survivors of this extermination

campaign had no choice but to take to the mountains, from where they undertook to fight those who, cheered by local secularists and condoned by the West, turned the dream of the Algerian people into a nightmare.

Another example that clearly shows that colonialism is responsible for the signs of *tawahush* in the Muslim world is the State of Israel, which was created, and continues to be sustained, by the West. The violence perpetrated by the Palestinians in Palestine is part of a legitimate struggle for national liberation to reverse a colonial project initiated by Britain and assisted by other Western countries who lend support to the Zionist entity out of the desire to expiate the sin of oppressing the Jews in Europe.

Whereas faith keeps the peace in Islamic civil society, and therefore the pacifying role of the state is kept to a minimum, in Western civil society the prevention of *tawahush*, or the maintenance of civilised standards, requires the dedication of enormous material resources in order to compensate for the erosion of the influence of religious deterrents. As religious values become increasingly insignificant, and consequently less influential, people's violence is principally checked using 'stick and carrot' policies. In the West, this has been made possible, on the one hand, by the state's monopoly of violence, and, on the other, by welfarism, the reward of the colonial pillage of other nations' resources, but not by the influence of civil sentiment. In other words, whereas religious values generate and cherish civil sentiment, liberalism, upon which the values of modern Western societies have been constructed, depresses it.

Liberalism is best seen as having two faces, one bright and one dark. The former, namely political liberalism, is exemplified by the democratic system and by the recognition and defence of rights and freedoms. The dark side is the philosophical dimension of liberalism which is based on the belief in the absolute ability of the mind to independently organise life; on giving precedence to the individual over the community; on excluding religious guidance and values from the organisation of economics, social relations, politics and international relations; and on ignoring the metaphysical component of man in favour of solely fulfilling his material needs.

As economic growth falters and states are compelled to shrink their welfare programmes, the absence of rewards will trigger *tawahush*. Today we are witnessing a decline in revenue. Cracks have started appearing in the matrix of Western society. As Ernest Gellner suggested in 1995 in a speech at the London School of Economics, when 'wolves' (states) are no longer able to leave 'dogs' (citizens) any more crumbs to feed on, the dogs will turn into wolves. By then, there will be nothing left to devour but society itself. Samples of this transformation were seen in the riots in Los Angeles, the disturbances in Brixton and Liverpool in Britain and the workers' strikes in France and Germany.

The incident of a number of Los Angeles policemen beating a black driver just because of the colour of his skin cannot be regarded as a feature of a long-lasting civil society. The incident and the riots associated with the trial of the policemen implicated in the attack were an expression of the injustices and frustrations of US civil society. The events are likely to be repeated. More riots could ensue in San Francisco, or in Chicago or in New York. The Palestinian uprising would seem very mild compared to the catastrophic consequences of future 'explosions' in the heartland of America or for that matter in the centres of big European cities such as London, Liverpool, Paris and Berlin. This is due to the factors promoting the emancipation of barbarity inherent in Western societies, what may be described as the 'remnants of natural society' that is founded on power and greed in lieu of truth and justice.

However, the existence of these impulses to barbarity should not prevent us from recognising that Western societies have within them impulses to civility too. The most notable manifestation of these impulses to civility is the existence of numerous voluntary organisations that defend human rights, combat racism and undertake a variety of benevolent activities. Western societies are pluralistic and complex, and significant sectors of people cherish values little different from those enjoined by Islam. However, the conflict between the impulses to civility and to *tawahush* may eventually lead to unfavourable results if religious values are not reinstated and individualistic tendencies curbed. When civil sentiment is deepened it provides a stronger and much more sound foundation for the respect and observance of the law. Good is recognised as good and evil as evil, and people would think of others as they would think of themselves, or as Kant put it 'act as if your action would be made universal.' However, when such lofty values are wrapped in materialistic philosophy and in atheism, as in the case of Western liberal societies, they become too idealistic.

Humans are instinctively inclined to think in terms of gains and losses. Most humans do good not because it is good, but because doing so may reap them some benefit or bring them a feeling of enjoyment or delight. Similarly, they avoid evil not because it is evil, but because they are keen to escape harm, pain or misery. It is true that there are those in the West who respect the law for the sake of the law; only a small, though highly distinguished, minority act in such fashion. The majority respect the law either for the benefit it brings them or to avoid punishment. Furthermore, while those who violate the law may be penalised, those who abide by it usually receive no reward.

In Islamic civil society, faith has authority over the conscience of individuals. In other words it has the power of a deterrent, discouraging individuals from violating the law. For the faithful, respecting the law brings immediate as well as deferred benefits. Here lies the significance of the Islamic concept of *taqwa*, understood as the constant presence of God in the life of the faithful. To a Muslim, observing the law is not only conscience-satisfying but is, above all, an act of worship to gain the pleasure of the Almighty. It would follow that in the Islamic state, worldly deterrents are not the only crime prevention measures available; abiding by the law, doing good and avoiding evil, or what may be summed up as civil sentiment, is reinforced by *taqwa*.

An Islamic civil society is one that is founded on the Prophetic maxim: 'None of you truly believes until he wishes for his brother what he wishes for himself.' It is a civil society in which good is done and evil is avoided not out of fear of the state but in response to the call of religious conscience, exemplified in another Prophetic tradition: 'God is compassionate to those who show compassion to his creatures on earth.' Civility here means liberating oneself from selfishness; a person's civility is a function of his ability to transcend his egoism and control his desires. In contrast to these Islamic values, one does not see in liberal philosophy a good answer to the question of why one should do good. Doing good because it brings you pleasure or protects you from harm is fair but not enough. One may ask, what good does it do me to sacrifice my pleasure, or to take the trouble to help my kin or my neighbour or give to the poor or charity? For many people, good is simply what brings pleasure, evil what causes pain.

Although it is true that in every community there are those who do good solely for the sake of doing it, they are the exception and not the norm. Most people fulfil obligations because in the end an interest is served, either in the form of gaining certain benefits or averting harm. In other words, humans are by nature more willing to satisfy their desires than gratify their conscience. Islam recognises this weakness and responds by imparting a dimension to interest or benefit that transcends the worldly and the material. Benefit is not restricted to this life. Whereas some reward may be collected before death, a more important, most valuable and eternal reward is collected in the life after death, hence the centrality of the concept of life-after-death to the Islamic way of life. Individuals are trained to sacrifice their own personal interests to serve the public interest; they do so because they are promised a great reward if they forfeit what is immediate and temporary in exchange for that which is delayed but everlasting.

Secularism: the bear and the fly

In light of the above, secularism may be considered an impediment to the preservation and development of civil society. In Western liberal societies, as a result of the marginalisation of religion, secularism has compounded the effect of individualism in reinforcing selfishness and encouraging a feverish drive to make profit and fulfill materialistic needs with little or no consideration for spiritual needs. In spite of the initial role played by secularism in consolidating civil society, it has ended doing the exact opposite. Allied with liberalism, which is a synonym for selfishness, greed and individualism, secularism will eventually do away not only with the notion of civil society but with society itself, turning it into terrifying isolated islets, conditions within which resemble those prevailing in today's big cities of the West. In the societies of Western cities one may see manifest signs of erosion, a great potential for the eruption of *tawahush*. What civility remains in Western cities, what warmth, what compassion? They have become isolated but crowded with millions of people. Inhabitants neighbour each other in body but not in soul. They fear each other, and some of them make a living out of terrorising their fellow citizens. A person may live twenty, thirty or even fifty years without knowing much about his closest neighbours, let alone communicating or cooperating with them.

Secularism is to blame for this serious deterioration in humanity. It is true it liberated man from the oppressive church, but it went too far and liberated man from the values of altruism and humanity. The effect of secularism on society may be likened to the example of the 'bear and the fly'. Instead of killing the fly, the bear ended up killing his fellow-bear whom he intended to rid of the annoying insect. It is true that secularism has emancipated the European mind and unleashed man's potentials, but it is turning him into a selfish beast that has no consideration for others and that endeavours to dedicate everything to his own interests. A clear example of this is what has befallen social relations. The family has become meaningless, and both maternity and paternity have lost their essence, which is based on sacrifice. Considering that setting up a family requires commitment and sacrifice, one finds no justification in the secularist logic for giving up pleasure and for losing physical beauty as a price for having children and caring for a family.

As Tunisian writer Muhsin Al-Mili put it, the culmination of secularism is the antithesis to the concept of civil society: it is the death of man.[10] Secularism views man as a body and set of material needs, thus eliminating the most important feature that distinguishes him from other creatures, his metaphysical dimension. Unlike animals, man is not content with appeasement, but searches for the aesthetic and metaphysical symbols in the very things that fulfil his desires. Man is motivated by curiosity and is thus constantly searching for answers to questions about the ontology, causality and teleology of the world. What secularism does is reify man, turn humans into material objects, and this is the death of man. Once this happens, and in spite of all the laws, the checks and

---

[10] Muhsin Al-Mili, *Al-'Ilmaniyah aw Falsafat Mawt al-Insan* (Secularism or the Philosophy of the Death of Man), Carthage: The Tunisian Press, 1986.

balances, man will be tempted, whenever possible, to escape the checks because man's motivation is to gain more or lose less, solely in material terms. The death of man means that society is not organised on the basis of civility but on the basis of Mafia-like competing interests that rob citizens and ravage society while covering each others' tails, sharing the spoils and bribing those in power. Hence, the secularist state, even in its democratic form, cannot survive without the exercise of a great deal of violence, much more than would be needed in an Islamic state.

In the past, secularist Western states exported many of their problems to their colonies, and it was there that much of this violence was exercised, both against communities in the colonies and against other colonial states over hegemony and over the spoils, some of which were dedicated to appease the public at home. The war effort meant more industrialisation, more employment, a higher standard of living and greater ability to provide social benefits to the population as a whole. The less a Western state is able to exercise violence abroad, the more violent it is likely to become at home, because with less carrots to placate the individual members of society, and in the absence of religious deterrence, the more sticks are needed to restrain them. In contrast, the Islamic state and society solve this problem through the concept of *taqwa*. The need for violence is significantly reduced when both the rulers and the ruled fear God, or to put it in another way, the level of violence is inversely proportional to the level of piety.

The erosion of the piety factor in Western democracies has, at the political level, manifested itself in the sharp deterioration in the reputation of politicians. A politician is no longer an exemplar of morality to whom citizens or future generations can look up. Today's shrewd politician is one who has a better ability to cheat and master the arts of fraud and hypocrisy. The shining mask of liberalism veils the wolf, whose main concern is to avoid scandal.

The predicament of Western liberal society is that no solution can be found within the secularist framework for the problem of reconciling altruism, a prerequisite of civil society, with the inborn human trait of selfishness. Such a problem has a solution only within a religious framework that is capable of extending the span of life beyond this world, and of setting up a system of justice that transcends earthly justice for divine justice that gives hope to those on earth to whom earthly justice is denied.

It must be stressed that no tension exists between recognising that secularism has in the West been associated with progress and democracy and considering it a promoter of barbarity. It is a philosophy of self-deception, barbarity, tyranny and alienation because in one of its most widespread definitions it means desacralising the world and viewing objects, ideas and values as usable things. Consequently, those who are more capable and more resourceful are in a better position to use these things. Power becomes the source of value and is used to legitimise every action undertaken by the powerful to achieve their objectives and desires. It is a philosophy of alienation because it strips man of his most important and unique characteristic: his ability to transcend nature. The more he transcends the more he fulfils his humanness. Religion is an indispensable source not only for transcending nature, but also for achieving a balance between the physical and the metaphysical in the life of man, a balance between heaven and earth, between clay and Divine Breath, between economics and ethics, between conscience and law. This is what renders secularism an oddity, an alienation from the profound longing within man for transcending nature and communicating with God. In this sense, secularism is a philosophy of solitude and bereavement. It leads to the severance of all social ties that can only be founded on man's transcendence of nature and his selfishness. Only through such transcendence will man experience altruism and compassion that are indispensable if family ties are to be maintained. Secularism, in as much as it means this worldly, restricts man and condemns him to that which contravenes his nature. Man is created to live in two realms. He is bigger than this world, and condemning him to imprisonment in it – which is the secularist disposition – is condemning him to estrangement and is a destruction of his greatest resource, his ability to transcend this world while existing in it.

At the same time, secularism is self-contradictory. For as it marginalises religion and desacralises the world, it offers itself as an alternative absolute and sacrosanct creed that employs every method of deception and violence to track and uproot the other. Evidence of this can be seen in the intolerant attitude of secularist societies toward religious minorities. An example of this is the banning of the head scarf, or denying a girl who wears it her right to education, in the oldest European secular society, France. This is a model of secularist self-contradiction. Within the same framework come the recent calls for the proclamation of 'the end of history' and the pillage perpetrated by the Western world during the colonial era. In the name of this new sanctity, peoples and civilisations were plundered and in its name nature was destroyed. Selfishness has replaced justice and compassion: millions of humans starve to death, yet the world's resources are controlled by an overfed minority that dumps millions of tonnes of food into the sea.

Acknowledging secularism's role as a progressive democratic movement is not contradicted by the above. For compared to theocracy and feudalism in the history of Europe and the sultanistic states in the history of the Muslims, secularism in the West has succeeded, notwithstanding its aforementioned evils, in awakening the Western mind from its theocratic slumber enabling it to take hold of the reins of power. Man's inalienable rights to life, to freedom of expression and to participate in administering public affairs were recognised. The sovereignty of the people was recognised, and for the first time since the eclipse of the short-lived Rightly Guided Caliphate peaceful alternation of power was accomplished. For the first time too, a constitutional framework to inhibit despotism, even if only in theory, was formulated and thus state power was restricted by the rule of law. The ruler has become an ordinary human being whose task is to serve his people. Equality was established and opportunities were created for empowering society through the formation of independent institutions that gave society a great deal of independence from the state and that enable it to pressure, rectify and replace governments.

No matter how critical one may be of secularism, it should not be denied its achievements as a progressive movement. One of the great accomplishments of secularism is the space it provides for pluralism and a reasonable degree of coexistence. Muslims should recognise that the presence of millions of them in the West today, for the first time in such big numbers, is the fruit of several factors including the secularist revolution which liberated the state from the hegemony of the church. In fact until an Islamic *shura* (consensual) system of government is established, the second best alternative for Muslims is a secular democratic regime which fulfils the category of the rule of reason, according to Ibn Khaldun. Under such a system of governance, it is agreed to respect the fundamental rights of all people without discrimination and without commitment to a religious frame of reference. What matters in such a system is that despotism is averted. A democratic secular system of government is less evil than a despotic system of government that claims to be Islamic.

SECULARISM, THE STATE AND
THE SOCIAL BOND
THE WITHERING AWAY OF THE FAMILY

Heba Raouf Ezzat

Defining secularism

'Who still believes in the myth of secularisation?' was the provocative question asked by the famous sociologist of religion Jose Casanova a few years ago.[1]

Quite a few sociologists of religion have abandoned the old paradigm that believed in the inevitability of a unilinear progress based on the separation between church and state that would lead to the privatisation of religion, and thence its decline. That was a paradigm which predicted the withering away of religion in an age of science and economic progress; a process assumed to be historical and irreversible.

Many sociologists, as well as philosophers, have testified, albeit not without astonishment, to the faltering of this process. The return of religion has become a central phenomenon in many societies, as well as a global trend that gains more strength with the unfolding process of globalisation.[2]

The renewed interest in secularisation, or de-secularisation, is seen in the works of two groups of scholars. The first consists of sociologists who study the phenomenon of the return of religion to the public sphere, described usually as the de-privatisation of religion. These sociologists focus on de-secularisation of the public sphere and the empowerment of religious groups or institutions. The other group consists of political scientists who focus on the politics of resurgence. They are interested in exploring relations between fundamentalists and the state. However, both groups are concerned primarily with 'the public' and very little interest, if any, is shown in what is happening to the private sphere, in its struggle to regain its role, function and centrality. Such neglect is the result of the classic definition and conceptualisation of secularism as a

---

[1] Jose Casanova, *Public Religions in the Modern World*, University of Chicago Press, 1994, p. 11.

[2] See, for example: Peter Beyer, *Religion and Globalisation*, London: Sage Publications, 1994; and Said Amir Arjomand (ed.), *The Political Dimensions of Religion*, Albany: NY, State Univ. of New York Press, 1993.

mere separation between church and state with the consequent supposition that secularisation processes are confined to the political and
economic realms. Yet an increasing number of scholars is arguing that
secularism is a comprehensive world outlook that operates on all levels
of reality through a large number of explicit and implicit mechanisms.

The secularist outlook is basically one that starts by neutralising, or
marginalising, God or even by announcing his death, and placing the
human being at the centre of the universe as its *logos*. The complex
duality of transcendental monotheism is replaced by a sharp dualism
of human beings and nature, one that manifests itself through a conflict
between the two. The problem, however, is eventually resolved in favour
of the 'natural'. The 'human' is thereby absorbed into, or reduced to, the
category of the 'natural', or sometimes to the category of the 'cultural'
(in the case of feminism for example). The initial humanism of secularism turns gradually into a naturalistic anti-humanism. The initial dualism
of the human being and nature is replaced by a thorough naturalistic
monism: the reduction of reality to one natural law, immanent in matter.
This is the epistemological basis for the process of deconstruction
and de-sanctification not only of nature but of the human being and all
related transcendental criteria.[3]

Sociologists like Glasner and Hill have tried to relate secularism to
the original Enlightenment project. In their analysis, the process occurs
at the institutional level: that includes the decline of religious institutions
and their role in society, the 'routineisation' of individual religious practices and the loss of their social significance, and the disengagement between
religion and other aspects of life.[4] At the normative level, secularism, according to them, evolves around the desacralisation of morals and values,
separating them from any absolutes in favour of a relative man-made
value system. The historical material context of these changes is highligh-
ted due to its importance for understanding the process of secularisation
and its conditions. The accompanying processes of urbanisation, industrialisation and modernisation are included in the studies.[5]

Other say of reaching a sophisticated understanding of secularism
have added to the increasing interest in comparative studies, widening
the scope for studying the relationship between the sacred and the
profane in other cultures and religions besides the Christian West.[6] Some

---

[3] Peter Glasner, *The Sociology of Secularisation: A Critique of a Concept*, London: Routledge
& Kegan Paul, 1977; and Abdel Wahab Elmessiri, 'Towards a more Comprehensive and
Explanatory Paradigm of Secularism' *Encounters*, vol. 2, no. 2, Sept. 1996.

[4] Susan Budd, *Sociologists and Religion*, London: Collier-Macmillan Publishers, 1973, p.
120.

[5] Michael Hill, *A Sociology of Religion*, London: Heinemann Educational Books, 1973,
pp. 19-43, 229-50; and Glasner, *The Sociology of Secularisation*.

[6] See, for example: Ninian Smart, *Dimensions of the Sacred: An Anatomy of the World's
Beliefs*, London: Fontana, 1996.

writers have suggested that the secularisation process started on the
material level first, unlike the common idea that it all started philoso-
phically with Enlightenment ideas, and was then applied to society.
Chadwick states that it was not the case that men first stopped believing
in God and in the authority of the church, and that they then began be-
having differently. He assumes that society had first lost any overall
social agreement as to the right ways to live together, and so ceased to
be able to make sense of any claims to moral authority.[7]

Western thought has reflected these ongoing changes but did not ini-
tiate them. With the decline of religion and the increasing role of science,
the latter was believed to be the tool for human control over human destiny.[8] It was believed to be value-free, not confronting society with any
ambivalent questions or critical choices. By the end of the nineteenth
century, medicine was replacing the church as moulder of public opinion.[9]

In social theory, Herbert Spencer and Parsons theorised about 'structural differentiation' – the process by which secular roles and institutions
become separated from religious ones. With the changes in material
(politico-economic) circumstances the term 'secularisation' was originally an emotive word, not far in its origin from the term 'anticlericalism'.
Sometimes it meant a freeing of the sciences, of learning and of the arts
from their theological origin or theological bias. Sometimes it meant the
declining influence of churches, or of religion, in modern society. The
process of secularisation was not restricted to thought and society, but
was accompanied by a process of secularisation of disciplines and of
the European mind as well. Modern sociologists have not always kept
the term to an unemotional plane. Sometimes they use the word in a
pejorative sense.[10] Yet this situation raised many moral questions. The
complicating fact for the late nineteenth century was the claim that you
could have morality without Christianity while the morality that you had
to have was Christian morality. Men were good Christian men morally
without necessarily possessing Christian faith.[11] As the logos became
the human being himself, cutting him off (freeing him or her) from
any transcendental dimensions of existence or sources of the self, the
modern notion of the self was related to a certain sense of inwardness.
People thought of their capacities or potentialities as 'inner', awaiting

[7] Chadwick; pp. 11-12.

[8] *Ibid.*, p. 233.

[9] David T. Evans, *Sexual Citizenship: The Material Construction of Sexualities*, London:
Routledge, 1993, p. 93.

[10] Budd, *Sociology of Religion*, pp. 142-6.

[11] Owen Chadwick, *The Secularisation of the European Mind in the 19th Century*,
Cambridge University Press, 1979, pp.120-3, 264; and Chadwick, p. 237.

the development that would manifest them, or realise them, in the public realm.[12]

The crisis in social values and institutions (religion, family and so on), and the 'embodiment' of the sources of the self, and the claim that they should be secular, forced sex to take up the slack, to become the sole mode of transcendence and the only touchstone of authenticity.[13]

The 1960s stand not as a single radical turning point but as a key moment in the secularisation/sexualisation process which has characterised the capitalist epoch, within which the heightened pre-occupation with sexuality in all manner of explicit, implicit and diverse forms has effectively saturated populations, structures and cultures with constellations of immanent sexual power/knowledge ripe for commodification.[14] The only visible aspect of continuity and of the cumulative effect of self-constitutive efforts is offered by the human body – seen as the sole constant factor among the protean and fickle identities: the material, tangible container, carrier and executor of all past, present and future identities.[15] People were encouraged to see themselves in terms of their sexuality, which is interpreted, as the core of the 'self'.[16]

The 'social construction of reality' as a starting point for sociologists in the 1960s ended up focusing on the 'social construction of sexuality'. The advance in reproductive technologies and genetic engineering fostered the status of science as the God of the secularist modern and postmodern era, and morality changed according to the ability to do something and became very relative and personal, reducing the notions of good and evil to the very narrow space of personal, individual choice. This was mainly reflected in issues like abortion, trans-sexuality, and homosexuality. The ideal is to be a swinger – sensitive to *ambi*sexual pleasures, capable of being aroused sexually with men and women.[17]

Other sensitive issues like pornography and prostitution moved from the area of condemnation to the area of ambiguity. Porn magazines, electric devices purchased by mail order or in local drug stores provide sexual gratification at a far cheaper price than the traditional path of (family) life long enslavement to marriage. The individual on his very own, with the help of instruments and chemicals, can possibly achieve his /her ultimate sexual self-fulfilment without even the need for hetero or homosexual affiliation. Sex was burdened with greater expectations

---

[12] Charles Taylor, *Sources of the Self: The Making of the Modern Identity*, Cambridge University Press,1989, p. 111 .

[13] Evans, *Sexual Citizenship*, p. 1.

[14] *Ibid.*, p.9.

[15] Zygmunt Bauman, *Intimations of Postmodernity*, London: Routledge, 1993, p. 194.

[16] Pat Caplan, *The Cultural Construction of Sexuality*, London: Routledge, 1993, p. 2.

[17] Evans, *Sexual Citizenship*, p. 96.

which were closely related to the stress on ideas of 'self-fulfilment' and 'personal actualisation'.[18]

While liberalism claimed that issues related to sex were a matter of personal choice, capitalism heavily incorporated them into the market economy, utilising every possible avenue, starting with movies and the media and ending with selling sex on the internet. If ours is a time of increasing demands for private and immediate gratification, this process occurred often without society realising how these values are, to a large extent, the product of modern consumer capitalism.[19]

The state, family and feminism

The enlightenment concepts of reason and knowledge led many people world-wide to believe that they could, and perhaps should, adopt a universalistic, culture-neutral, value-free standpoint on all cognitive, moral and political matters. This standpoint dictated a neutral, if not an actually hostile posture toward native cultural tradition.[20] This included family values.

The totalisation of the public sphere in modernist liberal civic culture produced what amounts to an informally established, state sponsored, 'secular' religion.[21] The state became the major actor on all scenes, and many functions were transferred to it from the declining extended family and from the increasingly shaky nuclear one. It also took over most of the activities once performed by religious institutions, and became the guardian of such spheres as education and morality – a secular morality without ethics.

Secularism involved the rise of the secular state and its gradual take-over of most of the activities once performed by religious institutions. It reflected a desire to disengage from any form of communal-based understanding and social regulations that are the elementary features of any form of *Gemeinschaft*. These are the foundations that provided group solidarity, binding society through common customs and beliefs. Glasner believes that in a *Gesellschaft* society the public role of religion becomes impossible because the relationships which religion sustained are no longer present – the binding of the group, the common heritage etc.[22] Common heritage and faith would be a hindrance in this situation since the individual becomes 'responsible for his own fate'. The new individu-ally-decided ethics are called the 'ethics of authenticity' and considered

[18] *Ibid.*, p. 271.

[19] *Ibid.*, p. 42.

[20] Thomas Bridges, *The Culture of Citizenship: Inventing Postmodern Civic Culture*, Albany: State University Press of New York, 1994, p. 142.

[21] *Ibid.*, p. 147.

[22] Glasner, *The Sociology of Secularisation*, p. 56.

to be one of the major achievements of modernity.[23] Citizens were taught to be more concerned with the contractual relationship to the state, establishing a 'civil society' with a 'social contract' that denounces any traditional non-secular bonds. The problem of 'enlightenment' began to turn into the new problem of 'secularisation'.[24]

Modernity spent most of its time and much of its energy on fighting communities, those larger-than-life groupings into which people are born, only to be held inside for the rest of life by 'the dead hand of tradition strengthened by collective surveillance and blackmail'. From the Enlightenment on, it has been seen as a commonsensical truth that human emancipation, the releasing of genuine human potential, required that the bounds of communities be broken and individuals set free from the circumstances of their birth.[25] As religion lay near loyalty to the family, religion lay near loyalty to the state and was usually an element constitutive of community and in the life of the state.[26]

The development of the welfare state has embodied a continual redrawing of lines between the public and the private, between the state and civil society, and in particular among the state, the market and the family. It is a phenomenon which has opened to public debate matters previously confined to privacy, raising new questions about the relationship between the state and civil society.[27]

Women's reform efforts were instrumental in the emergence of the modern welfare state and women were often the first to identify and respond to the welfare needs of women and children and to argue for state welfare programmes. On the other hand, welfare programmes empowered women and gave them the practical conditions for liberation in the public sphere.[28] 'Equality' emerged with the process of secularisation as a concept rooted in a naturalistic materialistic paradigm, giving it a quantitative meaning rather than adding other concepts, such as 'justice' or 'difference', to its analysis or conception in a more complex or profound context. This value was the starting point of the first wave of women's liberation, reducing equality to the 'material', and regarding economy as the arena for struggle and emancipation.

During this process of liberation and search for equality, especially in the marketplace, fundamental changes occurred to the notions of

---

[23] Charles Taylor, *Ethics of Authenticity*, Cambridge, MA: Harvard University Press, 1991, p. 1.

[24] Chadwick, *The Secularisation of the European Mind*, p. 7.

[25] Z. Bauman, *Life in Fragments: Essays in Postmodern Morality*, Oxford: Blackwell, 1995, p. 275.

[26] Chadwick, p. 114.

[27] Barbara L. Marshall, *Engendering Modernity: Feminism, Social Theory and Social Change*, Cambridge: Polity Press, 1994, pp. 132, 136.

[28] *Ibid.*, p. 133.

intimacy, domestic ideals and sexual politics as a result of industrialisation and the triumph of the market. To achieve a permanent deconstruction
of the family it was not sufficient to weaken it structurally, but a whole
discourse of relativity regarding the relation between males and females
emerged to support and legitimise these changes, redefining masculinity,
femininity, motherhood, fatherhood and the 'family' itself.

The strident and joyful rebirth of feminism in the Western women's
liberation movement at the close of the 1960s took off from a fundamental critique of the family. What troubled the feminists then was their
perception of women's dependent, undervalued and frequently isolated
miserable existence inside the family, especially when engaged in full-
time motherhood.[29] The growing interest a few years later in the maternal
nature of women's thinking, relating women to peace and accusing men
of causing war (hence assuming that women's political participation
would increase the chances of a world-wide peace) was not related at all
to the family. Later, even this 'myth' of motherhood was attacked.[30]

Definitions such as: 'the family is two or more individuals who maintain an intimate relationship that they expect will last indefinitely – or
in the case of a parent and a child until the child reaches adulthood – and
who live in the same household and pool their income and household
labour' started appearing in sociology books, supported by examples
and case studies that were provided in real life by homosexual and
bisexual relations.[31]

A new study area of 'non-traditional families' appeared including pre-
marital, ex-marital and one-parent families, communal living groups, and
single women who chose to become pregnant and stay single.[32] Not only
did a change in definition occur, but also a de-construction and separation between the different aspects and roles of the traditional family, such
as the 'assumptions' that children need two parents – one of each sex,
that mothers are more suited for child rearing, and that primary care for
young children should be provided by family members etc. These scientific, value-free advances led to a process of questioning and created the
will to experiment with social life. Economic, technological and institutional alternatives were sought as rights, especially by feminists, and
the legislative body of the state became the judge. Problems within the
family were even supposed to be policed by the authorities.[33]

[29] John Muncie *et al.*, *Understanding the Family*, London: Sage, 1995, p. 295.
[30] Brigitte Berger and Alan Carlson, *The Family: Is it Just Another Lifestyle Choice?*,
London: IEA Health and WelfareUnit (Choice in Welfare Series, 15), 1993.
[31] Andrew J. Cherlin, *Public and Private Families: An Introduction*, New York: McGraw
Hill, 1996, pp. 18, 21.
[32] Gary Becker, *A Treatise on the Family*, Cambridge, MA: Harvard University Press, 1981,
pp. 245, 251.
[33] Susan S.M. Edwards, *Policing Domestic Violence: Women, the Law and the State*, London: Sage, 1991.

On the political level the campaign for a fifty per cent quota in parliament as a declared goal of some feminists to indicate real equality is an example of this mechanical understanding of the concept of equality. The very demand of equality can even be questioned, on the theoretical level, by the increasing measures of 'positive discrimination', measures that made some people wonder about the real aim of some feminists: is it still women's liberation, or is it a quest for women's domination? In the last analysis, the term was carefully chosen: feminism. Some critics claim that it represents a further serious step on the path of secularisation. It is hence very important to understand the history and sociology of the family in the West in its relation to the history of secularisation and rationalisation.

Lifelong loyalties of marriage became no longer the norm. Divorce rates increased and nearly one-third of births now take place outside marriage, with many of the fathers playing little or no role further to their initial biological participation. The traditional family of mum, dad and the kids has become just another lifestyle choice. For the last thirty years or so many intellectuals have been scornful of the traditional family, condemning it as the prime source of repression. This hostility derives from the view that freedom is about overcoming obstacles to our desires, from which it follows that we are free when we surmount any barriers standing in our way. The most objectionable barrier of all is moral convention. Freedom means defiance of authority; it means rebellion against established values.

As the capitalist economy has developed, a major contributing factor to change in the perception of the family has been the growth in the earning power of women. A trend within the women's liberation movement encouraged women to reduce their childbearing, to raise their labour force participation, and (when necessary) to assert their independence by becoming head of their own household (by divorce if necessary). Some researchers believe that this trend within the movement was primarily a response to other forces that have dramatically changed the family in recent decades, especially the growth of the welfare state. Expenditure on social security, unemployment compensation, medical care and medical aid, assistance to mothers with dependant children, food stamps and other programs grew in real terms during the 1960s and the 1970s.[34] (Now that the state is retreating from the social services that enabled women to develop in the public sphere, they can no longer turn to the extended family which has already been deconstructed by the state.)

The language of liberation was also so loud in connection with the new sexual prescriptions for women, that commentators have assumed some obvious relationship between the 'sexual revolution' and improving living conditions for women. The high priests of sexology, helped by pornographers, progressive novelists and sex radicals continued to

[34] Evans, *Sexual Citizenship*, p. 270.

orchestrate woman's joyful embrace of her oppression through the creation of her sexual response.[35] Not only free sex, but also lesbianism became one of the main issues on the agenda of feminism, and its acceptance within the feminist movement even turned into a condition for real change.[36]

Trying to contextualise feminism and understand its archaeology is very much linked to the history of secularisation of the European mind and sciences. The mentality of generations of women's liberation activists and theoreticians was also shaped by the Marxist notions of patriarchy and position toward the family, as well – of course – as Marxist ideas regarding religion as a male-made set of oppressive ideas, especially when it comes to women. These ideas infiltrated even non-Marxist circles and became embedded in most feminist writings. The social contract on which the humanist enlightenment liberal approach based its equality notions was also deconstructed and an alternative sexual contract proposed.

Different schools of feminism developed self-referential/self-contained discourses, where the 'body' had become the *logos* of a *Weltanschauung* (world-view), pushing the 'naturalisation' of the human being as far as one can imagine, and achieving full lucidity in the questions of morals.[37]

Feminist thought and the feminist movement evolved, then, around the search for power, trying to become more and more 'empowered' and looking to the law as the tool for obtaining equal rights especially in the political sphere. Little attention was given to the announced 'death of the family', and even those who were not hostile to it were not encouraged by the radical feminist atmosphere to defend it.[38] The gains of modernity were considered far more numerous than the losses.[39]

[35] Berger and Carlson, *The Family*, p. vi.
[36] See for example: Sue Wilkinson and Celia Kitzinger, *Heterosexuality: A Feminism and Psychology Reader*, London: Sage, 1993.
[37] The lesbian writings claiming the moral high ground are interesting in this respect as an example that requires attention and deep analysis. It is worth mentioning that this was usually done by attacking 'traditional' notions of motherhood and basic values related to the family. There was no indication of diversity as they claim, but rather a harsh attack on heterosexuality and the classic definition of the 'family'. Related critical writings on sex, the body and 'reproduction' together form a picture of a counter ideology that aims at breaking down the 'family'. See for example: Sarah Lucia Hoagland, 'Lesbian Ethics and Female Agency' in Eve B. Cole and S. C. McQuin (eds), *Explorations in Feminist Ethics: Theory and Practice*, Indianapolis: Indiana UP, 1992, pp. 156-64; and Judith Butler, *Bodies That Matter – On the Discursive Limits of Sex*, London: Routledge, 1993.
[38] With the 'coming out' of the lesbian and gay movements, and the powerful theorisation on lesbian epistemology, many women became intimidated. In the last (secular) analysis one should not define the family according to fixed, biased, pre-modern measures. The mildest accusation would be 'homophobia', the most severe fundamentalism. See for example: Sandra Harding, *The Science Question in Feminism*, Ithaca, NY: Cornell University Press, 1986.
[39] Richard Rorty, 'Religion as a Conversation-Stopper', *Common Knowledge*, Spring 1994,

The shift from the modernist focus on the body politic to the enthusiastic feminist and postmodern interest in 'body politics' is also a historic secular moment.

As the two major problems for women, namely the patriarchal culture (family) and the lack of services and facilities, were solved by the state, it was easy for women to join the public sphere, thinking that they themselves had achieved that triumph, and for their own sake. Later, some women discovered that the rules of sexology remained unaltered. Behind the ballooned notions of liberation, the naked power politics of male supremacy – added to males' neglect of their family and paternal responsibilities – were being acted out. Yet very few feminists realised the other deception: the state's dominance over them as individuals along with all 'citizens', and the very important role it has played in the secularisation process that led to the fading away of many social bonds, and to the dominance of contractual relations.

The question remains as to whether a 'liberal state' is of necessity a 'secular state' if it is to be truly 'liberal', and to whether a 'liberal' mind must be, in a manner, a 'secular' mind. A sincere and serious evaluation of the benefits and the costs so far is inevitable.

One can trace an emerging revisionist discourse that is starting to rethink the concept of gender, the moral implications of reproductive technology and the basic assumptions of feminism. This discourse is trying to regain the family and redefine and investigate the established critique of so-called 'patriarchy'.[40]

Leading figures like Betty Friedan, whose book *The Feminist Mystique* sparked the American women's movement into being in the 1960s, acknowledges in her work *Beyond Gender* the disturbing paradox that women's rights have been granted at the expense of men. Right from the start there was a division. Instead of putting children and family as a collective unit first, the feminists put themselves first. Thus, redressing injustice turned into a sex war. Now she calls for a 'paradigm shift' beyond sexual and identity politics towards a new paradigm in which women and men are together fighting for the common good. What Friedan does not say is that feminism might have been terrific for single women, but failed completely to deal with motherhood, and was only satisfied to redefine it, attack it and deconstruct it, along with its wider context: the family.[41]

---

vol. 3, no. 7, p. 6.

[40] See, for example: Sidney Callahan, 'Gays, Lesbians, and the Use of Alternate Reproductive Technologies' in Hilde Lindeman Nelson (ed.), *Stories and their Limits: Narrative Approaches to Bioethics*, NY, Routledge, 1997, pp. 188-202; and Sara Ruddick, 'The Idea of Fatherhood' in *ibid.*, pp. 205-20.

[41] Betty Friedan, *Beyond Gender: The New Politics of Work and Family*, Baltimore, MD: Johns Hopkins University Press, 1998.

Heba Raouf Ezzat

Anthropologist David Phillips points out that contr-ary to received feminist wisdom, patriarchy and traditional family structures suited women as well as men. Most women look for long-term bonding to provide care and support for themselves and for their offspring. Patriarchal cultures bound men into families with long term obligations.[42]

Increasing attention is being paid to the argument that we may be seeing, in much contemporary behaviour, a clue to what may happen on a broad scale when men are both unemployed and detached from stable family life as compared to earlier periods when unemployment rates were higher and poverty deeper, but when both crime rates and the rates of family breakdown were dramatically lower. The variable that made and makes the difference is the incidence of stable nuclear families. 'A woman's right to choose' lays down with absolute clarity the freedom of the physical from the control of the word – be it the word of the church, the legal word, or the social word.[43]

Secularising the family: the case of Egypt

In the Islamic and Arab world the process of political secularisation (the dominance of the state) was not accompanied by the same degree of philosophical secularisation, or so-called 'rationalisation'. Nevertheless, the state, in the course of history, managed by law and economy to transfer the social functions of the family and the functions of religious institutions to its own realm. Although such a policy did indeed lead to the attenuation of these units, they survived in the public/social sphere. It was their survival that prevented the full accomplishment of secularisation on the philosophical and cultural levels. The secularisation of the 'self' did not gain ground, hence the unmistakable difference in discourse and concepts exhibited by the first wave of women's liberation. By the end of the nineteenth century, such movement was, to a great extent, rooted in religious values and committed to the family as an ideal and an established norm.[44]

Yet, at least on the level of discourse, the secular advocates of women's liberation (*vis-à-vis* the activist Islamist women) changed their agenda and ideas. In an age of globalisation, they moved from general demands ·of equality to increasingly adopting the broad international agenda of the feminists. Although they do not criticise religion as such, they are highly critical of what they regard as the 'male/patriarchal interpretation

---

[42] Geoff Dench (ed.), *Rewriting the Sexual Contract*, London: Institute of Community Studies, 1998.

[43] Berger and Carlson, *The Family*, pp. 4-6.

[44] See the following excellent study: Beth Baron, *The Woman's Awakening In Egypt: Culture, Society and the Press*; New Haven, CT: Yale University Press, 1994.

thereof'. Issues like redefining masculinity and femininity, the separation between sex and marriage, homosexuality etc. remain undiscussed due to the (still) powerful presence of religion and family in Arab and Muslim societies.

Although the legal domain had been one of its goals right from the beginning, the movement increasingly gave more weight to the legal approach to women's problems. The crisis of the family in modernising societies did not seem to be of equal concern.[45] The recent campaign by feminists, mainly professional lawyers, to change the marriage contract in Egypt to supplement it with conditions regarding the woman's rights to work, to travel etc., and their ongoing campaign to change the personal code to guarantee more 'equality' are very illustrative examples.[46]

The quest for equality within social structures that are facing increasing poverty and a deterioration in the basic conditions of life under the Structural Adjustment Programs dictated by the IMF and the World Bank might be open to criticism, but the crucial question of how to face capitalism and its secularist philosophical underpinnings, with a non-capitalist yet still secular frame of reference, is not even raised by the majority of Arab feminists. An answer would lead to a deeper discussion of the state's social and economic policies, but as these associations and groups are desperate to secure the state's approval of their agenda and to translate it into legal amendments, they would not wish to confront or oppose the regime.[47]

Political conditions impacting upon the legitimate feminist presence are restrictive. So far, the law, as a bargaining instrument, has been successfully abused by the state as well as by the feminists. Within that sensitive political balance, the secular women's liberation movement has been one of the allies of the regime against the 'fundamentalist' threat.[48]

[45] See, for example: The Report of the Committee for the Empowerment of Women in Society, as presented at the ICPD-UN Conference, Egypt, 1994; Dr. Hassan Abu Bakr, *Legal Status and Problems of Women in Urban and Rural Areas in Egypt*, Cairo: Amideast, 1997; Nadia Abdel Wahab and Amal Abdel Hadi (eds), *The Feminist Movement in the Arab World*, Cairo: New Woman Research Centre, 1995; and *Women, Law and Development*, Cairo: New Woman Research Centre, 1997.

[46] See the new marriage contract in Aziza Hussein *et al.*, *The Legal Rights of Egyptian Women between Theory and Practice*, Cairo: Women's Affairs Committee, 1992.

[47] On the theoretical and practical dilemmas of NGOs in the Middle East, especially in Egypt, see Nadia Sadig Al-Ali, 'Feminism and Contemporary Debates in Egypt' in Dawn Chatty and Annika Rabo, *Organizing Women: Formal and Informal Women's Groups in the Middle East*, Oxford: Berg, 1997.

[48] The intellectual expressions of the secularists have, within the political arena, been an intellectual support of the government regardless of its intentions. Unfortunately secularists have become scapegoats, at a certain point, in the state's non-committed role between different political trends as in the case of Nasr Hamed Abu Zeid. See for, example: Nasr Hamed Abu Zeid, 'Women: The Missing Dimension in Current Religious Discourse, *Cairo*, no. 123, Feb. 1993; Sanaa Al Masri, *Behind the Veil*, Cairo: Dar Sinai, 1989

The direct discussion (critique) of the question of the full application of *Shari'ah* had to be marginalised in their discourse in order not to lose the support of the masses of women who would not tolerate a direct attack on Islam. The epistemological and political approaches are therefore very important in understanding the real dilemmas of feminism in the Islamic world regarding the question of equality and the legal rights of women.

No profound understanding will be possible unless this analysis is also applied to the international level by addressing international law as well as the international network of NGOs and their role in North-South relations as agents of the New World Order.

What is of critical importance is to avoid falling into the same traps that no one could have foreseen when the enlightenment project started, yet that can be seen clearly now along with all their previously discussed social and moral paradoxes. We have a golden opportunity to construct our own modernity, having seen where things went wrong. The efforts made by sociologists in the West to carefully study the changing nature of social relations in the postmodern era produce an analysis that is highly important for us. We have the chance to reform our social structures, to make relations within them more 'equal' and more just, without having to lose them or helplessly watch them decay. We do not have to settle down with a form of togetherness if we can liberate women and still keep the family.[49] We do not have to turn the past of the West into a future for the Rest.

There are many complex aspects of women's lives that social scientists who are committed to political struggles for justice and human dignity need to explore. Recent socio-anthropological studies (which Western researchers have been able to resume while native researchers are usually not permitted to undertake) tried to approach the life of the majority of (supposedly oppressed and poor) women with the aim of discovering how they could take charge of their own destinies, make use of social and kinship ties to survive, and make their lives, as well as those of their children, better.[50] The importance of the household economy as an informal sector that women can use for their benefit is also under focus now.[51]

Many educated women in the Islamic world are rediscovering the liberating potential of their religious traditions. They demand respect, they

(Arabic); and Leila Abdel Wahab, 'The Influence of Islamic Movements on the Social Consciousness of Women' in Abdel Baki El Hermassi (ed.), *Religion in the Arab Society*, Beirut: Centre for Arab Unity Studies, 1990.

[49] On 'togetherness' in Western societies see Bauman, *Intimations of Postmodernity*.

[50] See, for example: Unni Wikan, *Tomorrow – God Willing*, University of Chicago Press, 1996.

[51] See, for example: Diane Singermann, *Avenues of Participation: Families, Politics and Networks in an Urban Quarter of Cairo*, Princeton University Press, 1995; and Diane Singermann and Homa Hoodfar, *Development, Change and Gender in Cairo: A View from the Household*, Indianapolis, IN: Indiana University Press.

already participate in economic and political processes, but they are also proud of motherhood as a value, they believe in the family as a social institution and regard themselves as the guardians of culture. Increasing numbers of them have chosen, sometimes against the wish of their own 'patriarchal' families to join the wider Islamic resurgence. They suffer from restrictions and discrimination and from the violation of their human rights by the authorities. Their lives are worth looking at and drawing lessons from, and to show, moreover, how simplistic approaches regarding their identity and consciousness need to be revised.

It is sad that many scholars insist on calling these women feminists, though they themselves choose not to define or identify themselves as such. This description only obscures the deep differences between such Islamic trends and the feminist epistemology/discourse regarding the issues of family, morality the scope and role of religion and many other questions.[52]

Some secularists have attempted to bridge the gap by deconstructing the religious tradition in the name of *ijtihad* and re-interpretation. Yet no parallel attempt has been made to study the sociological and philosophical limits of Western feminist discourse. It is simply accepted as egalitarian and liberating, with the assumption that it bears a cross-cultural validity that needs no proof. Almost no single scholar within the secular circles in the Arab world has even thought of expressing concern regarding the politics of feminism in the Third World, and the role of late capitalism in supporting it as a secular frame of reference among others.

While the very notion of citizenship is undergoing revision and deconstruction in current Western political theory, Arab feminists insist on placing their demands under the banner of 'equal citizenship', without offering a profound thesis about what they mean by the term, or about the wider political project they adopt for social change.[53]

Perhaps one should be very careful when criticising them. The feminists' failure to address these crucial notions, to produce new ideas on equality, participation and social justice, and to develop the tools needed to achieve the aspired change in our societies has been augmented by a political and cultural context that is in itself sterile.

[52] See, for example: Azza Karam, *Women, Islamism and the State: Contemporary Feminisms in Egypt*, London: Macmillan, 1998, pp. 4-13. Margot Badran calls all the writings from women in the Arab world for the last century 'feminist'. See for example: Margot Badran and Miriam Cook, *Opening the Gates: A Century of Arab Feminist Writings*, Indianapolis: Indiana University Press, 1990. Fatima Mernissi even extends the concept to women in early Islam! See for example: Fatima Mernissi, *Women's Rebellion and Islamic Memory*, London: Zed, 1996, pp. 113-15.

[53] See for example: Marlene Tadrus *et al.*, *Incomplete Citizenship*, Cairo: Centre for Legal and Human Rights Information and Research, 1995.

In an age of globalisation there is a real need to examine ideas and to compare the courses of the social changes that have taken place in other parts of the world. Our societies need not pay the heavy price that other societies have had to incur. At the same time we need to defuse the current polarisation by devising new forms of social organisation that are rooted in religious tradition. We also need to respond to the challenges of our time while observing full respect for the basic rights of individuals, social units and communities.

SECULARISM AND THE ARAB-MUSLIM CONDITION

Munir Shafiq

Secularism and religion in the West

The relationship between religion, state and society in the West is neither permeated by a realistic balance nor consistent with what is often described as a 'secularist West'. Many have attempted to present secularism as the most fundamental and outstanding feature of Western society at the level of the state, at the level of society and at the level of the individual. Yet, a careful examination of the situation leads to the observation that it is one thing to talk about the relationship between religion and the state and quite another to talk about that between religion and society.

The modern state in Europe emerged out of a bitter struggle against absolutist monarchical regimes and against the hegemony of the Catholic Church. The result of this encounter was a compromise, a historical reconciliation, between the state and the church. While the church was prohibited from transforming itself into a political party, it reserved the right to support a political party, or a political candidate, of its choice. The church was also granted freedom to conduct its proselytising activities in the society and to establish educational, social and economic institutions. On its part the church acceded that the people had the right to freedom of faith, including the freedom not to believe.

The relationship between the state and religious institutions in Western countries has not taken a single form. For instance, it is not the same in Britain as in Italy, Germany or the United States. Indeed, a variety of models came into effect. In Britain, for example, the monarch is head of church as well as of state. In contrast, the state in France after the 1789 Revolution was initially hostile to religion and religious institutions. But in the process of asserting its independence of the church, and thus the separation between religion and politics, the French state reached a historical rapprochement with the church ending the enmity between the two establishments and erecting numerous bridges of cooperation and mutual respect. Throughout Europe and North America, the pattern of state-church relationship varied from one country to another, with each experience giving rise to its own peculiarities.

With regard to the relationship between religion (or the church) and society, the majority of Western societies continue to be dominated by sentiments which are either Protestant or Catholic in origin. A degree of religiosity persists even though basic rites such as prayers are not regularly observed. It is very often clearly manifested at religious festivals and all other occasions when public opinion is tested. Western civilisation has, in general, preserved its Christian character. At the same time, secular non-religious, or anti-religious, trends in the West have been confined to small groups of intellectuals and middle, as well as upper, class citizens. Such trends have become especially popular among radical liberal, socialist and communist elites. In most Western European and North American countries, these elites have not played a decisive role in the adoption of crucial strategic policies or in influencing public opinion or public conduct, especially with regard to matters pertaining to morality and custom.

Accordingly, it would indeed be inappropriate to assert that secularism has exclusively commanded Europe and its leaders. European civilisation and culture are best viewed as a complex admixture of relationships among five components: secularism, the state, society, church and religion. In other words, one would be entirely mistaken to describe the current Western civilisation as non-religious, or to describe Western culture as a secular non-religious culture. In general it is a Christian civilisation suffused with a complex blend of Judaism, Greek and Roman paganism and irreligious liberalism, socialism and communism. The dominant tenor, including that of the state, includes religiosity, a characteristic clearly observed in the Anglo-Saxon part of the Western world. In the Catholic part, however, religion enjoys varying degrees of influence depending upon the nature of states and the historical development of regions.

Although secularism in the West has occupied a leading position in many universities, in the media and in the writings of many intellectuals, it has nevertheless not been able to assume absolute leadership or primacy. Very often it is obliged to make significant compromises. Thus, both state and society in the West have managed to avoid falling in the pitfall of irreligious secularism. The importance of this fact cannot be over emphasised. Compromise has always been a prerequisite of the integrity and cohesiveness of the West and its ability to resolve many of its problems. Had irreligious secularism, in any of its extreme liberal, socialist or communist forms, been given a free rein so as to stamp both state and society with its own imprint, the situation in the West would have been completely different. The equilibrium that took form as a result of conflict, re-alignment, compromise and balance of powers is what gives Western society its present shape. It has also been responsible for checking secularism and restraining its aspiration for exclusive command and its inclination toward hegemony. At the same time, it is this equilibrium which has, until now, saved secularism from total collapse in the West. Ever since it first appeared in its most flagrant form in France, secularism has been confronted with antagonists. The democratic system in the West has in its entirety, therefore, been established upon an equation governed by a definite balance of powers attained at all levels following a series of bitter conflicts, civil wars and revolutions. Secularism in the West has operated within the constraints of religion, tradition, church and public opinion. These constraints enabled it to limit all tendencies of extremism and intolerance. These restraints have continually prevented it from pursuing a radical trend and at the same time saved it from collapse when showing signs of bankruptcy.

Observations

Secularism has never attained a free hand and absolute command except in the shade of Bolshevik style socialist regimes, where oppression and despotism prevailed. The refusal of such regimes to accommodate the church (or the mosque) and tradition – in other words society's cultural and religious legacies – and the attempt to impose a purely secularist outlook – in politics, economics and social affairs – upon the state and society necessitated the use of violence and repression. This was inevitable since the only other alternative would have been for the secularist project to make a fundamental retreat if it were to adopt pluralism and democracy. In other words, it would have been compelled to make substantial concessions, reconciling itself with society's cultural underpinnings and recognising the necessity of power-sharing and redistribution of resources. In effect, the secularist project would have lost its exclusive, pure, secularist disposition. This was indeed what the Italian Communist party observed quite early when it called for a historic compromise with the Catholic Church. This is also what secularist liberal, socialist and communist parties in Russia, the Independent Republics and Eastern Europe are now endeavouring to achieve.

The contemporary Western experience with secularism has witnessed a concerted attempt by its proponents to implant a number of new values in society under the guise of modernisation and progress. These values are primarily concerned with issues such as the relationship between the sexes, family ties, education, raising children, crime and punishment and homosexuality. The secularist approach to these issues has been underscored by an absolute rejection of tradition and a call for severing all ties with the past. New ideas and values based on pure reason, and unrestricted by religion or tradition, are advocated instead. Wherever such ideas and values have prevailed, the result has been negative. The family as a social unit has been shattered. Indeed the very institution of marriage and family relationships have been disrupted, leaving behind a trail of dangerous consequences. Many of these are manifested in the increase in crime, drug addiction, individualism and isolationism. At the same time there has been an erosion of morality and compassion. The policy of lenient penalties and the endeavour to care for criminals more than victims have not only failed to reduce crime and assuage the pain of victims but have even led to a marked increase in crime.

In dealing with morality and social norms, secularism appears to be improvisatory, shallow and insubstantial. For even though it has managed to criticise and highlight discrepancies in traditional values, especially with regard to the family, women's issues and crime and punishment, its conclusions, which are based on severing ties with religion, tradition and the past, have not only failed in removing discrepancies, but have even provoked more serious shortcomings. Secularism disdains history, past human experience and the role of religion in society. It sees nothing in all of these but darkness. Such contempt for history is the outcome of a frivolous view of the historical experience of human societies. It is a perspective that fails to recognise that when societies adhere to certain values or traditions, they do so not out of ignorance or foolishness but as a result of a long experience, and as a consequence of having passed the arduous test of life. Some secularists seem not to observe that when peoples decide to adhere to certain traditions and values, in spite of the disadvantages inherent in them, they invariably do so after having been through some bitter historical experiences. In the course of history, human societies have experimented with conditions, some of which are not dissimilar to those liberal secularists are advocating today.

The problem with some secularists is that when they propose a particular pattern of behaviour which they deem objective, they do not realise that it must be empirically proven. Such ideas must be put to the test in people's lives. Their pros and cons can only be discovered in the course of time. Thus they should display respect to religious teachings and traditions which they so often oppose. They should also display greater humility concerning their own ideas, which are still at the level of improvisation and speculation; they have neither been tested nor proven to withstand trials and crises. They should, for example, treat the question of family cohesion with greater care. The family had been in the past a major source of defence in the face of disasters, crises and economic hardship. One can only imagine what would be the fate of individuals and societies when they are confronted by such trials in the absence of the family and the values that maintain its cohesion. Human societies have never before experienced existence in the absence of a coherent family unit. Where is the wisdom and rationality then in risking destroying what has proven to withstand the fiercest storms for the benefit of what is yet to be proven empirically? And who will be held responsible when all of society and posterity are made to pay the price of a failed experiment?

For these reasons, secularism has been generally incapable of striking the necessary balance in addressing the negative aspects of tradition, religion or religious institutions. Change, reform, modernisation and modernity should not, therefore, be realised by severing ties with the past, with history and with religion. Rather they should be achieved through a complex, steady and well-balanced process that is capable of accomplishing continuity through the elimination, or at least the attenuation, of imperfections and the generation of the 'new'. This 'new' will have to prove itself in the face of long-term trials brought about by social crises and successive changes in the balance of power.

Perhaps it is the composition of a contemporary Western civilisation of complex inter-relationships, involving secularism, religion, and tradition, that has enabled Western democracies to endure and strike a balance. Contrary to the opinion which attributes renaissance and democracy to secularism, it is this very composition which has made it possible for Western societies to democratise and accomplish renaissance. Striking a balance in Western societies has been the result not of a certain balanced procedure, as is the case in Islamic societies. It was rather realised through conflict, usually among unilateral positions, that leads to concessions which reflect the existing balance of powers.

It is important to note that this internal realignment with all its reconciliatory characteristics was brought about in Western Europe and the US as part of a broader rise to global domination. The colonial condition, which accompanied, provoked and fuelled the modern Western renaissance, did play a critical role in determining internal patterns of relationships and resolving various crises. It was this colonial condition which facilitated the accomplishment of internal concessions and reconciliation, permitting them to run their course far away from foreign intervention. It was this condition too which facilitated the inward flow of resources, thus stimulating economic growth, prosperity and progress. In many instances, the colonial condition also facilitated the export, or absorption, of internal crises through invasion and territorial expansion. Perhaps it is this condition of colonial empowerment which permits the West to enjoy the luxury of secularist improvisation, deconstructing here and there and experimenting with alternatives. If the West can afford to do so, weak, oppressed and downtrodden nations cannot afford the luxury of turning their societies into laboratories for theories designed primarily to deal with specific shortcomings rather than offer an alternative that is capable of passing the test of life.

Despite the defence mechanisms set up by sectors of Western societies, including the church, against some unbridled trends within liberal secularism – especially in areas such as education, the family, morality, values, delinquency and crime – the ill-effects of radical secularist ideas have pervaded Western societies, thus augmenting social crises. There has been a steady increase in crime, the family is disintegrating, sexual perversion is on the rise, drug addiction is spreading, and there has been a marked increase in the tendency toward individualism and the use of violence. This situation is like a double-edged sword. For on the one hand it has the potential of giving rise to a social backlash against irreligious secularism, thus increasing the hold of both church and religion on society; in short, it could instigate a return to core values, or 'back to basics', to use the expression of the former British Prime Minister John Major. On the other hand it could augment the deterioration of, and threaten, traditional social institutions, such as has been happening to 'Wasps' in the United States, to the advantage of radical minorities that espouse irreligious liberal secularism.

Hence, liberal secularism in Western societies is on the verge of a deep internal crisis with several possible outcomes, the most dangerous of which is the possibility of lapsing into a state of barbarism, especially if the serious rise in crime, drug addiction and violence, which have permeated the young, is not curbed. In this same context one may very well witness the increasing empowerment of trends, notwithstanding their marginality, that are extreme in their irreligious secularity. These trends are poised to rise to power having successfully intensified their hold over the media – including television, theatre and cinema – and as a result of the decline in society's traditional institutions, foremost of which is the family, precipitated by such influences.

Islam's civilisational model

The first Islamic model of the relationship between religion, state and society was moulded out of the experience of the Prophet and the four Rightly Guided Caliphs who succeeded him in leading the Muslim community. The Qur'an and the Sunnah formed together the constitution of the state whose frame of reference was Islamic in regard to its general goals, its method of government, and the theories underpinning its policy in politics, economy, war and international relations. At the helm of the state was a ruler who had a profound knowledge of jurisprudence, politics, economics and war, aided by advisors selected for their knowledge of, and expertise in, these fields. The objective was to win the pleasure of Allah through the implementation of his teachings in *'ibadah* (worship), *mu'amalah* (worldly dealings) and *da'wah* (calling to Islam). The state had a global mission, namely to invite mankind to Islam, the religion of pure monotheism, through the establishment of justice and by setting a good example. This is supposed to be achieved without resorting to oppression, coercion, or violence. The mission, in fact, is to free humans from the worship of idols, to free them from the servitude of power and caprice, and to guide them toward the worship of their Creator, the Almighty, alone. It is also the mission of the state to realise justice among all peoples without discrimination on the basis of colour, race, nationality or religion. The ruler and his advisers are expected, therefore, to comply fully with religious teachings and to pursue a policy that serves in the best possible way the interests of the community, humanity and the environment. In other words, they are not at liberty to choose, according to their own desires or personal interests, the policy to be pursued or the system of government to be set up.

The mind, which here appears to be restrained by the text – but is nevertheless given wide scope for innovation – is thus protected from the danger of being embroiled in the generation of theories or ideas designed to serve the private interests of the ruler or the ruling class. This is a chief difference between the Islamic model and objective irreligious secularism where the personal interests of the ruling class can be used to the detriment of the majority at home, or in the enslavement of other nations abroad.

It is important to note here that the model of a guided Islamic state cannot be described as a theocracy. It is rather a state whose frame of reference, the Qur'an and Sunnah, is religious. It is a model of state in which the ruler rises to power through *bay'ah* (pledge of allegiance) after having been freely elected by the community, to whose scrutiny and reckoning he is subjected. Furthermore, the community reserves the right to withhold its allegiance. The ruler in the Islamic state is an ordinary human being who is supposed to practice *shura* (council) and *ijtihad* (endeavouring to make the right judgement), and thus is liable to err; hence his opinions may be accepted or rejected.

One should also note here that the adherence of the Muslim mind to the textual frame of reference necessitates an interaction with life and reality from a strictly objective standpoint characterised by what typifies the scientific approach to learning and to the discovery of phenomena. The slogan of the Muslim mind therefore is: 'my Lord show me things as they really are'; 'my Lord enable me to see the truth as it is and help me to pursue it, and enable me to see falsehood as it is and help me to avoid it'. The difference between the Muslim mind and the secularist mind does not stem from seeing things as they are in reality, that is to say through a scientific and objective outlook, by which the secular mind cannot claim to be distinguished from the Islamic. The distinguishing feature between the two approaches stems rather from adherence to the truth and avoidance of falsehood so that the mind does not feel free to justify things that are oppressive, racist, colonialist, exploitative or extortionist, or to accommodate deviation, abnormality or crime.

Islamic history has been marked by a conflict between the *shari'ah* (canon law) on the one side and rulers, the state and people of wealth and influence on the other. Freedom from the restraints of *shari'ah* has been persistently sought by despotic rulers as well as by those who monopolise wealth and dedicate it to the achievement of their personal pleasure at the expense of the *ummah*. On the other hand, the call for a strict adherence to *shari'ah* has represented a continuous revolution against such rulers; it has been associated with the struggle by society to rid itself of corruption, degradation and the squandering of resources.

The profound influence on the lives and minds of Muslims by the Prophetic era and by the Rightly Guided Caliphate that succeeded it, and above all the justice and good example set by the first Islamic state model, has made it very difficult for any ruler to rebel against it. Any deviation by a ruler was considered as a great threat to the creed, histori- cal memories and future hopes of the *ummah*. Herein lies a major difference between the Islamic model, which offered scores of exemplary experi- ments over a period of 1,400 years, and the record of the church in the West. Whereas the Islamic experience was reflected in a period of renais- sance, justice, progress, equality and respect for freedom of expression, human dignity and human rights, the experience of the church has been associated with what many people would describe as the Dark Ages and the Inquisition. Thus the outlook on the past differs in the two instances. For this reason it has been possible for the separation of religion from the state to take place openly in the secularist irreligious West; while in the Islamic context, both in the past and the present, it has had to be approa- ched indirectly and using many masks.

Ever since the founding of the Umayyad Caliphate, the gap between the *'ulama* (scholars) and religion on the one hand and the state on the other gradually began to widen. The ruler no longer represented the Rightly Guided model (with the exception of the Umayyad Caliph 'Umar ibn 'Abdul 'Aziz whose rule was considered rightly guided). Since then, and until the end of the Ottoman period, the regime was described as the 'rule of avarice and conquest'.

During this time there emerged a tendency on the part of the rulers to distance their policies from the *shari'ah*, alienate the *'ulama* who genu- inely adhered to the principles of justice, and identify with persons known as *'ulama al-sultan* (scholars of rulers) in order to perpetuate an image of attachment to the *shari'ah*, which did not really exist. The pic- ture was as follows: rulers, supported by military personnel and scholars who shared their views, increasingly digressed from *shari'ah* and ruled, relying purely on reason, in a manner that served their own interests and desires. While spreading oppression and corruption, they preserved the caliphate, maintained a role for the *shari'ah* to play in personal mat- ters, and left for the *'ulama* the task of preserving religious symbols in society. The *'ulama* had become the authority to whom the people turned in times of crises and difficulties, when oppression and degradation became totally unbearable, or when disasters, crises or wars befell the country.

Some sort of a deal, a settlement, was struck between the *'ulama* and rulers. The *'ulama* did not incite rebellion against the rulers even though they despised the 'disagreeable' separation between the ruler and religion. At the same time, they did not condone deviant practices, and thus concentrated their efforts on consolidating the role and position of religion in society. In a sense the *'ulama* were the last line of defence for the people in times of crises and tribulation. While the rulers claimed to be the true protectors of religion in public, in reality they implemented their own laws and led in private a way of life that contradicted the basic tenets of religion. This condition did not remain stable throughout the past 1,400 years, for there were periods of conflict between the two sides. These were punctuated by periods of truce, violent suppression and open incitement to rebellion (a notable example was the case of Al-'Izz ibn 'Abdel Salam in Egypt). Not to mention of course the uprisings led by *'ulama'* during the last 200 years (Muhammad 'Abdel Wahab, 'Abdel Qadir Al-Jaza'iri, 'Umar Al-Mukhtar and Al-Mahdi, in addition to al-Azhar uprisings). Notwithstanding, the periods of settlement (truce without reconciliation in most cases) were the most prevalent throughout the centuries.

It is important to note that the trend in Islamic history, which disrupted the relationship between religion and the state (and thus brought an end to the model of the Rightly Guided Caliphate), bore the seeds of secularism in government, but it retained some ties with religion. The seeds of secularism germinated to produce despotism, injustice, immorality, misuse of public wealth, persecution of minorities and instigation of tribal and ethnic conflicts. The relationship between the ruler, his cohorts and military on the one hand and that of the *'ulama* and religion on the other vacillated between armistice and confrontation depending on changes in the balance of power. There was, quite naturally, no alternative to this cycle except the Rightly Guided Caliphate model.

The Muslim world knew Western-style secularism only when the global balance of power tilted in favour of the West which started interfering directly in the affairs of Muslims in order to impose on their societies its own brand of secularism.

The modern secularist states and the Arab-Islamic condition

Direct colonial intervention in most of the Arab and Islamic countries led to a serious internal imbalance. There was an attempt to create a new equilibrium based on the modern secularist state and a modern secularist army. Both of these were invariably formed in emulation of the colonialist authority and its army. The newly independent states were thus extensions of the colonial states and their institutions, including the army, the police, the intelligence services and legal system.

The state in the Arab and Muslim regions did not therefore emerge as a result of a domestic reconciliation, or resolution of internal conflicts. It was rather imposed upon the society from outside, and so does not represent the society. On the contrary it has representatives in society. It is isolated even from the elite who were trained in the missionary or secularist Western schools and universities. The monopolising of political power provokes the hostility of this elite in spite of its support for the alienation of Islam from the state and its acceptance of the Western model of secularism. However, accepting the Western model of secularism necessitates taking into consideration the equilibrium which exists in Western societies between the state and religion. This dimension has been completely shrouded in the Arab secularist model because its presence would create an opportunity for Islam and the *'ulama* to play a role. Secularist dictatorship and its alienation of society have led to severe crises in most modern Arab and Muslim states. In search of a way out of this predicament, the ruling secularist elite enhanced its subordination to foreign powers and intensified its dictatorial attitude toward society, thus alienating itself even further.

The first attack launched against society by the modern state took place during the colonial era and was directed against traditional Islamic institutions. To start with, the *awqaf* (endowment trusts) were seized and placed under government control, thereby denying them the independence they had enjoyed for many centuries. Similar measures were taken against religious educational institutions in an attempt to impose control on them or marginalise their role.

But the real war was waged after independence to the extent that all religious institutions and associations were stripped of their independence and all their activities placed under the direct control of the authorities, including the appointment of *imams* (prayer leaders in mosques), determining the opening and closing times of mosques for prayer and proscribing the convening of classes inside the mosque after prayer. Whereas in the West the relationship between secularism, the church, religion and the state stabilised through an historic accord that left the church and its charitable, educational and media institutions completely independent, the secularist authorities in the Muslim world have not agreed to any settlement with Islam and its institutions; instead, they have sought to eliminate Islamic rivals or at least subdue them through a process known as 'drying of the springs'. It is interesting to note that these same secularist authorities have not dealt with the Christian church in the same manner. Instead, the church has been left completely independent and fully in charge of its endowments and schools.

In dealing with the Islamic religion and Islamic institutions, the secularist authorities in the Arab and Muslim countries have followed the Bolshevik model even though they may be far removed from social-ism and communism. Certain states, which previously maintained positive relations with religion and religious institutions, either for reasons to do with their cultural foundation or because of the era of their struggle against communism, have now begun to constrain this positive attitude and incline toward practices characteristic of the Bolshevik model.

It is worth observing that Western liberal secularism, which agreed to a settlement and accepts the church and religion, is now encouraging Arab and Muslim countries to continue in their war against religion to the end. What is more compelling to observe is the position of the church and traditional religious institutions in the West toward the secu-larist genocidal campaigns against Islamic religious establishments and the marginalisation of the role of religion in Muslim societies. On the other hand, it is necessary to observe that a secularist-Christian alliance exists in the West aimed not only at encouraging the secularist endeavour to combat Islam and Islamic institutions, but also at encou-raging Christian missionary activities, endowing Christian missionaries with special concessions in the Muslim countries where Islamic activities are being restricted.

The continuation of this condition of external and internal warfare will lead inevitably to the prevalence of one of three options in the future. The first option would be for the despotic state of repression, subordination and perversion to endure and emerge as the secularist model for the Arab and Islamic countries. The other alternative would be the eruption of civil war and the emergence of an Islamic state which is likely to sink in the quagmire of trying to suppress its own rivals. The third option would be to reach some kind of truce, settlement or reconciliation in order to create a more balanced situation regardless of whether it is under the leadership of the Islamists, the nationalists or the Arabists. This option though is like swimming against the tide which gains force from the Western winds.

Conclusion

Modern states in most Arab and Islamic countries espouse secularism without any consideration for the historic conditions that led to its development in the West, nor for the concessions, reconciliations and settlements struck internally with religion, the church and the Western Christian civilisational legacy, nor for the prevailing global hegemony of the West and what such a condition entails. The consequence of such failure in observing these important criteria has inevitably led to the adoption of a path different from that pursed by the Europeans, whose model Arab and Muslim secularists allege to emulate. Thus the claims of Arab and Muslim secularists that their own model is based upon the Western model, and that they seek progress by pursuing the Western path, are essentially baseless. For instead of building a tolerant state that adopts multi-party democracy, an intolerant and parochial, and in some countries sectarian, autocratic state has been created. Instead of a vivid and empowered civil society, we find a society of coercion in which basic rights and civil liberties are denied. Rather than independence, a condition of subservience to external powers prevails accompanied by an acute case of internal alienation.

It will be impossible, in the Arab and Muslim countries, to consolidate the values of pluralism, tolerance, freedom of expression and belief, sovereignty of civil society and acceptance of free polling results as a final arbitration unless Islam is recognised as a frame of reference, unless a historic reconciliation is struck among various domestic social powers and political groups, and unless an equilibrium emanating from an internal balance of powers rather than from foreign intervention and compulsion is attained. It remains to be said that reforming the current situation in the Arab and Muslim regions requires a revision of perception not only by Muslims of the West but also by the West of Islam and the Muslims.

RATIONALITY OF POLITICS AND POLITICS OF RATIONALITY

DEMOCRATISATION AND THE INFLUENCE OF ISLAMIC RELIGIOUS TRADITIONS

Abdelwahab El-Affendi

If we are to believe Ernest Gellner, then the Muslim world has no hope of democratisation if it sticks to its traditions. In his discussion of what he sees as the absence of civil society in the Islamic world, he argues that 'Muslim polities are pervaded by clientelism. There is government-by-network. Law governs the details of daily life, but not the institutions of power.'[1] As a result, the Muslim World 'exemplifies a social order which seems to lack much capacity to provide political countervailing institutions and associations, which is atomized without much individualism, and operates effectively without intellectual pluralism'.[2] The root of this problem, in Gellner's view, is that Islamic tradition has influenced Muslims to the extent that, even though they may be 'severe and fastidious about the implementation of the sacred prescriptions' they are, nevertheless, 'not otherwise over-sensitive about the internal organisation of political authority, nor greatly perturbed by its clientelist structure and its unfastidious methods and partiality. Nothing else is expected of politics. Authority is accountable to God for the implementation of religious-legal rules, but not to man for the practice of some civil ideal.'[3] The same notion is picked up by Arkoun in an earlier intervention, arguing that the idea of 'supreme divine authority' in Islam has been both relegated to the realm of the 'unthinkable' and violently manipulated both by 'ulama (who were keen to preserve their 'authority') and by rulers who wanted to exploit the halo of religious legitimacy.[4] Both authors thus see the problem in the dichotomy of 'authority' which is divine in origin and ascription, and 'power' which is divorced from it and accountable to no one in practice. Muslim societies, Gellner argues, resemble

---

[1] Ernest Gellner, *Conditions of Liberty: Civil Society and its Rivals*, London: Harmondsworth: Penguin Books, 1996, p. 26.

[2] *Ibid.*, p. 29.

[3] *Ibid.*, pp. 22-3.

[4] Muhammad Arkoun, *Tarikhiyyat al-Fikr al-Islami*, Beirut: Markaz al-Inma' al-Qawmi, 1996, pp. 165-92.

151

ancient communities which 'sometimes escape the tyranny of kings, but only at the cost of falling under the tyranny of cousins, and of ritual'.[5] They also share with communism and ancient Sparta the characteristics of being a 'moral order', intent on imposing virtue on the members of the community, regardless of what an individual member may think.[6]

The politics of rationality

Reading these comments one would think that Gellner is speaking of a Muslim world which has no relation whatsover to the one we know, where, if anything, both power and authority appear to be strongly, even violently, contested on a daily basis. But we will leave our comments on his theses for later. For the moment, we would like to register his point which seems to emphasise the role of doctrine and tradition in shaping modern Muslim practices, including the absence of democracy in most Muslim countries. This central point contradicts the conclusion of another scholar who undertook a careful examination of the roots of Muslim intellectual tradition. In his pioneering – if controversial – analysis of the evolution of classical Islamic thought, the Moroccan philosopher, Muhammad Abid Al-Jabiri, espouses a diametrically opposed view to that of Gellner's: it is politics which subverted the Muslim intellectual endeavour, and not the other way round. In other words, power has been so vehemently contested that the whole edifice of Islamic thought had been shaped by struggles for power. The present crisis in Arab-Islamic thought, therefore, has its origins in political manipulations which stunted the development of rational thought processes, causing the history of Muslim thought to be dominated by irrational influences emanating from Neo-Platonic and other Hellenistic philosophical traditions.[7] Al-Jabiri believes that his study has 'emphasised sufficiently the principal role played by politics in directing Arab-Islamic thought,' showing the (mainly Shi'i) opposition to have been instrumental in importing 'irrational' elements of Hellenistic thought into Muslim discourse as a weapon in its struggle for power, inducing a counter-reaction from the state which tried to foster rationalism as a counter-tactic. This had led first to the politicisation of religion and, later, philosophy or, to use Al-Jabiri's words, 'the conduct of politics through religion, which evolved to become also the conduct of politics through philosophy'.[8]

---

[5] Gellner, *Conditions of Liberty*, p. 7.

[6] *Ibid.*, pp. 50-3, 137.

[7] Muhammad Abid Al-Jabiri, *Naq al-'Aql al-'Arabi: I. Takwin al-'Aql al-'Arabi* (Critique of the Arab Mind, vol. I: The Formation of the Arab Mind), Beirut: Dar al-Tali'ah, 1984.

[8] *Ibid.*, pp. 346-7.

Now I am not about to join the growing band of Al-Jabiri's detractors. Quite the reverse, in fact. But while recording al-Jabiri's pioneering effort and rich insights, I seek leave to stand him on his head on this particular point and, at least in one aspect, side with Gellner. I believe that the causal chain should be reversed and could be more accurately construed the other way round: it is the abiding irrationality which infected Muslim thought early on that created the political muddle, and not the reverse. And it was not just the long-term failure to comprehend the essence of Greek rationalism that was the problem. The methods of reading and interpreting the Islamic heritage itself also suffered from serious lapses. These reflected themselves in doctrinal splits and political and intellectual muddles. The endemic political instability which continues to infect the Muslim political landscape until this day cannot be delinked from the intellectual muddles which characterised Muslim political thought (and Muslim thought in general) through the ages. It goes without saying that any attempt at genuine reform and democratisation will be fruitless unless the root causes of the current stagnation are addressed. And the root causes can be found in the confusion at the core of Muslim thinking, traditional and modern. But this does not mean that Gellner's diagnosis was correct, as we will show presently.

Al-Jabiri's 'archaeological' approach: a beginning

Al-Jabiri's method of analysing the evolution of Muslim thought reflects some elements of Foucault's 'archaeology of knowledge' approach, in that it seeks to discover the underlying basic trends which infuse all thought processes and branches of knowledge in a certain epoch.[9] In his reckoning, the originality of Arab-Islamic thought during its formative period lay in what could be called *al-bayan* (exposition or elucidation) and its central concern had been the Text, whether religious or linguistic. Islamic thought occupied itself in that early period with the elaboration of linguistic sciences: grammar, rhetoric etc. and, of course, with the preservation, transmission and study of religious texts: the Qur'an, the *sunna* (Prophetic traditions) and the sciences that crystallised around them, in particular Islamic historiography. All these 'original' sciences were united by one over-arching epistemological principle which governed all their operations: the principle of *qiyas* (deduction by analogy) in grammar and *fiqh* (jurisprudence). Closely related to this is the principle of *istidlal* (deduction) in *kalam* (theology) or (which is the same

[9] For an overview of Foucault's work see Alan Sheridan, *Michael Foucault: the Will to Truth*, London: Tavistock Publications, 1980. Interestingly, Jabiri's characterisation of classical Islamic thought as one ruled by *qiyas* (analogy) is echoed in Foucault's description of the Renaissance vision as similarly that of a 'world held together by resemblance', where it was 'resemblance that largely guided exegesis and the interpretation of texts' (*ibid.*, p. 51).

thing) simile in rhetoric. What we face here is one predominant 'thought mechanism', which seeks to comprehend and pigeonhole the individual incident or occurrence by relating it to a fixed origin or source through analogical reasoning. Emergent experience had to be ordered by relating it to well-defined elements in earlier experience.[10] It is with this view that one must appreciate the revolutionary character of the Andalusian revolt against *qiyas*, spearheaded by Ibn Hazm Al-Andalusi (AH 384-456/ 994-1064 CE) and his *zahiriyah* (literalist) school. By rejecting *qiyas*, Ibn Hazm substituted reason for it as the fourth legislative principle in Islamic law (together with Qur'an, *sunna* and *ijma'* (consensus)), and thus set the stage for the full maturity of Muslim rationalism.[11]

Before going on to discuss the import of this insight for our topic, we need to fully understand the character of the activity we are looking at here, i.e. the formative period of Muslim thought in its original phase. For the Muslim enterprise of that period could not be properly understood or analysed without understanding its proper goals and objectives as perceived by the participants themselves. The core of Muslim intellectual activity during that early period had been directed towards one cardinal objective: to reconstruct the early Islamic (and even the immediately antecedent pre-Islamic) period through painstaking 'archaeological' research. Attempts to reconstruct and critically analyse this activity, especially of the type attempted by al-Jabiri, Arkoun and others, could be construed, therefore, as the 'archaeology of an archaeology', or a 'meta-archaeology of knowledge'. And herein lies the complexity of the exercise.

The motive of the early Muslim scholars, when they embarked on a reconstruction of the historical period in question, was the eagerness to fully understand the divine message. Their reasoning in this, as elucidated by Al-Shafi'i, was simple: the Qur'an has been revealed in the Arabic tongue, to a specific community of people, at a particular historical juncture. To fully understand it, one needed to fully comprehend not only the language as it was spoken then, but also the historical, social and intellectual climate that reigned at the time. Al-Jabiri finds several faults with this approach (as do many others, like Arkoun)[12]. First of all, he agrees with many commentators in affirming that the subsequent reconstruction of the early period had been coloured by the climate (including the political conditions) that reigned at the time. In particular,

[10] Al-Jabiri, *op. cit.*, pp., 120, 128-31.

[11] Al-Jabiri, *op. cit.*, pp., 299-328.

[12] Muhammad Arkoun, *Min al-Ijtihad ila Naqd al-'Aql al-Islami* (From *ijtihad* to the Critique of Islamic Reason) trans. Hashim Salih, London: Al Saqi, 1991, in particular pp. 38, 55, 67, where he accused traditional jurists of opportunism, manipulation of reports and manufacturing or manipulation of evidence.

Al-Jabiri argues that the reconstruction of the Arab past was a direct political response to the challenge posed by the non-Arab majority which constituted the Muslim masses, and who were mounting a bid for power. This explains the conflicting images of the pre-Islamic era in the literature, being condemned in some contexts, and glorified in others.[13] Another problem is the insistence on 'purifying' the Arabic language from any accretions perceived to be of foreign origin, thus ossifying and restricting the language, and imprisoning it in its 'Bedouin' and primitive past.[14]

This claim suggests that the purpose of the reconstruction was mainly political, implying that there were other, more scientific, ways of performing this task. Looked at from the perspective of the objective of the enterprise in question, however, it is difficult to see how the task could have been carried out otherwise. The rigour (the *scientific* rigour) and diligence manifested by the early generation of Muslim linguists, grammarians, *hadith* collectors and jurists when they applied themselves to researching the facts and authenticating reports, is difficult to duplicate, even today. Al-Jabiri's affirmation, following Sir Hamilton Gibb, that the very completeness of the sciences in question was a recipe for stagnation, since nothing could be added to them,[15] is a praise in disguise for the enterprise. For it is ridiculous to blame someone for doing a job too well and ascribe subsequent stagnation to this very excellence! Indeed, what is admirable in the enterprise of pioneering Muslim scholars was the conscientiousness with which they attempted to rise above their prejudices and apply rigorous scientific criteria when it came to reporting of *hadith* or historical incidents. Far from succumbing to the temptations of power and material incentives, the majority of leading scholars actually adopted a consistent stance of resistance to the powers that be, a point to which we shall return. This shows that although it is legitimate to say that the recording of history and *hadith* could not have escaped the influence of the reigning intellectual, social and political climate (how could it?), it is safe to say that the concerned scholars did all that was humanly possible to free themselves from these constraints, with admirable success. If this is the case, where does the problem lie then?

The crisis of political thought in Islam: genesis

We are not concerned here with the totality of Muslim thought, so we are going to restrict ourselves to its political dimension. And as soon as we turn our attention to this area, the most glaring flaw of classical methodology becomes fully apparent. If Islamic thought, as many claim, had

[13] Al-Jabiri, *op. cit.*, pp., 58-60.

[14] *Ibid.*, pp., 78-94.

[15] *Ibid.*, pp., 342-3.

been coloured in all its manifestations by politics, the most incontestable evidence for this would naturally be found in the area of political thought. But if we look closely, we will find that, although this is unquestionably the case in many instances, the views expressed on each topic were diverse enough to make the charge of predominant political bias untenable. It is thus the area of the overall methodology of classical thought that needs to be looked at. Even in politics, therefore, the problem is epistemological and methodological, not political, at least not in the narrow sense of the term.

If we were to identify the most problematic feature of traditional Islamic thought in general, and political thought in particular, we could call it 'textualism', that is, the tendency to seek solutions (only) within the confines of earlier precedents or explicitly sanctioned conduct. This is partially the import of *qiyas*, 'the derivation on the basis of an earlier example', as the jurists put it. *Qiyas*, however, involves not one, but two acts, even three. The first is to ascertain the existence of a precedent; second, a general rule is derived from that precedent; and, third, this rule is applied to the case in question. One does not start from, nor look for, general principles which reason could then be allowed to freely apply to a variety of cases. The scholars were thus busy looking for individual incidents and occurrences, which they then quickly generalised.

In political thought, this has been done with a vengeance. And it is particularly in this area that this methodology was confronted with a maddeningly recalcitrant reality, represented by the almost complete absence of explicit injunctions and clear precedents which would save the thinking man the trouble of racking his brains for genuinely original solutions. Al-Jabiri finds it remarkable that, even though the question of the *khilafah* (caliphate) had been the central issue of contention between various Muslim political groups, theorisation on the *khilafah* only began at least a century after the institution was inaugurated. The debate was initiated by the Shi'i minority from an oppositional perspective, with the Sunnis reacting much later to the theses of their adversaries.[16] Al-Jabiri also points to the supreme irony that, although the basic schism within the community was between a minority that insisted that the *khilafah* question has been resolved by explicit injunctions determining who should assume the office (the Shi'a) and a majority that regarded it as a matter of discretion left for the judgement of the community at large (the Sunnis), we find the first group relies exclusively on rational arguments to demonstrate that the *khilafah* could not be left for reason alone to determine, but must be resolved by appeals to specific injunctions, while the latter relied mainly on historical precedents and 'texts' to prove that

---

[16] *Ibid.*, pp., 107-8. Cf. Abdelwahab El-Affendi, *Who Needs an Islamic State?* London: Grey Seal Books, 1991, pp. 22-6.

the issue has not been resolved by explicit textual injunctions, but has been left to reason to determine![17]

The problem is that only the *khawarij* (a tiny minority of militant dissidents opposed to all main schools of thought) consistently maintained a rational stance on the issue, arguing that the institution of the *khilafah* was a discretionary one, which is not even essential or mandatory if justice could be maintained without it. The others went on meticulous archaeological expeditions to sift through each and every individual action by the early generation of Muslims to try to derive from it rules for later application. Even the *khawarij*, however, were rational only in theory, since their uncompromising and violent 'idealism' was the epitome of irrationality. The way the movement self-destructed and disintegrated into a myriad factions fighting each other and everybody else was not exactly a recommendation of reason's ability to resolve such matters.

The methodology adopted by the majority, however, had created more problems than it solved. The way it went about reasoning was usually like this: Omar has nominated Abu Bakr (the first caliph) for *khilafah* and pledged allegiance to him (in the face of opposition from many others), and his choice was endorsed by five men, leading to Abu Bakr being declared Caliph. It is therefore lawful for five men to declare another Caliph, and his tenure would become lawful on the basis of this alone.[18] Even more telling, as Al-Mawardi reports, others said that three people could install the supreme political leader of the Muslims, with one of them to declare him *imam* and two to witness, on the analogy of marriage, where it is deemed sufficient for the guardian of the bride to contract her marriage in the presence of two witnesses.[19] The analogy with marriage is carried further when it is used to argue that you cannot have more than one ruler, nor can a council of two men or more assume the post, since two men could not be allowed to marry the same woman.[20] On another point, it has been recorded that Abu-Bakr did appoint Omar as successor, and his choice was endorsed by the community. Therefore, it is lawful for the ruler to appoint his own successor. The question then arises: what if the ruler appoints a relative, such as his son, as successor? And one answer given was that this was perfectly lawful, since it was his prerogative as the supreme authority, and he does not even need to have his choice endorsed by the majority (or by anyone else for that matter) to be valid.[21] Another question arises: can he appoint a number of

---

[17] Al-Jabiri, *op. cit.*, p. 108.
[18] Abu'l-Hassan al-Mawardi, *Al-Ahkam al-Sultaniyyah*, Cairo: Maktabat al-Babi al-Halabi, 1973, p. 7.
[19] *Ibid.*, p. 7.
[20] *Ibid.*, p. 9.
[21] *Ibid.*, p. 10.

successors according to a defined order of succession? Answer: of course
he can. Was there not this incident when the Prophet – peace be upon him
– sent a military expedition and appointed Zayd ibn Harithah as commander, with the stipulation that if he were to be killed in battle, then
Jaafar ibn Abi Talib was to succeed him, and if the latter were also to die,
then the commander was to be Abdullah ibn Abi Rawaha. If all three
were to die, then the expedition should choose its own commander.[22]
This precedent (with the significant omission of the final proviso of the
community choosing its leader) was used to endorse the decision by the
Abbasid ruler, Haroun Al-Rashid, to appoint his three sons as successors
according to a prescribed order of seniority.

What is the problem with this approach, then? To start with, the recourse to precedent instead of appeal to over-arching principles obscures
the overall picture and leaves itself open to manipulation, a continuously
present danger in political matters. Second, this meticulous running after
even the most obscure and irrelevant of precedents tends to obscure the
most important fact about political thought in Islam: the acknowledged
fact that not much specific guidance in the form of clear injunctions exists in this field. In other words, it tends to obscure the cardinal fact that
the political organisation of the Muslim community and the conduct of
its affairs has been left to its discretion, something which seems to terrify
many who, like the people described in the famous parable of the cow
in the second sura in the Qur'an, insist on desperately digging for clues
where none are needed. The parable in question tells the story of the
Israelites who were requested by Moses to slaughter a cow for a certain
ritual function. Instead of picking the first suitable cow and thus comply-
ing with a clear and straightforward injunction, they kept asking: what
type of cow? When they were given an answer, they demanded again:
What colour? No sooner was an answer given than they were again
complaining that apparently too many cows fitted the description, and
asking for additional criteria, which were again supplied.[23] And the moral
of that story is: if the believers receive an injunction, they are to act upon
it according to their discretion, and not keep delaying action by looking
for irrelevant guidance. This lesson was not left vague, but was clearly
delineated in unequivocal terms in the Qur'an.[24] The essence of this advice is for believers to use their discretion where no specific advice is
given, and not keep asking for more guidance in lieu of exercising their

[22] Mawardi, op. cit., p. 13.

[23] See Qur'an, 2: 67-71.

[24] 'O ye who believe! Ask not questions about things which, if made plain to you, may
cause you trouble. But if ye ask about things when the Quran is being revealed, they will
be made plain to you, Allah will forgive those: For Allah is Oft-Forgiving, most Forbear-
ing. Some people before you did ask such questions, and on that account lost their faith.'
(The Holy Qur'an, 5: 101-102)

judgement. After all, the exercise of reason is the whole point of human existence on earth. Had God wanted to, he could have populated the earth with automatons that only functioned if fed instructions. But he chose not to do so. And we have to live with this fact.

Unfortunately, theoreticians in the field of *khilafah* (and many other areas as well) chose to employ the exact reverse of this advice. Here was an area where specific injunctions about the formation of government and its conduct were so scarce that a significant section of the community thought it appropriate to argue that the formation of a government was not even necessary. When the early Muslim community was confronted by the leadership vacuum that appeared after the death of the Prophet, it did the sensible thing and resorted to *ad hoc* solutions to the problem dictated by circumstances. But instead of departing from this starting point and trying to think and act rationally about the question of political organisation, a curious anomaly emerged: the community, in later years, usually *acted* rationally on the issue, but consistently *thought* irrationally about it. After some costly struggles at the beginning, fed by idealism, the community usually adopted in practice the least costly, i.e. the rational, solution, but refused to endorse it in theory. This was the root of this dangerous dislocation between theory and practice, which exists to this day: with theory having no chance of becoming reality, while reality is devoid from any ethical and legal basis.

Another major flaw of the methodology in question, which manifested itself mainly in the realm of political reasoning, was to take all precedents out of context. For example, the famous incident where the Khalifah Omar was forced to withdraw a ruling he made limiting dowers in marriage because a woman protested against it, is usually related by narrators as if Omar and the lady in question were the only two persons in the mosque. A similar treatment is given to all decisions and rulings issued by the khalifah. But what the incident in question shows is something more important: that the rulings made by the khalifah were not their personal decisions as a matter of fiat, but were habitually made and announced in the mosque, which was attended by all the adult population of Medina, men and women, five times a day. The objection of a single individual in that congregation, man or woman, would have invalidated the ruling or caused it to be revised. To take decisions of this character out of context, and thus equate, for example, the decision of Abu Bakr to appoint Omar as successor in full consultation with the whole community, without a single recorded objection, with (the first Umayyad Caliph) Mu'awiyah's decision to appoint his son as successor and treat the two as different expressions of the same principle is a basic methodological flaw. For Mu'awiyah's decision was not only opposed by the majority, but actually led to a series of costly civil wars. It goes without saying this defective methodology of reading precedents has to be radically reconsidered.

Democracy and its instability

In order to appreciate the nature of the Muslim predicament in this regard, one has to look at the wider picture of the overall human endeavour. Al-Jabiri discusses, following Festugiere, what he calls the 'self-destructiveness of Greek rationality', a feature duplicated in the Islamic experience where the Hellenised philosophers in Islam became the main purveyors of irrationality.[25] This is a very interesting phenomenon in its own right, with parallels even in our times. But what is of more relevance to the present inquiry is the self-destructiveness of democratic polities, that is, of rationally organised consensual political systems, a phenomenon (i.e. this self-destructiveness) that, until recently, has been the norm rather the exception. The way in which the Medina city-state degenerated quickly into an authoritarian system displays close parallels with the history of Athens and later Rome. The common factor in all three was imperial expansion in conditions of primitive communications. The rise of empires, the expansion of military activities and institutions, in addition to the sheer size of the state and bewildering diversity of the populations, meant that political institutions suitable for the running of a city-state democracy were no longer appropriate. Conservatism in political thought precluded a speedy adaptation of political philosophy to accommodate the new demands, while practice could not wait for theory. Ambitious and successful military commanders, competent administrators, or others with suitable qualifications stepped in to fill the vacuum. Then they started making the rules. Meanwhile, the faithful theoreticians continued to live in the past, refusing to see or hear, condemning the present to permanent illegality, without ever dreaming of adapting theory to practice. Those who did, when they did, tried to justify what happened retrospectively by selectively fishing for precedents and anecdotes. By the time men like Ibn Khaldun began the attempt to *explain* rather than justify, the political developments of their time, there was little left to explain, since the disintegration was almost complete by then.

In pre-modern times, democratic or semi-democratic orders were characterised by their short life span, due to their inherent instability. City states, where democracies usually flourished, were vulnerable to more powerful predators from abroad, as well as to ambitious individuals from within. Most modern democracies have not evolved consciously as 'virtuous cities' according to pre-conceived utopian plans, but were actually the end result of an intense, and often prolonged, struggle for power within elites. This was the case even in the US which, more than any other country, had utopianism as an in-built component in its struggle for existence.

---

[25] Al-Jabiri, *op. cit.*, pp. 166-7, 267-8.

Modern democracies can best be seen, as Gellner suggests, as the outcome of a 'political stalemate' which allowed civil society to evolve and maintain its viability outside the political realm, and then exert influence over it.[26] Understanding this important dimension of the evolution of modern democracies is indispensable if the benefits of the experience are to be generalised elsewhere. If the misunderstandings which characterised the classical Islamic political theories and the modern readings of them, were to be compounded by a third level of misunderstanding about the nature and essence of modern democracy, then the muddle will become truly hopeless. The fact that the modern democratic experience is in essence a balance of power equilibrium, rather than an ideal-type approximation of utopia, can be confirmed by (and helps to explain) many historical facts that would otherwise be regarded as anomalous. The fact that democracy in America was able to coexist with slavery, the active extermination of indigeneous inhabitants and the disenfranchisement of many citizens could be understood in this context, as could the apparent juxtaposition of Western democracies with imperialism and the prolonged disenfranchisement of women and the lower classes in these democracies. The very character of the institutions of modern democracy (parliaments, parties, the media, pressure groups, unions etc.) indicates that they were so constructed as to cater for the powerful and those who could assert themselves and acquire a voice. The confrontational nature of the democratic process is a living embodiment of the advice given by one US president for those who cannot stand the heat to stay out of the kitchen. The working classes in the West had literally to fight for their place in the modern democracies, and so had people of colour in the US. Today, with the unions weakened and the state and powerful economic interests on the ascendant, the poor are again feeling the pinch, and acute poverty amid plenty is again becoming tolerated in many Western and other democracies.

The object of this analysis is to understand, not to condemn. Many Muslims today, and not only despots, use the criticism of modern democracy as a justification of their own prejudices or of defective systems. Whatever maybe the shortcomings of modern democracy, its advantages are clear for all to see. And a better system has yet to be devised. Although the media and common parlance discuss political struggles in terms reminiscent of the olden days, ('he is fighting for his political life', 'the knives are out for so and so' etc.) it remains true that the way the game of politics is played within modern democracies, at least in internal politics, is generally relatively civilised, and blood is usually not spilt.[27]

---

[26] Gellner, *Conditions of Liberty*, p. 48. Cf. Adam Przeworski, 'Democracy as a Contingent Outcome of Conflicts' in John Elster and Rune Slagstad (eds), *Constitutionalism and Democracy*, Cambridge University Press, 1988, 58-80.

[27] See Helmut Kuzmics, 'The Civilizing Process' in John Keane (ed.) *Civil Society and the*

The losers do not go to the gallows, and are even permitted to continue to contribute to political and intellectual life. Thus while relative power is what determines the outcome in the process (and even the rules of the game), there are a number of basic rules which are generally observed by all. In the past two centuries, attempts have been made to expand the areas covered by such norms: national and international legislation on human rights, guarantees for civil and political rights, legislation protecting workers, children etc.

However, the bottom-line guarantee has always been the balance of power within each country. In particular, the effectiveness of civil society in limiting the authority of the state constitutes one of the essential features of modern democracy. This explains the failure of democratic experiments in newly formed countries in Africa, Asia and Latin America. These countries had, immediately on independence, promulgated constitutions modelled on foreign imports, sanctioning political arrangements and procedures that bore no relation to the prevailing balance of power within the countries in question. When this balance began to reassert itself, the disjunction between the moral-legal basis of the system and the actual reality caused the system to be sapped of legitimacy, opening the way for further decline, especially since no alternative approach to harmonising institutions, values and reality was forthcoming. Revolutionaries who wanted to remould whole communities and force their nations into the strait-jackets of the modern centralising state did much more damage.

For the Muslim world, this development represented just one crisis too many, the proverbial final straw which was the last thing the overburdened camel needed. It is no surprise, therefore, that this part of the world remains today a barren wilderness in a world which is becoming covered at a precipitate rate with the green pastures of democracy. The way out is to proceed by peeling these layers of crises like an onion, starting with the latest.

I do not here even want to dignify with an answer the arguments which deny that democracy conforms to Islamic values. What is incontestable is that none of its alternatives does. The most sacred duty of all politically active Muslims is, therefore, to try to work hard to replace these systems, and to ensure that democracy must not only prevail in all Muslim lands, but must also put in deep roots. Proposals for democratisation must, however, be based on a deep understanding of the communities for which they are designed. The above arguments regarding the nature of modern democracy imply that democracy can only be safeguarded if its starting point is the prevalent balance of power. It does not need to endorse this balance of forces, but it has to take it into account and enlist

State: New European Perspectives, London: Verso, 1988, pp. 149-78.

the support, or at least the acquiescence, of the influential for the cause of democracy. It also means that the forces which benefit from democracy need to be organised, mobilised and strengthened. In other words, to have democracy one must first have an active, diverse and involved civil society. The suspiciously fashionable idea these days of advocating 'democracy without democrats'[28] in the Muslim world is thus plainly a non-starter.

Of course when one speaks of a 'balance of power' situation, the international arena is immediately conjured up, since the term originates there. It goes without saying that the international balance is an integral element in modern internal arrangements. After all, the current outbreak of democratisation is the direct result of a major shift in the international balance of forces, an indication, if any was needed, that the international balance of power can make or break democracies. As it happens, a central reason why the old order survives in the Muslim world and defies the tide of democracy, especially in the Middle East, is precisely that the major international players are happy with things this way. But it would be simplistic to claim that foreign support for dictatorships is the sole reason why they persist. In fact, the foreign actors benefit immensely by this relation, which means that they are as dependent on it as it is on them. But what this calls for is a close examination of the relation between foreign support for authoritarian regimes and the marginalisation of civil society in many Muslim countries. Algeria is just one example where a foreign-backed ruling elite is able to ignore all major strands of local opinion and rule according to its own narrowly based vision. But it is not the only one, nor is it even in a minority among Muslim countries.

This stance by the major international actors, by which we mean major western powers, is another manifestation of the irrationality of modern 'rationalism'. The main motive for the current policy regarding democracy in the Muslim world is the 'rational' one of achieving maximum gains at the lowest cost. We have mentioned above the self-destructiveness of rationality, and the self-destructive tendency of democracy. Here, we have the apparent mutual destructiveness of rationalism and democracy. The rational impulse dictates the appeasement of the powerful and the neglect of the weak, until the latter become strong enough or turn violent. It abhors dogmatic idealism in favour of pragmatism and what Popper called the 'piecemeal engineering'. This tendency puts it into direct conflict with the ideals of democracy, which call for justice, equality and maximum freedoms for all. It also provides an implicit encouragement to violence and the unprincipled pursuit of power, aspects of which have become integral to the modern experience, as we see in the arms race, political violence, terrorism and war.

[28] See Ghassan Salame (ed.), *Democracy without Democrats? The Renewal of Politics in the Muslim World*, London: IB Tauris, 1994.

Again this is not an indictment, but an attempt to understand the human predicament, of which the Muslim predicament is one example.

Reconstructing Muslim political thought

The starting point for the reconstruction of Muslim political thought is thus the flawed one of rationality. There is little specific guidance on the matter in the authoritative sources which, as we have stated above, leave the whole matter to discretion and reason. The approach of classical theoreticians, which sought to reconstruct a theoretical edifice out of meticulous archaeological digging, was uncalled for and has proved problematic. The right starting point would have been the basic principles enjoined by Islam: the pursuit of justice and respect for the Law and fundamental values of Islam, which are also basically human and universal in character. Any system which responds to these criteria is the correct one. And it goes without saying that more than one system could do so.

One must not neglect the ethical dimension here, though. There are those modern thinkers who believe that the reform of Islamic thought could be achieved through divorcing the 'reverential attitude' towards the texts from the sober evaluation of their import and the critique of traditional procedures and approaches.[29] This is to miss the whole point of Islamic thought. For the Islamic sources are an inspiration only to those who view them with reverence. Otherwise, what is the point of seeking guidance in them? The ethical dimension has thus never been absent from the Islamic intellectual endeavour, even in its scientific part. The leaders of the main jurisitc schools did not attain influence solely on account of their erudition, but chiefly because of the public perception of their moral rectitude and verifiable commitment to Islamic values. The founders of the six major juristic schools in Islam have all suffered persecution of some sort. Far from being power seekers, as some imply, they forcefully rejected any attempts by the powers that be to ensnare them into their embrace, and they suffered as a result. Some scholars would carry this insistence on moral probity to fastidious extremes, as illustrated by the story of the *hadith* collector who had travelled hundreds of miles to meet a person and listen to some of his reports. When he came upon the man, he found him carrying an empty sack which he brandished to his horse to lure it to him, on the false expectation that food was being offered. The traveller returned without accepting any *hadith* from that person, arguing that a man that did not shrink from deceiving an animal could not be trusted to be meticulous in reporting and verifying *hadith*!

We do not share Al-Jabiri's (and others') critique of the spirit which guided the early generations of Muslim scholars who thought reveren-

---

[29] See for example Arkoun, *Min al-Ijtihad*, pp. 82-6.

tially and meticulously to reconstruct the landscape on which Islam had dawned. Theirs was a labour of love which we fully understand and greatly respect. They were attached to what they saw as the source of divine light, and cherished every aspect of it. They were not, as Al-Jabiri claimed, propelled into this enterprise by Arab chauvinism (most of them were *not* even Arabs!) but by a genuine scientific spirit and an ethical imperative. We cannot hope to outdo them on either score. In fact our critique of the flaws of their work can only rely on the work itself and its findings.

This said, however, our task is different from theirs. The first generation of Muslims to confront the question of political leadership after the departure of the Prophet did not have much specific guidance to go on. They were aware of the general principles and basic injunctions, and they employed reason as best they could to set up an admirably successful working system. Later generations used this as an excuse to absolve themselves from the burden of thinking and reasoning. Instead of acting rationally as God intended from them, observing the basic principles of which they were aware, and using the rational faculties with which they have been endowed, to see to it that those principles found expression in practice, they allowed themselves to be lost in the maze of precedents that were usually taken out of context and were quickly becoming irrelevant.

Today, Muslims do not have the same excuses. We have a rich historical experience in front of our eyes. We have seen the Islamic experience start from uncompromising idealistic premises which soon collapsed under the heavy weight of reality; we have also seen, from another perspective, the Western experience, which started from quite the reverse: a stark realism which took its name from its first expositor: a certain Niccolo Machiavelli of Florence, and evolved into something resembling idealism (but which, we have seen, is *not* really idealism), and approximating the early Muslim 'democratic' model in a surprising way. These two lessons of success and of failure are instructive in their convergence. Somewhere in between we could find what we are looking for.

The challenge of democratisation

Going back to Gellner's diagnosis for what lies behind the failure of democracy to take root in Muslim lands, I would first like to agree with him on one point at least. For years now, I have been chastising Islamic movements and thinkers on precisely this point: their over-preoccupation with partial, even trivial, legal matters, such as alcohol consumption, or the way women dress or behave, while neglecting the central issues pertaining to the constitution of the very authority which is supposed to oversee the implementation of these rules.[30] We have seen Islamists and venerable *'ulama* backing despotic regimes which murder and torture innocent people, but ban alcohol and mixed dancing! I am not alone in inviting Muslims to have a sense of perspective on these issues. There is an anecdote about Abdullah ibn Abbas, who was asked by Iraqi pilgrims about whether it was lawful to kill a mosquito in pilgrimage (the killing of most animals is prohibited during pilgrimage). His answer: 'You Iraqis have murdered the Prophet's grandson and are too fussy about killing a mosquito?' The root cause of this lack of proportion is due to the 'textualism' I have pointed to earlier. It so happens that there are clear textual references to alcohol and dress, but none to political organisation. Modern Islamic writers, chief among whom are Abu'l Ala Al-Maududi and Sayyid Qutb, have contributed to this confusion, especially by emphasising the notion of 'God's authority' within the Islamic state. They seem to create, by this formula, the illusion that the conflicts taking place in Muslim polities are between God and some people, and not, as has always been the case, between different groups of people, none of whom disputes God's authority, but all dispute that of each other. To say, as the *khawarij* did, that 'authority belongs to God alone', is to bypass the basic question at issue: who should exercise this authority here and now?

Part of this confusion and lack of perspective is of relatively recent origin. Early Muslims were quite fussy about these matters. The great schism in the Muslim community (that of *sunna* and *shi'a*) was over the organisation of political authority. The schools of *kalam* (theology) emerged over disputes on political issues. Very costly wars, some of them going on for generation after generation, were fought over the issue. At the same time, to try to link the alleged absence of a viable civil society in Muslim polities to religion or ideology represents a double misunderstanding. Civil society refers, of course, to the institutions of society which are engaged in fulfilling functions other than the politico-military one or, to put in other words, non-state actors. It implies a 'distinction between the state (and its military, policing, legal, administrative, productive and cultural organs) and the non-state (market-regulated, privately controlled or voluntarily organised) realm of civil society'.[31] Since the main business of modern societies had tended to be economic, there has been a tendency, since Marx, to emphasise the economic component of civil society. This tends to obscure the complexity of the socio-economic dimension of civil society, as well as the actual diversity of societies and their structure, and peddles the implicit ethnocentric notion that all societies have to conform to a certain historical ideal. Secondly, and

[30] See El-Affendi, *Who Needs an Islamic State?*

[31] John Keane (ed.), *Civil Society and the State: New European Perspectives*, London: Verso, 1988, p. 1.

on the basis of this mistaken conception, the past and actual vibrancy of Muslim civil society is thus overlooked. Even as Gellner affirms the lack of diversity in Muslim communities, his own arguments unwittingly marshal many examples which contradict his own arguments![32]

The whole history of Islam has been of a vibrant civil society which defied state control, especially in the intellectual sphere. There is some truth in the claim that the Muslim *ummah*, as a self-defined religious community, is one that is, in theory at least, committed to an 'uncompromising devotion to virtue'.[33] As such, the constitution of civil society within it did reflect this tendency. However, a closer look at Muslim societies reflects the fact that, whatever their problems, their distinguishing mark is their singular ability to safeguard the basic orientation of society against state encroachment, be it foreign or local. Gellner may regard this capacity as the problem, rather than the solution, since it meant that civil society does exert a limiting influence over individual freedoms.[34] This is an arguable point which need not detain us here, for the strength of Muslim solidarity has manifested itself chiefly in opposing oppression, not in oppressing individuals. The question which is occupying us is securing democracy and freedoms for Muslim communities such as they are, and not as they are supposed to be according to this or that vision. And the truth is that Muslim societies do have the capacity to develop and sustain structures to defend freedoms against oppressive state mechanisms.

On the other hand, to claim that the Muslim community distinguishes itself by displaying 'a strong tendency towards the establishment of an *ummah*, an overall community based on the shared faith and the implementation of its law',[35] is to fall in a double trap of essentialism and orientalistic oversimplification, and especially the tendency, which I have criticised elsewhere,[36] of taking common sense terms (such as *ummah*, or community) out of context, and building false theories around them. On the other hand, to claim that the Muslim community is unique on being 'based on a shared faith', is manifestly false. The very definition of a community involves some shared values or 'faith' on which it is based. And, finally, to equate communist societies and Muslim communities and use the rubric '*ummah*' for both is another manifest error. While the Muslim community is precisely a 'civil society' before becoming a political community, the communist order has been imposed on preexisting civil societies from outside by a 'faithful' minority. This is why

---

[32] See his discussion of diverse sects and the contrast between city and countryside in *Conditions of Liberty*, pp. 15-24.

[33] *Ibid.*, p. 69.

[34] *Ibid.*, pp., 8-11.

[35] *Ibid.*, p. 26.

[36] El-Affendi, *op. cit.*, pp. 69-70.

the communist order did not survive the state from which it derived its
existence, while the Muslim community survived the Mongol genocides,
the Crusades, colonialist domination, and all sorts of assorted disasters
and calamities.

The current weakness of the structures of civil society in most
Muslim polities has nothing to do with the intrinsic qualities of these
societies, nor with any ideological influences. This is, rather, a dynamic
reality which is being created and recreated daily in front of our very
eyes. At this very moment, 'civilised' acts of oppression are taking place
in tens of Muslim capitals and countless other cities, where a frontal as-
sault is being launched on the organs of civil society: schools, private
associations, civic organisations etc., under this pretext or that. The destruction of civil society in Muslim lands is, to reiterate, not a relic of
history nor is it the consequence of culture or ideology. It is an outright
act of vandalism which is reproducing itself daily, with increasing violence. Intellectual contributions which neglect this glaring fact, and try
to justify what is going on by appeal to farfetched theories, are nothing
less than complicit in the ongoing genocide.

This brings us to our main point: that the reconstruction of Muslim
society must start from the unwavering commitment to democratisation
and respect for freedom, especially the freedom of association. And when
I say democracy, I mean exactly that: democracy, the self-rule of the
people through their freely chosen institutions and representatives. Not
the rule of God, nor *shura*, nor 'Islamic democracy'. Just democracy.
Give the Muslim people the right to decide how they want to be ruled,
and the power to hold their rulers accountable. It goes without saying
that the Muslim people would want to rule themselves according to the
values of Islam, according to one understanding of these. But it is the
people who decide what these values are. The moment we start saying
that the authority in a polity is for God and not for the Muslims, or allow
a class of people to determine for others what the values of Islam are, this
means that someone, other than the community (and above it) must
decide what the will of God is. Experience has shown that this a recipe
for bringing to power despots for whom the will of God is the last thing
on their minds.

Conclusion

I could have skipped all the foregoing arguments and just summarised
all that needs to be said about Islam and politics in two principles:
appeal to reason and an unwavering ethical commitment. It is the rational
dimension that has been sidelined in the Muslim experience. The ethical
dimension has always been alive. But, as we have seen, reason by itself
is no guarantee for success or virtue. Modern totalitarianism has been

amazing and very instructive in its irrational 'rationality'. One could only marvel at the efficiency and 'rationality' with which the death and labour camps were being administered. To say nothing of the 'rational' basis of systems like the communist experiments in Eastern Europe and elsewhere. 'Reason', after all, is as good as the input it gets. The early Muslim philosophers juggled the irrational theses of Neo-Platonism and the supra-rational given of divine revelation with admirable dexterity. But the output of this admirably rational exercise could only have been wild irrationality. To achieve its maximum potential, rationality must be guided by ethics. We have no fears on that regard, however. The Muslim community has always heeded the ethical imperative. Throughout the ages, Muslims continued to refuse to be swayed by abstract scientific pontification that obscured or neglected the ethical dimension. They would still not succumb to such an inducement, neither today, nor tomorrow. We would not want it any other way. The men of reason, if they want to be heard, must also try to be men of ethics, if not virtue. It is the synthesis of the rational and ethical imperatives which will point the way out. Our current problem stems from the long-term divorce between the two in the Muslim experience.

PHILOSOPHICAL AND INSTITUTIONAL DIMENSIONS OF SECULARISATION

A COMPARATIVE ANALYSIS

Ahmet Davutoglu

Modernisation: 'civilisational conversion' or universal process?

Basil Mathews, a missionary who travelled throughout the Muslim world in the second decade of this century, wrote a book in 1926, *Young Islam on Trek: A Study in the Clash of Civilisations*, whose title prefigured that of Huntington's famous article. His analysis of civilisational transformation in the Muslim world immediately after the collapse of the Caliphate, in its approach towards modernisation and inter-civilisational relations, demonstrates a degree of imaginative continuity with Huntington's own theorising.[1] The difference of their backgrounds as a Christian missionary and a secular academician does not appear to have made much difference.

The modernisers of Turkey in the early decades of this century adopted the process of modernisation in the belief that it was an inevitable universal phenomenon, with secularisation as its rational essence. Mustafa Kemal Atatürk, political leader and leading moderniser, emphasised the absolute necessity of modernisation for the survival of the nation in a speech commemorating the anniversary of the War of Independence: 'Surviving in the world of modern civilisation depends upon changing ourselves. This is the sole law of any progress in the social, economic and scientific spheres of life. Changing the rules of life in accordance with the times is an absolute necessity.'[2]

The correlation between secularisation and survival of the nation was underlined by other leading Turkish intellectuals of the same period:

---

[1] In this article, I compare these two texts from the perspective of modernisation and secularisation. A comparison from the perspective of inter-civilisational relations can be found in my paper 'Civilisational Self-perception and Pluralistic Co-existence: A Critical Examination of the Image of the *Other*', *International Seminar on Western Perceptions of Muslims; Muslim Perceptions of the West*, The Centre for Muslim-Christian Understanding, Georgetown University and Islamic Research Institute, IIUP, Islamabad, 4-6 October, 1997.

[2] *Türk Yurdu*, no.1 (1924). Cited in Niyazi Berkes, *The Development of Secularism in Turkey*, London: C. Hurst & Co., 1999, p. 464.

'There are now two roads for us to follow: to accept defeat and annihilation or to accept the same principles which have created contemporary Western civilisation. If we want to survive, we have to secularise our view of religion, morality, social relations and law.'[3] It is significant to note that 'the principles, which have created contemporary Western civilisation,' were accepted by them as universally valid necessities for the development of any society regardless of its civilisational background.

The same process of modernisation, however, was seen as a *conversion* by Mathews:

It is a symbol of the deeper and even more significant fact that young feminine Turkey is turning her eyes too toward the West. And it is Christendom and not Christianity to which young Turkey is looking. They want national power, commercial expansion, a place of pride among the peoples, a richer, fuller life. [...] We are watching, then, one of the rarest and most moving vital events in history – *a national conversion*. The word 'conversion' is here used in its true sense of turning round and moving in another direction. The present Turkish revolution is the abandonment of one way of life or civilisation and the adoption of another. [...] They openly say that the supreme mistake of the Turkish people was the adoption of Islam seven hundred years ago – an adoption which has led them out of the path of progress and civilisation up a *cul-de-sac*.[4]

It is interesting that Huntington, too, used the term *convert* for Turkey:

Some other countries have a fair degree of cultural homogeneity but are divided over whether their society belongs to one civilisation or another. These are torn countries. Their leaders typically wish to pursue a bandwagoning strategy and to make their countries members of the West, but the history, culture and traditions of their countries are non-Western. [...] In addition the elite of Turkey has defined Turkey as a Western society, the elite of the West refuses to accept Turkey as such. [...] Historically Turkey has been the most profoundly torn country. [...] To redefine its civilisation identity, a torn country must meet three requirements. First, its political and economic elite has to be generally supportive of and enthusiastic about this move. Second, its public has to be willing to acquiesce in the redefinition. Third the dominant groups in the recipient civilisation have to be willing to embrace the *convert*. All three requirements in large part exist with respect to Mexico. The first two in large part exist with respect to Turkey.'[5]

So, in Huntington's conceptualisation a 'torn country' represents a half-conversion in comparison to Mathew's full and radical conversion. So there is a vital question related to the process of modernisation: is it an irreversible and universal process, as held by the modernisers of

[3] Ahmed A ao lu, Üç Medeniyet (Ankara, 1928), cited in Berkes, *Development of Secularism in Turkey*, p. 464.

[4] Basil Mathews, *Young Islam on Trek: A Study in the Clash of Civilisations*, London: Church Missionary Society, 1926, pp. 82-3.

[5] Samuel Huntington, 'The Clash of Civilisations', *Foreign Affairs*, Summer 1993, pp. 42-4.

172 *Ahmet Davutoglu*

non-Western societies, or is it a civilisational conversion which equates modernisation with Westernisation, as perceived by the representatives of the *recipient civilisation* (using Huntington's concept for Western civilisation).

If the former is true, we have to concentrate on the universality of this process, which implies a specific discussion of universal human nature rather then civilisational presuppositions. If the idea of conversion is true, then the discussion necessarily tends towards a culture-bound exclusion made by the power structure of the hegemonic civilisation.

Mathews' and Huntington's conceptualisation of conversion necessarily creates a clear-cut polarisation between the West as the subject having the power to lead history and the Rest as the passive objects of this historical process. The concept of *recipient civilisation*, itself, reflects an egocentric self-perception that is powerful enough to accept or reject the conversion of others.

At the beginning of this century Mathews' understanding of the modernisation attempts in the Muslim world as a process of conversion and equally Huntington's 'West-Rest' polarisation at the end of the century, are reflections of the same civilisational self-perception arising from an 'egocentric illusion'. Toynbee provides a clear challenge to Mathews and Huntington when he reveals the illusions their theories are founded on:

But apart from illusion due to the world-wide success of the Western civilisation in the material sphere, the misconception of 'the unity of history' – involving the assumption that there is only one river of civilisation, our own, that all others are either tributary to it or else lost in the desert sands – may be traced to three roots: the egocentric illusion, the illusion of 'the unchanging East', and the illusion of progress as a movement that proceeds in a straight line.[6]

This egocentric illusion creates its own imagination to understand the 'other'. The conceptual framework of modernisation and its relevance to the historical conditions of non-Western societies must be re-examined to understand the dilemmas and crisis of this process.

Secularisation: a 'misnomer' or a historical reality?

Attempts at civilisational transformation in non-Western societies as a response to the power-centric Western hegemony have been variously conceptualised as modernisation, secularisation, Westernisation and Europeanisation. Modernisation and secularisation appear to carry a more objective and universal character while Westernisation and Europeanisation reflect the subject-object relation of this change.

[6] Arnold J. Toynbee, *A Study of History*, New York: Oxford University Press, 1965, vol. 1, p. 55.

The concept of modernisation 'performs two abstractions on Weber's concept of modernity', as Habermas underlines: dissociating 'modernity' from its modern European origins through stylising it into a spatio-temporally neutral model for processes of social development in general, while breaking the internal connections between modernity and the historical context of Western rationalism, so that processes of modernisation can no longer be conceived of as rationalisation, as the historical objectification of rational structures.[7] Modernisation, as a time-bound and epochal concept based on the idea of unilinear historical progress, and secularisation, as a philosophical and political concept being used for epistemic and institutional bi-compartmentalisation of human consciousness and socio-political life, can be applied to Western societies. Westernisation and Europeanisation can only be used for non-Western societies. Therefore, modernisation and secularisation are seen as complementary counterparts of the same phenomenon whereas Westernisation and Europeanisation always substitute each other.

There are two significant critiques of the concept of secularisation; the first addresses the reality of the concept, and the second examines the historical validity of this process. The representatives of the first approach argue that secularisation only exists in the minds of those who wish it to occur. For them it is a term of propaganda and dogma rather than a real sociological phenomenon. David Martin has even suggested erasing this concept from the sociological lexicon because of its speculative and dogmatic character: 'God is dead. Therefore secularisation must be occurring. Therefore secularisation is a coherent notion.' The whole concept appears as a tool of counter-religious ideologies which identify the "real" element in religion for polemical purposes and then arbitrarily relate it to the notion of a unitary and irreversible process.'[8]

The followers of the second approach question the historic demarcation between non-secular and secular periods. Chadwick argues that postulating a dream-society that once upon a time was not secular contradicts scientific methodology in historical studies:

you can be aware that there was never a world that was not secular. And yet you need to beware of defining your religion in narrow terms with the object of enabling yourself thereafter to plead that 'true' religion never declined, and so to make the quest for secularisation into a quest for a misnomer. When describing a historical process you may easily place your unproven axiom at the end of the process as at the beginning.[9]

[7] Jurgen Habermas, *Philosophical Discourse of Modernity* (trans. by F. Lawrence), Cambridge: Polity Press, 1985, p. 2.

[8] David Martin, *The Religious and the Secular*, London:Routledge, 1969, pp. 1, 16, 22, cited in Owen Chadwick, *The Secularization of the European Mind in the 19th Century*, Cambridge University Press, 1975, p. 2.

[9] Chadwick, *Secularization*, p. 4.

The concept of secularisation and its relation to the pre-modern and Christian value system is still under discussion. Blumenberg's critique of Löwith's theory that the central modern phenomena are products of the secularisation of Christian ideals demonstrates the continuing dispute over this conceptualisation: 'one must regard the secularisation thesis as an indirectly theological exploitation of the historiographical difficulties that have arisen with regard to the philosophical attempt at a beginning of the modern age.'[10]

Chadwick's question as to whether secularisation is a process concerned only with religion in its broad sense or a process inseparable from the decline of Christianity highlights misconceptions over the conversion of theological frameworks: 'Could Christianity slowly turn into Islam without the world becoming in the least "secularised" in the process, as once, two thousand years ago Judaism begat Christianity? Or if, as observers like Raymond Aron have thought, Communism is a modern form of religion, could Christianity slowly change into Communism without "any secularisation" on its way thither?'[11] Such a conceptualisation necessarily brings theological frameworks back to the agenda because as Chadwick underlines, 'if secularisation is supposed to mean a growing tendency in mankind to do without religion, presumably we need to know just what it is which he is supposed to be doing without'.[12]

This ambiguity on the concept of secularisation within the Western tradition becomes more evident when it is applied to non-Western historical traditions. The differences between religious traditions and their different social functions and roles make the situation even more complex. The question of the objectivity and universality of the process of modernisation and secularisation persists. Is modernity a static objective to be reached or an 'unfinished project' as it has been described by Jurgen Habermas?[13] If it is an unfinished project, what will be the role of non-Western civilisations, which have been the object of this project, in its next phase? Is secularisation an irreversible part of this universal project or a culture-bound counterpart of one form of modernity specific to a particular civilisation? Can there be alternative reflections of this project congruent with the authentic traditions of non-Western societies, or is deconstruction of the authenticity of non-Western civilisations a natural and irresistible pre-condition for the completion

[10] Hans Blumenberg, *The Legitimacy of the Modern Age*, trans. by Robert M. Wallace, (Cambridge, MA: MIT Press, 1983), p.75..

[11] Chadwick, *Secularization*, p. 16.

[12] *Ibid.*, p.17.

[13] 'Modernity-an Unfinished Project' was the title of Habermas' speech in September 1980 upon accepting the Adorno Prize. See Jurgen Habermas, 'Modernity versus Postmodernity', *New German Critique*, 22 (1981), pp. 3-14 and his *Philosophical Discourse of Modernity*, p. xx.

of this project? If deconstruction is inevitable, will there remain any historicity to non-Western civilisations in the future? Without historicity, what does the rhetoric of pluralism mean?

It was easy to answer these questions in the early decades of the twentieth century when Arnold Toynbee declared 'the last agonies of non-Western civilisations'.[14] The expectation in those decades was a natural vaporisation of authentic cultures and civilisations as a result of the universal project of modernisation and secularisation supported by the power-centric hegemony of Western civilisation.

The situation at the end of this century, however, is quite different from two perspectives. First, the finality of these projects is being questioned by Western intellectuals, and this intra-civilisational self-critique has become an inter-civilisational crisis in response to the resistance and revival of the authentic self-perceptions of non-Western civilisations. Today neither the question nor the process is one-dimensional and one-directional. The validity of the over-optimistic futurism of the theories declaring one-directional finality of this process, such as 'the end of history', has been challenged by the dialectics of history. For example, the Bosnian crisis became the end of 'the end of history' because it revealed the imbalances of Western civilisation and the deformities of the existing world order.

Huntington's thesis of the clash of civilisation, from this perspective, is a product of the post-Bosnian context, whereas Fukuyama's thesis is an over-optimistic evaluation of the historical context of the post-Soviet/pre-Bosnian era. The end of 'the end of history' led Huntington to use the revival of non-Western civilisational entities to formulate a new strategy for the Western powers.

The analytical purpose of his strategic pragmatism is to define new areas of conflict, rather than to understand the existential dilemma of non-Western civilisational and cultural entities. The sharp contrast between West and the Rest reflects the culture-bound and strategy-oriented character of his analysis. It also demonstrates a Western self-perception based on a subconsciousness of being the *subject* of history: the West has a mission to lead and specify history and therefore has the legitimate right to develop necessary strategies against the Rest are supposed to be the *object* of the specified flow of history.

---

[14] In the 1930s, Arnold Toynbee wrote that out of twenty-six civilisations no less than sixteen were dead and buried including the Egyptian, the Andean, the Sinic, the Minoan, the Sumeric, the Mayan, the Indic, the Hittite, the Syriac, the Hellenic, the Babylonic, the Mexican, the Arabic, the Yucatec, the Spartan and the Ottoman. He concluded that the remaining ten surviving civilisations – the Christian Near East, the Islamic, the Christian Russian, the Hindu, the Far Eastern Chinese, the Japanese, the Polynesian, the Eskimo and the Nomadic – were in their last agonies being under the threat of either annihilation or assimilation by Western civilisation. See Arnold J. Toynbee, *A Study of History*, vol. 2, pp. 286-8.

Such a pragmatic approach cannot provide us with the methodology and concepts to develop a framework for the analysis of civilisational revival and its relation to modernisation and secularisation. Gellner's argument, however, that modernity for Muslims has not led to an erosion of their historic essence, but on the contrary, to its renewal under new conditions might be a meaningful strategic point:

To say that secularisation prevails in Islam is not contentious. It is simply false. Islam is as strong now as it was a century ago. In some ways, it is probably much stronger. At the end of the Middle Ages, the Old World contained four major civilisations. Of these, three are now, in one measure or another, secularised. Christian doctrine is bowdlerised by its own theologians, and deep, literal conviction is not conspicuous by its presence. In the Sinic World, a secular faith has become formally established and its religious predecessors disavowed. In the Indian World, a state and the elite are neutral vis-à-vis what is a pervasive folk religion, even if practices such as astrology continue to be widespread. But in one of the four civilisations, the Islamic, the situation is altogether different. Why should one particular religion be so markedly secularisation-resistant?[15]

The success of the process of secularisation in the Sinic and Indian traditions is debatable; but his question why Islam is a secularisation-resistant religion is key to understanding Islamic civilisation and its response to the process of secularisation. It is difficult to comprehend the psycho-ontological, intellectual, historical and political crisis in the Muslim world without answering this question.

Secularisation and ontological consciousness

Civilisational self-perception and secularisation. There are two distinct analytical levels of secularisation in the sense of a process of separation. The separation of institutional structures – namely the separation of church and state as organised and institutional forms of religious and political authorities – is one level. However, it is difficult to explain the secularisation-resistant character of Islamic civilisation from this perspective because, unlike the church in Christianity, there has been no organised class of clergy in the form of a religious institution throughout the history of Muslim societies.

The more fruitful level of analysis, with regard to the Muslim experience, is that of ontological existence. Consciousness of ontological existence and of its meaning in the political and social sphere are the most critical issues if a comparison is to be made between the Islamic and Western tradition. I have dealt with this theme extensively in *Alternative Paradigms*.[16] What follows is a summary of the basic arguments I make there.

[15] Ernest Gellner, *Postmodernism, Reason and Religion,* London: Routledge, 1992, p. 6.
[16] Ahmet Davutoglu, *Alternative Paradigms: The Impact of Islamic and Western Weltanschauungs on Political Theory,* Lanham: University Press of America, 1994.

Ontological consciousness demands an understanding of the self in its triadic relations with God, the universe and other human beings. In pantheistic and materialistic worldviews, for example, there is an identification of God and the universe which conditions ontological consciousness of the self.

Such an analysis of the dimensions of the ontological consciousness of the self provides the foundation for understanding the formative parameters of civilisational self-perception in Western and Islamic civilisations. The philosophical and political process of secularisation and its consequences are reflections of these imaginations of civilisational self-perceptions.[17]

The Husserlian conceptualisation of *Selbstverständnis* (self-perception)[18] can be used to develop a comparative analysis of self-perception as the imaginative reflections of civilisational prototypes and its relation to *Lebenswelt* as the world of common experience. Civilisational confrontation takes place between these alternative *Selbstverständnis*es. For example, a confrontational relation between traditional masses and modernising elites developed when modernisation attempts in Muslim societies aimed at weakening traditional civilisational self-perception or at replacing it with a new civilisational self-perception. The contrast between the ordinary Muslim's *Selbstverständnis* and the conjectural/ material *Selbstverständnis* of modernisers in an age of Western supremacy was one of the main causes of crises in Muslim societies.

It is important to examine continuity rather than discontinuity in order to understand the internal consistency of historical traditions of self-perception. Western ontological proximity and Islamic absolute monotheism – as two alternative paradigmatic bases – reflect two alternative modes of ontological consciousness which directly effect the imaginative and theoretical link between ontological and socio-political existence:

---

[17] I am using identity and self-perception as two different states of consciousness. Identity, in a relational sense, might be seen as a way of social recognition which needs two parties; while self-perception is purely a consciousness of individuality. An identity might be given or imposed by some authorities and therefore may be arbitrary and artificially dependent on other social and political factors; for instance, the Yugoslav state gave an identity to its citizens which was dependent on the existing political structure, but, when this structure dissolved, their real identities (in fact self-identities) as a reflection of self-perceptions revived. So, a self-perception necessarily implies an identity while the opposite is not always true. An identity might be transformed into a self-perception only if it fits the authentic internalised elements of the personality. Self-realisation and self-consciousness are essential dimensions of self-perception. See my *Civilisational Transformation and the Muslim World* (Kuala Lumpur: Quill, 1994) for a more comprehensive discussion on this difference between self-perception and identity.

[18] Husserl's definition of this concept can be found in his masterpiece *Die Krises der Europäischen Wissenschaften und die Transzendentale Phänomenologie*, W. Biemel (ed.), The Hague, 1954, pp. 275-80.

The irreconcilability of the philosophical and theoretical bases of Western and Islamic political theories, images, and cultures might be analysed only within a well-defined framework of the interconnections among ontology, epistemology, axiology, and politics. The origins of the problem should be sought in the root paradigms of two alternative *Weltanschauungs*. The originality of the Islamic paradigm is related to its theocentric ontology based on the belief of *tawḥid* supported by the principle of *tanzih*. The differentiation of ontological levels via ontological hierarchy and ontologically defined epistemology are the cornerstones of the process from its *imago mundi* to the axiological foundations of political images and culture. The Western paradigm around proximity of ontological levels through a particularisation of divinity supported by intrinsically polytheist and pantheist elements, is the philosophical origin of the secularisation of life via rationalistic axiology. This is a specific character of the Western philosophical tradition based on epistemologically-defined ontology which has led to a relativised and subjectivised religion.[19]

Western paradigm: ontological proximity and particularisation. Ontological proximity and particularisation are common to both religious and secular self-perception in Western tradition. These two elements have a history running from ancient mythology and philosophy to Christian theology and from Christian theology to modern philosophy. Particularisation of divinity in ancient mythology and Christian theology, led ultimately to a proximity and identification on the ontological level between God, man and nature.

From the perspective of ontological and epistemological proximity and particularisation, secularism derives from Christian theology although it has shaken off its dogma and institutional structures. The best example of the continuity of ontological proximity is

the parallelism between the images of Olympic gods in Homer, 'like-God' interpretations of Plato in *Theaetetus*, the belief of *homoiosis* in early Christian theology, and Aquinas' assumption of 'God-like' perfection in the *Summa Contra Gentiles*. [...] The origins of the deification of 'the technological man' (in the form of superman) and his ontological crisis leading to discussions of the existential value of human beings might be examined within this context.[20]

Such ontological proximity necessarily leads to an image of the semi-divine being as an intermediary ontological category. The divine character of Christ and its immanence in the Christian Church provided an ontologico-theological justification for the special mission and status of the clerical class. These were then transformed into an intellectual and political control mechanism led by the clergy throughout the medieval centuries. All difference was then necessarily heresy. Secularisation can be seen as a process towards egalitarianism through its elimination of

---

[19] Davutoglu, *Alternative Paradigms*, p. 196.
[20] *Ibid.*, p.14.

the semi-divine ontological category of the clergy. But as a consequence of ontological proximity this category continued in secular form. The image of a mission assigned to a superior race, from Kipling's *White Man's Burden* to the Nazis, was justified as an ontological category.

Religious symbols and rites have been replaced by secular ones, but the category of ontological superiority has survived, be it in the form of a new caste system as guardians of a national mission, such as SS officers in Nazi Germany or as revolutionary pioneers, like the *apparatchiks* of the Soviet regime.[21] Transformation from a semi-divine religious category of special ontological status to a secular/ideological image of Promethean man[22] exposes the continuing versions of ontological proximity in Western tradition. In short, God died in secular/Western imagination, but semi-divine or super-human beings continued to survive either as an ontologico-theological or as an ontologico-philosophical image.

The theological and philosophical versions of ontological proximity were synthesised by Hegelian idealism. The Hegelian reconciliation of Hegel and Christian theology bore some significant characteristics of ontological proximity: particularisation of divinity, deification of the human being, pantheistic tendencies, and the imposition of logical categories for God (although Hegel does state that there is only one God). Hegel's understanding of God in his *Lectures on the Philosophy of Religion*[23] as a universal Spirit which particularises itself and his

[21] David Martin's analysis related to the image and status of leadership between Orthodox Russia and Socialist Soviet regime clarifies this element of continuity: 'Peter the Great made the Orthodox Church a state department and when the revolution came it simply stood Caesaro-Papism on its head. The Orthodox Church was still treated as a department of state but under the autocratic control of an atheist Caesar.' David Martin, *A General Theory of Secularization*, New York: Harper and Row, 1978, p. 22.

[22] A striking example of this transformation might be observed in the emergence of the new secular symbols after the Soviet revolution: 'Promethean man and his machines were natural emblems in the conversion process. In a rapturous eulogy of man, the jurist Mikhail Reisner promised that with "its steel beasts, machines," mankind would build a "magnificent garden all over the earth" after declaring war on gods. The atheist tractor appeared in the 1930s, described in a pamphlet called *Prayers on a Tractor* and used in posters showing the tractor fighting the cross. The railroad was another potent symbol. Before the Revolution, the antimodernist Leontiev's parable of a long black train blocking a religious procession had been a metaphor for modern evil. After the Revolution, agit-trains sped into the vastness of Russia with their good news of a godless universe. One of them was actually called 'The Godless Express'...the party... recommended communist public festivals and private rituals. As to the first, Yaroslavsky promoted "revolutionary counter-celebrations" sober and joyous, processions with revolutionary songs and music, lectures and reports, and reasonable games – all timed for the cycles of the seasons to compete with Church holidays.' R. Stites, *Revolutionary Dreams: Utopian Vision and Experimental Life in the Russian Revolution*, New York: Oxford University Press, 1989, pp. 108-10.

[23] G.W.F. Hegel, *Lectures on the Philosophy of Religion together with a Work on the Proofs of the Existence of God*, 3 vols. Reprint from the first publication in 1895, trans. by E.B. Speirs and J. B. Sanderson, London: Routledge and Kegan Paul, 1968, vol. 3, p. 10.

re-interpretation of the Trinity are clearly particularisation of divinity; and his image of Christ as the God-human establishes ontological proximity and identification between divine being and humanity.[24]

The dualistic character of Christianity in theology and politics has its philosophical origins in the Stoic assumption that the world is a product of two interacting principles: the one active and determinant, the other passive and determined. The blending of Stoic matter/spirit and body/soul dualities with the thoroughgoing dualism of Ptolemean gnosis – between the image of the divine (*pleroma*) and material world – affected cosmological and ontological thinking throughout medieval centuries.

This dualism supported by ontological particularisation created a separation of axiological and political spheres. Stoic doctrine 'that every human being is a member of two commonwealths, the civil state of which he is a subject and a greater universal state, composed of all rational beings, to which he belongs by virtue of his humanity' was transformed into the Augustinian *Two Swords* within which political and religious authorities were legitimised through a process of separation between state as a natural and legitimate human institution and the church as a superior and universal divine institution.

This separation survived throughout centuries of secularisation. The struggle among political and religious authorities was not over the image and concept of separation but largely over the legitimation of the superior authority within this context of separation. Both parties tried to legitimise their struggle for political control and superiority over the other by means of arguments based on ontological proximity. For example, James I stated during his struggle against the Pope that the monarchy was supreme on earth—that not only were kings God's lieutenants upon earth sitting upon his throne, but they were called gods even by God himself. Blumenberg's reference, in his *Legitimacy of the Modern Age*, to Overbeck's argument that 'theology itself is nothing but a piece of the secularisation [*Verweltlichung*: rendering worldly] of Christianity'[25] is very interesting from this perspective.

Secular ontology of post-historic man and the 'divided self'. This institutional separation, was in fact a separation of the ontological and sociopolitical levels of existence for each individual. For this reason the question of *self* became the core issue of modernity. Lewis Mumford's concept of 'mechanical post-historic man who left the human behind

---

[24] For the details of the impact of Hegelian synthesis see Davutoglu, *Alternative Paradigms*, p. 31.

[25] Hans Blumenberg, *The Legitimacy of the Modern Age*, trans. by Robert M. Wallace, Cambridge, MA: MIT Press, 1983, p. 119.

him' and his search for the creation of a new self is a good example of the critical approach towards modern self-perception.[26]

Two alternative approaches emerged in order to solve this dilemma of 'divided self': re-defining self-perception on the basis of a mechanical, body-oriented and materialised secular ontology; and a categorical differentiation of the assumptions of self-existence from the mechanism of socio-political existence.

The first approach is an extreme version of ontological proximity through which the individual sees godly, divine and natural qualities in himself. Christopher Lasch's characterisation of the 'narcissistic personality of our times'[27] is one of the best psychological analyses of this secular ontology. The myth of Narcissus' worship of his own appearance has been reinvented as a new pure form of secular ontology.

Secular ontology must confront two dilemmas. One is the inner clash between narcissistic self-assertion and the limits of physical capability. Lasch's conclusion that narcissism is a defensive strategy in response to the threatening nature of the modern world is the best expression of this inner clash between a super-ego and its limits. The narcissist subject, who assumes all supernatural qualities in himself, is frustrated by observing the limits of his physical existence, which necessarily leads to a crisis of ontological insecurity. When he realises the weakness of his body, the narcissist becomes alienated from the body, leading to an unembodied self. Laing's analysis of divided self[28] is a striking analysis of this psychological extreme and its relation to ontological insecurity.

The other dilemma of secular ontology is the legitimacy of moral values. Objective moral values lose their binding character when they are linked to the narcissistic self-perception of the subject who wants to maximise his ontological security and freedom. So, this narcissistic self-perception creates its own threat and anxiety. A moral dearth becomes inevitable as a consequence of this dilemma, as is stressed by Philip Rieff who relates the rise of the therapy culture to secularisation as

---

[26] 'In the post-historic scheme, then, man becomes a machine, reduced as far as possible to a bundle of reflexes: rebuilt at the educational factory to conform to the needs of other machines... None of the characteristic activities of post-historic man, except perhaps the exercise of pure intelligence, has anything to do with the service of life or the culture of what is veritably human. Post-historic man has already, theoretically, left the human behind him... Man's principal task today is to create a new self, adequate to command the forces that now operate so aimlessly and yet so compulsively. This self will necessarily take as its province the entire world, known and knowable, and will seek, not to impose a mechanical uniformity, but to bring about an organic unity, based upon the fullest utilisation of all the varied resources that both nature and history have revealed to modern man...' Lewis Mumford, *The Transformations of Man*, London: George Allan and Unwin, 1957, pp. 129,138.

[27] Christopher Lasch, *The Culture of Narcissis*, London: Abacus, 1980, p. 74.

[28] R. D. Laing, *The Divided Self*, Harmondsworth: Penguin, 1966.

a process of weakening traditional religion.[29] Anthony Giddens uses these psychological analyses[30] in his work *Modernity and Self-Identity* in order to show the impact of secularisation on self-identity: 'Capitalism creates consumers, who have differentiated (and cultivated needs), secularisation has the effect of narrowing down moral meaning to the immediacy of sensation and perception. "Personality" replaces the earlier Enlightenment belief in natural "character". Personality differentiates between people, and suggests that their behaviour is the clue to their inner selves.'[31]

The reflection of this narcissistic secular ontology in international relations are racist and ultra-nationalistic actions which idealise national self-perception to such an extreme as to permit the claim that all other human beings should serve, or even be sacrificed, for the maximisation of the ontological freedom, security and superiority of a specific group of human beings. Discrimination, racism and ethnic cleansing can only be justified by means of a narcissistic self-perception. The concepts of 'chosen nation', 'white man's burden', 'west-rest', 'white-black' are all reflections of the subject-oriented and value-free self-identity of secular ontology: the ultimate version of ontological proximity. This is the most fundamental dilemma of the secular foundations of Western democracies.

The second approach to healing the divided self is the categoric differentiation between ontological and political spheres that can be observed in radical interpretations of secularism. Such a radical separation implies two categorically detached sets of premises: one for the subject's sphere of ontological existence, the other for the social, economic and political spheres of his life. This requires the subject to forget his own ontological premises in the relational sphere of social existence.

This begs the question of whether such a categorical separation is possible and, if so, what authority will set the limits of these two categories. The historic experience of such a radical separation of two existences in France shows us the power-centric character of its legitimation. The absence of religious symbols and values in public life did not mean absolute neutrality towards religion. On the contrary, religion has been replaced by a set of ontological premises and socio-political values specified by the existing power structure.

---

[29] Philip Rieff, *The Triumph of the Therapeutic*, Harmondsworth: Penguin, 1966.

[30] 'What he [Rieff] calls "therapeutic control" operates to preserve a certain level of "adequate social functioning" in settings where religion no longer supplies binding guidelines. Formerly if people were miserable, they sought the solace of the church; now they turn to the nearest available therapist. By means of therapy a person aims to become "the sane self in a mad world, the integrated personality in the age of nuclear fission, the quiet answer to loud explosions".' Anthony Giddens, *Modernity and Self-Identity*, Cambridge: Polity Press, 1996, p. 177.

[31] *Ibid.*, p. 171.

Absolute privatisation of religion as a natural result of this categoric separation creates a vacuum between the private and public spheres. This in turn causes a schism between the ontological and socio-political consciousness of the individual. Either secular religions or systematic/totalist ideologies attempt to bridge this schism. The Comtean secular religion of humanity is a striking example. It replaced 'revealed religion' with 'proven religion', which was supposed to be based on positive science.

First, wishing to replace 'revealed religion' by ' proven religion', he substitutes for the supernatural God of Christianity a new deity, 'humanity', now re-named *le Grand Etre*. Instead of worshipping an imaginary god, separate from the world and human activity, men will devote themselves to a deity that unquestionably exists and that demands no less reverence and service than the gods of the past ... positivist religion thus satisfies the intellect in that its object is real, not illusory. [...] He established a cult of 'sociolatry' with a logically ordered list of festivals celebrating the 'fundamental social relations' (humanity, marriage, the paternal, filial and fraternal relations and that of master and servant), the 'preparatory states' of man's religious development (fetishism, including festival of animals, fire, the sun and iron, polytheism and monotheism) and the 'normal functions' (women, the priesthood, the patriciate – the capitalists – and the proletariat.[32]

These secular religions and totalist secular ideologies became as militant as religious monopolism in pre-secular Christianity, as has been rightly underlined by David Martin: 'The character of a given religion matters a great deal. For example the whole preceding analysis implies that a Catholic or Orthodox monopoly creates a militant counter-image of itself. The nexus of French Enlightenment doctrines resembles a Catholicism inverted and the secular religions produced by France are sometimes a form of Catholicism without Christianity.'[33]

Islamic paradigm: ontological hierarchy and unity. The fundamental difference between Western and Islamic traditions should be sought from the perspectives of the root-paradigms of Western secularism. Both pillars supporting Western secularism, ontological proximity and particularisation are alien to the Muslim ontological consciousness and self-perception.

The absolute monotheistic character of the Islamic belief system prevented ontological proximity and the emergence of any intermediary ontological category, the life of which became the theological source of

---

[32] Comte introduced a new calendar with months named after Aristotle and Archimedes and starting from 1788. He even planned to convert first Europe, then Russia, the Muslim World, the Hindus and the Africans. For a summary of the basic creeds and rituals of his religion of humanity see D. G.. Charlton, *Secular Religions in France 1815-1870*, New York: Oxford University Press, 1970, pp. 87-95.

[33] Martin, *General Theory of Secularization*, p. 24.

legitimacy for the established church in Christian centuries in the form of the historic Body of Christ[34] and the communion of saints (*communio sanctorum*), as well as for the modern state in the form of 'the divine march in history' in the Hegelian system. In Islamic ontological consciousness neither church nor state can have divine status as an intermediary ontological category. Equally, there also cannot be absolute ontological particularisation among divine beings with its reflection in socio-political separation (*Entzweiung* in the Hegelian sense) between church and state.

On the contrary, the concept of *maratib al-mawjudat* (hierarchy of beings) and its relation to Absolute Being (Allah) necessitates a direct ontological self-consciousness on the part of the individual human being independent from religious and socio-political authorities. This independence eliminates the role of these institutions in the process of the re-production of individual self-perception.

Four significant counterparts to the Islamic paradigm of ontological hierarchy and unity underline the unique characteristics of the religious and historic experience of Muslim societies: first, the direct, well-defined, easily understandable ontological and epistemological relationship between God and man in the form of a revealed text; second, the rational/human tradition of the re-interpretation of this revelation through a methodology of individual and collective rationality embodied in the consensus of the community; third, the historicity of both the revealed text and the religious leadership of prophecy; and fourth, a firm link between the ontological and socio-political levels of existence of the individual. The four factors form the basis of a rational legitimation process in Islamic civilisation, which prevented both the emergence of a sacred clergy and consequently secular exclusion of religion.

The very concept of a divine message in Islam[35] is greatly different from other religious traditions from the perspective of rational legitimation. It is *divine* in the sense of its origin and means of revelation. However, it has a human dimension as an object of rational epistemological analysis in the process of its collection and in its interpretation as a text. Objective testimonies of the companions of the Prophet were the sole criterion in establishing the canonical text of the divine message. In even more systematised fashion, objective testimony was the basis for the collection and classification of *hadith*, the second legitimate source of religion.

---

[34] 'For the Church is His body, as the apostle's teaching shows us; and it is even called His spouse. His body, then, which has many members and all performing different functions, He holds together in the bond of unity and love, which is its true health. Moreover He exercises it in the present time...' Saint Augustine, *On Christian Doctrine* (Great Books of the Western World, vol. 16), Chicago: Encyclopedia Britannica, 1990, p. 708.

[35] I mean mainstream Sunni Islam when I use Islam without any specification. Other sects have some differences in this regard. The common ground of Islamic belief, however, made these approaches closer to each other after a process of interactive transformation.

It is no exaggeration to say that Islamic civilisation is the unique experience of the transformation of an oral religious tradition in textualised form. Unlike many other religious traditions, superstitions, dreams and mystical/subjective experiences were not used to legitimate the divine religious text. The role of human/rational criteria in this process of transformation from verbal to textual tradition is a reason why a sacred class of clergy did not emerge in Islamic civilisation.

The same rational legitimation process was used in interpreting the revealed divine text. The human, and therefore subjective, dimension of interpretation prevented the formation of a church organisation monopolising judgement. Therefore the *sharh* and *tafsir* traditions of commentary emerged in Islamic intellectual history as opposed to the *dictatus papae* in the history of Catholicism.

For the same reason there is a tradition of individual, and refutable, *ijtihad* in Islam, rather than a tradition of religious councils composed of privileged clerics having the right to specify the final word on behalf of God as credo as well as set the limits of human rationality. These were the limits that brought about the need for secularisation as a process of intellectual freedom and rational legitimation. This was not the case in Islamic experience. The irrational elements in Islamic thought have never been the mainstream of the intellectual discourse.

Ijtihad and *ijma'* as epistemological and methodological tools for the legitimate re-interpretation of the divine text and for producing new non-divine intellectual frameworks created a suitable atmosphere for developing individual and collective rationality – whose absence was another factor leading to the process of secularisation in Western tradition. Therefore, many Muslim thinkers referred to classical concepts in order to overcome the challenges of modernity through re-establishing new foundations for religious and political legitimacy without alienating authentic ways of legitimation. Iqbal's concept of republican spirit is an illuminating example of these attempts:

It is, however, extremely satisfactory to note that the pressure of new world forces and the political experience of European nations are impressing on the mind of modern Islam the value and possibilities of the idea of *jma'*. The growth of republican spirit and the gradual formation of legislative assemblies in Muslim lands constitutes a great step in advance. The transfer of the power of *ijtihad* from individual representatives of schools to a Muslim legislative assembly which, in view of the growth of opposing sects, is the only possible form *ijma'* can take in modern times, will secure contributions to legal discussion from laymen who happen to possess a keen insight into affair.[36]

Another fundamental difference between the Western and Islamic tradition from this perspective revolves around the historicity of prophecy

[36] Muhammad Iqbal, *The Reconstruction of Religious Thought in Islam*, Lahore: Iqbal Academy, 1989, p. 138.

and religious leadership. The dual character of the begetter of Christianity, Jesus as the historic founder of the religion and the metahistoric personality of Christ as part of a theological deity did not only create a complex set of dogmas, but also an inevitable question of religious and socio-political legitimation.

The question 'who represents the metahistoric personality of Christ?' has been the fundamental dilemma of the Christian tradition, which evolved in the very syncretic atmosphere of *Pax Romana*. The legitimate foundation of St Paul's authority in religious affairs did not have a socio-political power dimension, while Charlemagne's imperial-political power could not have legitimised itself without referring to the religious authority of the Pope. The consent of the people or rational argumentation over authority were not relevant sources of legitimacy either for religious or for political authority.

This is not the case in the Islamic tradition. The undivided historic personality of the Prophet made it possible to establish a united concept of authority based on rational legitimacy. The uniqueness of the Prophet's authority derived from its epistemological foundation as divine message, not because of the Prophet's special ontological status. Therefore, rationalisation of religious and socio-political legitimacy started immediately upon the death of the Prophet, which marked the completion of the divine message and the end of the epistemological legitimacy of authority.

This is one of the main differences between Islamic and Western/ Christian tradition. A comparison between St Paul's and Abu Bakr's historical experiences may make this split clearer. St Paul did not have any historical or rational relationship with Jesus. Therefore, his authority as the second founder of Christianity had a metahistoric dimension representing the special ontological status of Christ as a divine (and human) being. That metahistoric dimension to the legitimacy of religious and socio-political authority was transferred to the metaphysical personality of the church and to the meta-human personality of the Pope. A rational mode of legitimacy could not develop within such a tradition. Therefore, secularisation emerged as a means to the rational legitimacy of political authority in the Western tradition.

Unlike St Paul, Abu Bakr had a historical, direct and well-documented relationship with Prophet Muhammad. The split after the death of the Prophet between Omar who argued that 'the Prophet did not die and was merely absent in the spirit and that he would return', and Abu Bakr who argued that 'the Prophet died like any other human being and would not come back',[37] was the most critical issue throughout Islamic history. Abu

---

[37] For a descriptive summary of this discussion see Martin Lings, *Muhammad: his life based on the earliest sources*, London: Islamic Texts Society/George Allen & Unwin, 1983, p. 342.

Bakr's response was the starting point of a rationally legitimised authority in religious and political affairs. It marked the end of the unique epistemological authority of the Prophet and the beginning of the human authority of Abu Bakr. There was no need to establish a church as a spiritual institution mediating between human beings and a living prophet in the form of an invisible spirit or semi-divine ontological being. A church with a power of metahistoric legitimacy could have emerged, only if there was a belief in the deity of the founder of the religion.

Therefore, unlike Christianity, the rationalisation of religious and socio-political authority in Islam, especially in Sunni Islam, started immediately after the death of the Prophet and survived throughout Islamic history. The authority of Abu Bakr was established and legitimised after logical argumentation, rather than a metaphysical experience. His wars against false prophets were to protect such authority against pseudo-epistemological authorities.

Rapid and early political success, unlike Christianity as Gellner underlines, strengthened the institutionalisation of rational legitimacy of authority and prevented church/state dualism: 'Islam knew rapid and early political success, which is perhaps one of the reasons why a church/state dualism never emerged in it: the original charismatic community had no need to define itself as against a state which still remained alien. It was the state from the very start.'[38]

The emergence of Islamic civilisation was the product of a new ontological self-perception in a specific time/space dimension of a geographical and historical context. The geographical location (space dimension) of this civilisational formation was the cradle of all authentic civilisations from India to Egypt. Its historical context (time dimension), on the other hand, was a dynamic process of intercivilisational synthesis. The evolution of an Islamic mentality occurred in parallel with a direct historical experience, as opposed to the tension between the metahistoric character of the Catholic Church and the hostile environment of the Roman empire. Therefore, the Western Christian and secular dichotomies such as ideal/real, normative/positive, religious/secular, heavenly/earthly – the first of each pair representing the metaphysical and metahistorical, the second the observable and historical – did not occur to the Islamic intellectual and socio-political imagination. Neither utopic idealism nor Machiavellistic realism has been in the mainstream of Islamic tradition. Even the concept of the golden age of Islam refers to the historical period of the Prophet and first four Caliphs unlike the metahistoric character of the Christian concept of the 'Kingdom of Heaven'.

Muslims, throughout their history, have tried to reconcile this ontological self-perception with historical reality by reflecting the

---

[38] Gellner, *Postmodernism, Reason and Religion*, p. 9.

ethico-axiological values of religion in the institutional forms of socio-political life. Different faces of Islamic civilisation such as the Abbasids in the central Arab lands, Andalusia in Spain, the Ottomans in Euro-Asia and the Mughals in India are testament to this civilisational vivacity.

Persistence of ontological consciousness and 'socio-political divided self'
The most significant consequence of the Western challenge in the modern era was the break between ontological self-perception based on religious imagination and socio-political institutionalisation based on a secular Western construct. For the first time in history, the Muslim mind had to divorce the ontological and political level of existence. This necessarily resulted in a comprehensive crisis; the Muslim version of the 'divided self'.

This question of divided self was not taken seriously by the early forerunners of modernisation who assumed that the secular transformation was an inevitable and universal phenomenon. This assumption was based on a new imagination of history consistent with the idea of progress. For them, the traditional assumptions of the ontological self had to be sacrificed to allow the emergence of a new socio-political one imposed by the irresistible forces of a new civilisation. The process of secularisation was presented as the formulation of a new identity, while modernisation was seen as a civilisational conversion by the likes of Mathews and Huntington.

It is significant to note at this point that the fundamental dynamic of the process of secularisation in non-Western societies in general and in the Muslim World in particular has been the mismatch between the traditional way of legitimation through a religious value system and attempts to re-establish all spheres of social life by a process of legitimation based on a rhetoric of the values of ideological positivism. Modernisers in the Muslim world tried to overcome this hurdle either by eliminating the role of religion in public life or by transforming religion from within via a process of reform. The first method was used in those countries where a totalist ideology has replaced religion, while the second was used in those countries where a secular religion consistent with ideological positivism was attempted by transforming traditional religious values.

The basic assumption of both these methods was the idea of progress as an outcome of the secularisation of history, which presupposes a natural transition from religiosity to secularism and from tradition to modernity. Therefore, the basic parameters of traditional civilisations, including Islamic civilisation, have been dissolved and reshaped by the comprehensive influence of modern Western civilisation. The philosophical, spiritual, logical and institutional links between the structures and forms of traditional civilisations have been severed by this deconstructing influence of the Western challenge.

The unifying character of the idea of progress implies a theoretical, phenomenological and historical parallelism between traditions of Western and Islamic civilisation. The differences, however, especially those related to the ontological consciousness of the individual, created severe discord between the surviving structures of traditional civilisations and the new superstructures of the political and economic institutions on the one hand and between the secular culture of the elite and popular traditional/religious mass culture on the other.

The modernists expected that the new institutional framework would necessarily transform the traditional self-perception and mentality of the Islamic civilisation. This expectation, however, did not come true. On the contrary, self-confidence has grown and Islamic identity has revived using modern forms and structures.

The main reason for this is the difficulty in penetrating the individual Muslim's self-perception through reforms and changes in the institutional and social network. For example, a significant cornerstone of the secularisation process in Europe was the denial of the divine essence of the church after the conciliar period in the fifteenth century. Accepting the church as a human institution directly affected the ontological self-consciousness of an individual Christian because the ontological consciousness of each Christian was defined by the mediation of the institution of the Church.

This was not the case in the institutional secular reforms in the Muslim World. They could not affect the individual ontological self-consciousness of a Muslim because these institutions were not part of the essence of this consciousness; rather they were seen as its outcomes or counterparts. There was no theologically justified human knowledge due to the absence of a divine religious institution. The Muslim mind did not have much difficulty in reconciling ontological consciousness with the findings of science in the absence of a theological dogma opposed to science, as happened throughout the process of secularisation in the West. The Muslim mind, however, had great difficulty in re-defining the ontological self through the dictates of a secular institution, because the self had not been defined by their religious institutions before. An institutional definition of the ontological self was alien to the Muslim imagination throughout the classical period of Islamic civilisation.

The secularisation process in the Muslim world was not able to change the worldview in the mind of a Muslim, and this could be easily reproduced either by the individual himself, by the family or by traditional small group dynamics due to its simple and readily conceivable character. Sherif Mardin's analysis of the Turkish experience of secularisation clarifies this tension between socio-political secularisation and traditional building of personal identity:

...Kemalism did not understand the role played by Islam for Turks in the building of personal identity. After all, Islam had an aspect that addressed itself to man's being in this world, to his basic ontological insecurity, which enabled it to fasten itself on to psychological drives. It is a truism, but still one worth emphasising, that Islam has become stronger in Turkey becausê social mobilisation had not decreased but on the contrary increased the insecurity of the men who have been projected out of their traditional setting. [...] The revitalisation of Islam in modern Turkey is a very complex occurrence, part of which is structured at the personal level, part of which relates to the attempt to bring back the full glory of Islam, and part of which is political. It is a pity that positivism, which played such a large part in the elaboration of Kemalism, did not choose in its Turkish version to remember Auguste Comte's warning: '*L'Humanite se substitute definitivement a Dieu, sans oublier jamais ses services provisoires.*'[39]

Secularisation and time-consciousness: history and de-traditionalisation

Secular history and the idea of progress. One of the most critical aspects of the process of secularisation is the re-construction of time-consciousness within a new framework of historical imagination. The essential issue here is the relationship between a metahistoric divinity and historical reality. The questions of how divine or semi-divine beings intervene in history, through which ontological imaginations effect historic realities, have been the fundamental problematic of religious and secular re-construction of time and history.

The transitions from pagan mythology to religious divinisation of history and from re-historisation of religion to the understanding of secular history are the cornerstones of Western time-consciousness. Pagan mythology established a relation between a meta-human imagination of being and a meta-historical imagination of time. This being-time consciousness was transformed into the divinisation of history in Judaeo-Christian theology that gave a special ontological status to the historic existence of a nation, the Chosen Nation, and of a person, Jesus Christ.

These transitions have been the most problematic issue in the analysis of the formation of the modern mind, especially the question of time-being consciousness. The categoric separatiorí of the pagan, Christian and modern minds as three impenetrably subsequent consciousnesses made it impossible to see the process of the transformation of the imagination of time and history in Western civilisation. Blumenberg's critique of Löwith who argues that 'the modern mind has not made up its mind whether it should be Christian or pagan'[40] carries this dilemma of categoric separation: 'The bastard nature of the idea of progress – a pattern

[39] Sherif Mardin, 'Religion and Secularism in Turkey' in Albert Hourani, Philip S. Khoury and Mary C. Wilson (eds), *The Modern Middle East: A Reader*, London: I.B. Tauris, 1993, pp. 372-3.

[40] Karl Löwith, *Meaning in History*, University of Chicago Press, 1949, p. 207.

whose true meaning is Christian and Jewish but whose modern form is non-Christian and non-Jewish, that is "pagan" – is seen as characteristic of the modern mind in general.'[41] Although Blumenberg criticises Löwith's view on the secularisation process as a transformation from Christianity to modernity, he also admits the continuity of the tradition in terms of questions and problems, rather than solutions and answers.

Secularisation of history in the sense of freeing historical understanding from theological bias or axioms,[42] was a response to the divinisation of history through the imagination of a divine penetration into history through semi-divine ontological beings, such as Chosen Nation, Christ or church. This was a process 'in which Christianity becomes historised and history secularised.'[43]

Historisation of Christianity meant reformulation of its relation with paganism and modernity on the one hand, and re-interpretation of the historicity of Christ on the other. Reformulation of the historical relationship between pre-Christian paganism, Christianity and post-Christian modernity necessarily brought about the question of continuity because a rhetoric of a revolutionary sudden break could mean a new meta-human penetration.[44] The question of the historicity of Christ, on the other hand, created theological disputes[45] related to the consciousness of being, parallel to the historical disputes on the consciousness of time.

So, the internal consistency of time-being consciousness of the Western mind has been shaken despite elements of continuity. The distinction made by German theologians between *Historie* and *Geschichte* was an attempt to re-establish this internal consistency: 'thus the resurrection, for example, is no longer to be understood as *historisch* (that is, as an event in external, scientifically ascertainable history) but rather as *geschichtlich* (that is, as an event in the existential history of the individual)'.[46]

[41] Blumenberg, *Legitimacy of the Modern Age*, p. xvi.

[42] Chadwick, *The Secularization of the European Mind in the 19th Century*, p.193

[43] Eric Voegelin, *From Enlightenment to Revolution*, John H.Hallowell (ed.) (Durham, NC: Duke University Press, 1975), p.18.

[44] Jean Seznec stresses this element of continuity from the perspective of theological imagination as well: 'As the Middle Ages and the Renaissance come to be better known, the traditional antithesis between them grows less marked. The medieval period appears 'less dark and static' and the Renaissance 'less bright and less sudden'. Above all, it is now recognized that pagan antiquity, far from experiencing a 'rebirth' in fifteenth century Italy, had remained alive within the culture and art of the Middle Ages. Even the gods were not *restored* to life, for they had never disappeared from the memory or imagination of man.' Jean Seznec, *The Survival of the Pagan Gods*, Princeton University Press, 1972, p. 3.

[45] Theologians such as A. Drews in Germany and W. B. Smith and J. M. Robertson in England denied even the historical reality of Jesus while Bruno Bauer asserted in 1840 that Jesus was a myth, the personified form of a cult evolved in the second century from a fusion of Jewish, Greek and Roman heritages. For these discussions see J. M. Robertson, *Short Story of Free Thought*, 2 vols. London: G. P. Putnam's Son, 1914.

[46] Peter L. Berger, *The Social Reality of Religion*, Harmondsworth: Penguin, 1973, p. 169.

Berger interprets this change in time-consciousness as a process of translation within which 'theology adapts itself to the reality presuppositions of modern secularised thought'. A split between religious and historical imagination emerged during this process of translation because 'the *realissimum* to which religion refers is transposed from the cosmos or from history to individual consciousness. Cosmology becomes psychology. History becomes biography'.[47]

This process has been the anchor point for the transformation of the Western mind from a divinised conception of history to a secularised history within a framework of continuity. Secularisation of time-being consciousness occurred at the historical juncture when the understanding of profane nature and profane history emerged as two pillars of modern being-time consciousness. The process in which God became immanent in nature and nature was profaned within a secular cosmology was realised through the mediating role of Spinoza's pantheism. Similarly, God became immanent in history and history was profaned within a secular time-consciousness through the deterministic grand theories of history which assumed a determining essence of history such as Adam Smith's invisible hand or Hegel's spirit.

Hegelian philosophy of history was a sophisticated attempt to synthesise this transformation with the continuity from pre-Christian Roman paganism and German polytheism to Christian divinisation of history and from the historisation of Christianity to the secularisation of history. This Hegelian synthesis has been used for the philosophical justification of the idea of unilinear progress within a deterministic framework that became a new form of impenetrable meta-human history. From this perspective, Marxist atheistic determinism shares the common historical heritage with the divinised history of Christianity. Löwith's interpretation of modern philosophies of history as outcomes of a 'process of "secularisation" of the eschatological pattern set up by the Jewish and Christian religions' and his example that 'Marx's idea of communism is "really" a secularised version of the biblical paradise or the coming of the messiah' is very interesting from this perspective.[48]

It is not surprising that several theories of endism,[49] including Fukuyama's end of history as their last version, share the same time-consciousness which underlies their imaginative and theoretical construction. Fukuyama re-interprets the Hegelian definition of history as 'the progress of man to higher levels of rationality and freedom' which 'had a logical terminal

---

[47] *Ibid.*, p. 168.

[48] For a summary and critique of Löwith's argument see Blumenberg, *Legitimacy of the Modern Age*, pp. xv-xvi.

[49] For the analysis and critique of these theories see the introductory chapter, 'The Fallacy of Endism' in my book *Civilisational Transformation and the Muslim World*, pp. 1-9.

point in the achievement of the absolute self-consciousness'[50] in order to legitimise his own concept of history as man's search for a single universally congenial political system. This is the lastest descriptive example of a time-consciousness based on a synthesis of Christian (coming of the Messiah) and secular futurism as the final stage in the unilinear progress of history.

So, the Marxist utopia of a classless society and Fukuyama's declaration of the ultimate victory of the liberal/capitalist system as the end of history share a common background of time-consciousness. The best definition of this time-consciousness has been given by Johann Galtung in his analysis of the *Randbedingungen* (constraints under which perception takes place) of the mind of *homo occidentalis*: 'time: that social processes are unidirectional, with progress from low to high and so forth, but also with crisis to be overcome, possibly ending well, with a positive *Endzustand* (state of end).'[51]

This process of the secularisation of time-consciousness did not have any relevance for the Muslim mind because there was neither a question of the divinisation of history nor a need for the re-historisation of the religion in the formation of Muslim time-consciousness. The time-consciousness of the traditional Muslim mind might be summarised as follows:

that time can not be conceived by serial and categorically separated periodisation; rather it can beconceived by the continuity of social processes which may also have a circular character. There is a constancy related to the basic characteristics of *Haqq* (Truth) and *Batil* (Falsehood), so there is always the possibility of a positive and negative *Endzustand* (state of end) which is the examination of human being in this world. Additionally there should be a positive *Anfangzustand* (state of beginning) as well as the intention of a positive *Endzustand* (state of end).[52]

As has been clarified before, the historicity both of the revealed text and the religious leadership of prophecy did prevent the divinisation of history as well as the re-historisation of religion in the Islamic tradition. No nation, person or institution has been absolutised as the determining subject of time and history. Unlike Christianity, neither the Prophet of Islam nor his followers or institutions claimed a meta-historic existence. They acted in history and within the rules of history. The miracles of the Prophet were accepted as exceptional indications of God's power rather than

---

[50] Francis Fukuyama, *The End of History and the Last Man*, New York: The Free Press, 1992, p. 64.

[51] Johann Galtung, 'On the Dialectic between Crisis and Crisis perception' in S. Musto and C. F. Pinkele (eds), *Europe at the Crossroads*, New York: Praeger, 1985, p. 11.

[52] For a comparative analysis of Galtung's conceptualisation of *homo occidentalis* and this time–consciousness see my *Civilisational Transformation and the Muslim World*, pp. 65-70.

permanent manifestations of divine intervention. It is also important to underline that the most significant miracle of the Prophet is the divine text of the Qur'an as an understandable, interpretable and visible source of knowledge.

As history and divinity were not absolutely identified in the Muslim mind, there was no need for an absolute split of these two as happened in the secularisation of time-consciousness. Re-historisation of the religion was not a necessity for the Muslim mind in order to develop a rational construction of history. Using Chadwick's description, 'freeing historical understanding from theological bias or axioms' was not a fundamental problematic even for the classical Islamic historians.

Ibn Khaldun's objective methodology of history is not only his personal achievement, but also the product of his cultural milieu and its conceptualisation of time and history. It is a balanced approach when compared to the absolute divinisation of Christian historiography and absolute rational mechanisation of secular historiography in the Western tradition. Ibn Khaldun, who underlines, as an objective historian, in the first sentences of his *Muqaddimah* that 'history makes us acquainted with the conditions of past nations as they are reflected in their national character'[53] and that 'the writing of history requires numerous sources, greatly varied knowledge, speculative mind and thoroughness',[54] reminds the reader frequently, as well, that 'God is the guide to that which is correct'[55] or that 'the final outcome of things is up to God'.[56] He, however, did not need a process of re-historisation of religion for the construction of a rational analysis of history:

History is a discipline widely cultivated among nations and races. [...] Both the learned and ignorant are able to understand it. For on the surface history is no more than information about political events, dynasties and occurrences of the remote past, elegantly presented and spiced with proverbs. [...] The inner meaning of history, on the other hand, involves speculation and an attempt to get at the truth, subtle explanation of the causes and origins of existing things, and deep knowledge of the how and why of events...[57]

So, the Muslim mind did not have a problem regarding historicity in the classical era. In consequence, it was very difficult for the Muslim mind to grasp the philosophical dilemma created by the process of secularisation of time-consciousness as experienced by the Western mind. The time-consciousness of *homo occidentalis*, as it has been

[53] Ibn Khaldun, *The Muqaddimah: An Introduction to History*, trans. by Franz Rosenthal, 3 vols., London: Routledge and Kegan Paul, 1986, vol. 1, p. 15.

[54] *Ibid.*, p. 15

[55] *Ibid.*, pp. 25, 55 etc.

[56] *Ibid.*, p. 56.

[57] *Ibid.*, p. 6.

described by Johann Galtung, has created three very significant problematics for the Muslim mind throughout the process of modernisation and secularisation.

First is the place of time within the self-perception of the individual being. The secular definition of time within the framework of unidirectionality and progress makes it a static absolute which functions according to its own mechanistic rules. This time-consciousness of modernity has created a dilemma in the Muslim mind that sees time-consciousness as a meaningful and dynamic dimension of the relation between God as the ultimate reality and man's ontological existence. Historical flow in this sense is not a static, mechanistic and unconscious unidirectionality, rather it is a reflection of man's perception of ultimate reality in the dimension of time-consciousness. Muhammad Iqbal, the great thinker who tried to restructure the Muslim mind against the challenges of Western civilisation, resolves this dilemma of time-consciousness and ontological existence as follows:

Personally, I am inclined to think that time is an essential element in reality. But real time is not serial time to which the distinction of past, present, and future is essential; it is pure duration, i.e. change without succession. [...] Serial time is pure duration pulverised by thought – a kind of device by which Reality exposes its ceaseless creative activity to quantitative measurement. It is in this sense that the Qur'an says: 'And of Him is the change of the night and of the day'.[58]

The second problematic for the Muslim mind in relation to the secular time-consciousness of modernity is its value dimension. The assumption of the secular time-consciousness 'that social processes are unidirectional, with progress from low to high and so forth' necessarily gives an absolute status to the values of the latest period of serial time which, in fact, means relativisation of human values. Relativisation of human values according to the unidirectional mechanism of serial time reduces the values of the past to a lower status on one hand and creates an ambiguity toward the values of the future on the other. Internalisation of such a relativisation of values is very difficult for the Muslim mind, which presupposes the trans-historic permanence and persistence of the basic values of humanity.

There is a very significant dimension of political economy to this dilemma. Such an understanding creates a causal relationship between the political economy of the hegemonic civilisation, the serial time within which it dominates and the values imposed by this dominance. (The existing parameters of the dominant economic mechanism at the latest historic stage impose their preferences as the universal set of values for humanity.) This in fact means a power-centric value formation and its

---

[58] Iqbal, *Reconstruction of Religious Thought*, p. 47.

justification through a universalised time-consciousness. Such a dependency threatens the historical validity of the values of non-Western civilisations, as will be discussed in the following pages.

The third problematic for the Muslim mind related to secular time-consciousness is the illusion of comprehending history. The logical consequence of the unilinearity of time and the end of history is the assumption of the perfectibility of the hegemonic civilisation. This is Toynbee's 'egocentric illusion'. Muslims had no difficulty in legitimising and internalising the transfer of science and technology, either in the past when they sifted the pre-Islamic heritage or during the challenge of modernity. Such interaction and transfer started in Muslim societies in the eighteenth century, almost at the same period as Russia and earlier than Japan.

Muslim societies had theoretical religious justification and historical experience to this end because Muslims, throughout history, have been concerned with the substance of knowledge rather than with the historical and civilisational origin of it. Muslims, without any hesitation, took philosophical and logical concepts from Greek civilisation and a mathematical notation from Indian civilisation. They could then easily re-construct all these elements in a new paradigm. Such actions have been given support and legitimacy by several hadiths of the Prophet, such as 'the word of wisdom is the lost property of a believer; he has the right over it [takes it] wherever he finds it'.[59]

So, transfer of knowledge, science or technology did not create a problem of legitimacy in the process of the modernisation of Muslim societies. The assumption of the perfectibility of the hegemonic civilisation, however, did create a psycho-historic tension, which could not be internalised by the strong civilisational self-perception of the Muslim individual. The identification of the human heritage with the subjective historical experience of Western civilisation and the declaration of the perfectibility of the last stage of this experience has been a blow to the integrity of Muslim self-perception in its being-knowledge-value dimension. It is difficult to reconcile the idea of progress with the fundamental *a priori* of the Muslim mind that the perfectibility of the knowledge and values of the prophetic tradition goes back to the beginning of history.

This persistence of the value system in the Muslim mind is based on the historicity of ethical ideals and of perfectibility, unlike Christian meta-historic ideals and secular models of the state of nature. A comparison between the Ottoman concept of *kanun-u kadim* (eternal tradition/

---

[59] There are several versions of this hadith. For two of the most famous versions see, *Sunan al-Tirmidhi, Kitab al-Ilm* (19/2687), vol.5 (Istanbul: Cagri, 1981), p. 51 and *Sunan Ibn Majah, Kitab al-Zuhd* (15/4169), vol.2, Istanbul: Cagri, 1981, p. 1395. This hadith is widely known and used especially pro the legitimacy of inter-cultural and inter-civilisational exchange, despite discussions over its authenticity.

ancient law) as one of the basic concepts of political, cultural and social legitimacy and the secular concept of *state of nature* may clarify this difference between Islamic and Christian/secular time-consciousness. The Ottoman concept of *kanun-u kadim* is the reflection of common human rationality in the form of the historic traditions which have developed in tandem and is consistent with prophetic knowledge (*kelam-u kadîm*). The Hobbesian or Marxist *state of nature*, on the other hand, is a hypothetical assumption related to the pre-historic time from which historic dynamism and dialectics started. Thus, the Muslim mind assumes that the ethical ideal and perfectibility are reflected in the continuity of the eternal tradition from the past through the present to the future while the secular idea of progress justifies the break between past and present and glorifies the future.

This is the fundamental factor why Ottoman statesmen and intellectuals saw the supremacy of Western civilisation as a power-centric challenge rather than a philosophical or ethical one. They tried to preserve their own paradigm in the sphere of *Weltanschauung* and social legitimacy although they realised that there was a need for a technological transfer in order to overcome the power-centric challenge of Western civilisation. For them, science was a tool rather than a new foundation for a new *Weltanschauung*. For them, power-centric supremacy did not mean the perfectibility of the being-knowledge-value system which, according to them, had been realised by the eternal tradition and historised at the hands of the Ottomans. Therefore, they concentrated on military modernisation rather than on philosophical secularisation in the sense of a paradigmatic change in the ontological, epistemological and axiological foundations of individual self-perception, which later modernisers saw as the backbone of civilisational survival.

The real culture shock of modernisation in Ottoman history came when a new elite fell under the influence of Western time-consciousness of the idea of progress (*terakki*) in the late nineteenth century. This meant a radical change in defining historic past and identity. Penetration of secular time-consciousness was transformed into a crisis of identity and self-perception. This resulted in tension between the positivistic idea of progress which degrades the past – eternal tradition – and the resistance of traditional time-consciousness which links the Muslim mind to it. The clash between elite and popular culture on the one hand and hierarchical political will versus civil/family values on the other might be seen as natural consequences of this tension created by the gap between two alternative time-consciousness.

Secularisation and de-traditionalisation. The process of secularisation in the West is the product of a historico-cultural continuity. Therefore the dichotomy of 'modernity' and 'tradition' in Western civilisation is a methodological tool of historical and sociological analysis, rather than a persistent and prevailing phenomenon which creates dual social imaginings and realities. As Wagner puts it in referring to Abrams,[60] *'traditional society* is largely a sociological construct that was developed as a tool of comparison when trying to grasp the present'.[61]

Therefore, theoretical frameworks on the dichotomy of tradition and modernity or discussions on the process of secularisation and de-traditionalisation did not create a crisis of time-consciousness nor raise the question of historicity in the Western mind. Taking Edward Shils' definition of tradition as *traditum*,[62] that is anything which is transmitted or handed down from the past, it can even be argued that modernity has created its own tradition in its later periods. Seeing modernity as a product of a post-traditional era in its reference to tradition, and at the same time a determining predecessor in its reference to postmodernity shows an element of continuity. Tradition, early modernity, late modernity and postmodernism might be seen as several stages of the same historic continuity. Tradition, in this sense, loses its pre-modern character especially from the perspective of postmodernism, which could be accepted as a reaction to the traditionalisation of modernity.

Eclectic concepts, such as 'pre-modern era', 'post-traditional society' or 'post-modern religion', in fact reflect this element of continuity in their descriptive character. The unexpected revival of religious identities in the later stages of modernity, despite the effects of a massive process of secularisation, made these eclectic concepts inevitable tools to describe existing phenomena. It was impossible for a Comtean mind to accept a synthesis of religion and postmodernity, since the former represents the irrational pre-modern era, while the latter an advanced rationality, the natural result of an absolute process of secularisation. The concept of postmodern religion itself symbolises a process of 'back into the future'[63] which necessarily contradicts the essential idea of progress. This also highlights current re-traditionalisation[64] (the re-emergence of religiosity)

---

[60] 'A sociological past has been worked up, a past which is linked to the present not by carefully observed and temporally located social interaction by inferentially necessary connections between concepts', Philip Abrams, 'The Sense of the Past and the Origins of Sociology', *Past and Present*, 1971:55, p. 20.

[61] Peter Wagner, *A Sociology of Modernity: Liberty and Discipline*, London: Routledge, 1994, p. 38.

[62] Edward Shils, *Tradition*, London: Faber and Faber, 1981, p. 12.

[63] See Zygmunt Baumann, 'Postmodern Religion?' in Paul Heelas (ed.), *Religion, Modernity and Postmodernity*, Oxford: Blackwell, 1998, p. 72.

[64] Ninian Smart's reference to new traditions is very significant from this perspective of re-traditionalisation: 'some traditions, however, are perceived as relatively new: royal France was replaced by revolutionary France – the one being as it were the Old Testament and the other the New. The USA sees itself as a young country. The Soviet Union was seen as a new revolutionary creation, replacing decadent Tsarism. But even these new traditions

and an element of de-traditionalisation[65] (the re-formation of the religious traditions).

The absolute identification of modernisation with secularisation is proven groundless from the perspective of de-traditionalisation and re-traditionalisation. The interacting process of these two phenomena effects a new combination of religious and secular elements, which results in a new balance and continuity in the historical imagination of the Western mind. De-traditionalisation as a consequence of secularisation, in this regard, never did function as a one way process due to its always being intrinsic to Western civilisation. The surviving substance of religion has been reproduced in this circular and reactive process of de- and re-traditionalisation[66] during the process of secularisation.

In non-Western societies, however, the dichotomy of modernity and tradition has taken root due to the fact that secularisation has not been a natural and intrinsic process created by native social forces and legitimised by society's symbols and values. Rather, it has been the product of the political will of an elite at the political centre. This process of secularisation as a guided and imposed change led to a process of de-traditionalisation, rather than a simple separation of religion and state. Traditions have been seen as barriers to modernisation by the elite of modernisers while radical secularisation has been seen as a threat to traditional socio-cultural values by conservatives.

This tension between the centre having the political power to transform society through a process of secularisation and the periphery trying to preserve traditional culture has produced two significant consequences. First, the process of secularisation has been presented as a radical civilisational conversion by an elite that paints the discontinuity of de-traditionalisation as an inevitable part of the historical flow from tradition to modernity, from religion to secularism and from superstition to science. These binary oppositions of ideological positivism destroyed the time-consciousness and historicity of non-Western traditions. The de-Confucianisation in Maoist China or the de-Islamisation in the radical process of secularisation in the Muslim world did not only aim to

---

are, or were, traditional. In short we may see the modern world as involving re-traditonalisation.', Ninian Smart, 'Tradition, Retrospective Perception, Nationalism and Modernism', in Heelas, *Religion, Modernity and Postmodernity*, p. 79.

[65] As Thompson underlines, 'those who use the term de-traditionalization generally argue not that traditions have altogether disappeared from the modern world, but their status has changed in certain ways: they have become less taken-for-granted and less secure, as they have become increasingly exposed to the corrosive impact of public scrutiny and debate', 'Tradition and Self in a Mediated World', in P. Heelas, S. Lasch and P. Morris (eds), *Detraditionalization*, Oxford: Blackwell, 1996, p. 90.

[66] David Martin's analysis of the patterns of secularisation is a striking example for the surviving socio-cultural substance of religious traditions and their impact on the process of secularisation; see David Martin, *General Theory of Secularization*.

peripheralise religion in the socio-political sphere, but also tried to restart the time-consciousness of these societies to coincide with the beginning of modernity.

So, the process of secularisation, which in its Western application has historicised Christianity, in non-Western civilisations tried to de-historicise religion and tradition. The reconstruction of time-consciousness and history necessarily resulted in a discontinuity in the sense of a break in historical flow and imagination. Egyptian references to the pre-Islamic Pharaonic period, Turkish references to pre-Islamic Anatolian civilisations and Iraqi references to pre-Islamic Babylonia as the golden periods of these nations are striking examples of the process of the reconstruction of history in order to formulate an official secular ideology of territorial nationalism with a reference to pre-religious and pre-traditional history.

The second important consequence of this interpretation of secularisation as an absolute de-traditionalisation and de-historicisation is the absence of collective rationality, which can only be reflected in surviving traditions. Modernisation was sought by transferring the collective rationality and historic experience of another nation rather than by reforming existing indigenous and authentic traditions. The only exception to this is Japanese modernisation, which tried to establish a logical, symbolic, institutional and historic correlation between authentic tradition and new forces of modernity in order to respond to the Western challenge.

Disputes over the meaning of secularism in non-Western societies reflect this process of de-traditionalisation. Secularism may mean the absence of religious symbols, beliefs and values in public life. This is typical of Jacobean French secularism of the Third Republic (1871-1942). In this case the aim is to eliminate all visible aspects of religious traditions, values and beliefs. Such a radical break creates an oscillation between two versions of the sacred, one religious and the other secular. David Martin describes it thus:

The third cultural area worthy of scrutiny in any discussion of religion and modernity is the Middle East. In this case the imports from Europe are much more significant than those from North America. European models of the unitary secular state have so far had more impact than American models of competitive voluntarism. Turkey offers a prime instance of European influence. The country oscillates between two versions of the sacred, one provided by Islam, the other by Kemal Atatürk. Religion is simultaneously blamed as the source of backwardness and defeat, and lauded as the fount of everyday values. Tunisia and Egypt also offer evidence of a partial secularisation in the sphere of the state owing much to the European model.[67]

---

[67] David Martin, 'The Secularization Issue: Prospect and Retrospect', *The British Journal of Sociology*, 1991:42(3), p. 472.

An alternative approach defines secularism within the framework of freedom of religion and follows Anglo-Saxon or American traditions, which synthesise the idea of separation of state and church with the idea of religious freedom. This approach, which would have established a constructive link between tradition and modernity was not followed by the modernisers of Muslim societies in the Middle East, as also pointed out by David Martin.

Secular education and historical existentiality of non-Western civilisations.

The egocentric illusion of Western civilisation has become a universal phenomenon after the educational paradigm of this civilisation became the global standard to be applied to all the different civilisational entities. Two significant results have emerged as a consequence of this standardisation through a hegemonic educational paradigm: the denial of the contributions of non-Western civilisations to human culture and the alienation of the new generations of non-Western societies from their own historical heritage and natural environment.[68]

Thomas Kuhn underlines in *The Structure of Scientific Revolutions* that there is a relationship of dependency between educational textbooks and existing scientific paradigms:

As the source of authority, I have in mind principally textbooks of science together with both the popularisations and the philosophical works modeled on them. [...] Textbooks thus begin by truncating the scientist's sense of his discipline's history and then proceed to supply a substitute for what they have eliminated. Characteristically, textbooks of science contain just a bit of history, either in an introductory chapter or, more often, in scattered references to the great heroes of an earlier age. [...] For reasons that are both obvious and highly functional, science textbooks (and too many of the older histories of science) refer only to that part of the work of past scientists that can easily be viewed as contributions to the statement and solution of the texts' paradigm problems. Partly by selection and partly by distortion, the scientists of earlier ages are implicitly represented as having worked upon the same set of fixed problems and in accordance with the same set of fixed canons that the most recent revolution in scientific theory and method has made seem scientific. No wonder those textbooks and the historical tradition they imply have to be rewritten after each scientific revolution. And no wonder that, as they are rewritten, science once again comes to seem largely cumulative.[69]

[68] For the impact of this educational paradigm on inter-civilisational relations see my paper 'Global Culture Versus Cultural Pluralism: Civilisational Hegemony or Civilisational Dialogue and Interaction', *Civilisational •Dialogue: Present Realities, Future Possibilities,* Centre for Civilisational Dialogue, University of Malaya, Kuala Lumpur, 15-17 Eylül 1997.

[69] Thomas S. Kuhn, *The Structure of Scientific Revolutions*, 2nd edn. (University of Chicago Press, 1970, pp. 136-8.

So, each scientific revolution produces its own textbooks. These textbooks, which were the means to revolutionary change, begin to be a conservative factor in following stages of the reproduction of the existing paradigm. The paradigm, which starts with a revolutionary change, transforms itself into the *status quo* after being established as a standard. The continuity and reproduction of the existing paradigm is achieved through using standard educational means.

There is a similar relationship between the existing civilisational hegemony and its educational paradigm. Similarly, each civilisational hegemony produces its own textbooks in order to prove and reproduce its own paradigm of history. This is especially true in the process of the intellectual transformation after a shift of power among civilisations. The hegemonic character of Western civilisation made this phenomenon more global and monolithic. Colonialism, as a political and military hegemony, used education as a means of the reconstruction of the historical imagination of the colonised people.

The idea of unilinear historical progress has justified this manipulative process in order to identify the history of mankind with the history of Europe. The Eurocentric imagination of time and history necessarily excluded the contributions of other civilisations. History of Philosophy, History of Economic Thought, History of Political Thought, History of Science and all other textbooks and educational standards put in the minds of individuals from different civilisations the same monolithic sequence and periodisation of the historical progress of mankind: Ancient Greece, Roman Empire, Medieval Era, Renaissance, Enlightenment, Modern Age. The sequence from Plato and Aristotle to Cicero and Seneca, from St Augustine and St Thomas Aquinas to Machiavelli, Spinoza and Hobbes, from Locke and Rousseau to Hegel and Kant has been used as an absolute chain of continuity in the history of ideas.

The cultural and intellectual heritage of other civilisations are accepted as part of the historical flow only within the framework of their contribution and attachment to the existing hegemonic paradigm of Western civilisation. To rewrite Kuhn's statement on textbooks: For reasons that are both obvious and highly functional, culture-bound textbooks (and too many of the older histories of ideas) refer only to that part of the heritage of other civilisations that can easily be viewed as contributions to the monolithic assumptions and conclusions of the historical paradigm of the hegemonic civilisation.

Eurocentric education continued to be the only global standard even after the end of the colonial era. So, the Chinese, Indian, Muslim or African student becomes convinced by this globalised assumption that his ancestors did not contribute anything to the history of mankind because there is no place for Confucius, Farabi, Ibn Rushd, Liang Shu Ming, Iqbal, Gandhi or Radhakrishnan in this historical continuity. And even if there is, the role of these thinkers is presented as valid for the locality of their particular civilisation, rather than as a globally valid contribution to humanity. Today, an educated Chinese knows more of Plato than of Confucius, an educated Muslim knows more of St Thomas Aquinas than of Imam Ghazzali.

Levi's analysis of Wilhelm Windelband's influential and widely read method in the history of philosophy underlines this self-centred approach: 'Windelband begins broadly enough: for him the history of philosophy "is the process in which European humanity has embodied in scientific conceptions its views of the world and its judgments of life".'[70] The Comtean unilinear intellectual process from theological to metaphysical and scientific stages together with this Eurocentric view of history implies that non-Western civilisations as the products of non-scientific factors, are dead traditions which can not be reproduced in a historically meaningful framework. The ultimate version of this understanding is the idea of the end of history, which assumes that history started with the West and came to an end with the West. The name of William McNeill's *magnum opus* on the history of civilisations reflects the same imagination despite the fact that it is one of the most objective textbooks on the subject: *The Rise of the West: A History of the Human Community.*[71]

Even the concept of *objective knowledge* should be re-examined within this framework of the culture-bound global education. For example, maps which are being taught and used as objective and scientific reflections of geographical realities, are, in fact, a culture-dependent imagination of a specific civilisation.

Fernand Braudel says 'maps tell the essential story'[72] in his analysis of the role of geography in the formation of Islamic civilisation. This statement can be extended to civilisational constructs in a more comprehensive framework. Every civilisation has produced its own map reflecting its imagination of the world. These maps have been used to prove that the subjective image of the civilisation-builders or the centrality of their civilisation is objective geographical fact.

We know that the planet is a globe; so there should not be categories such as up/down or centre/periphery regarding the earth. At the same time, however, we assume that north is always up and south is always down or that Europe and the Mediterranean is always in the centre and that the Far East or sub-Saharan Africa are always on the periphery.

For example, Japan and England are two islands with similar geographical locations in relation to the Eurasian continent; one is a small island

[70] Albert William Levi, *Philosophy as Social Expression*, University of Chicago Press, 1974, p. 17.

[71] William McNeill, *The Rise of the West: A History of the Human Community*, University of Chicago Press, 1963.

[72] Fernand Braudel, *A History of Civilisations*, New York: Penguin, 1993, p. 55.

to the east of Eurasia, the other to the west of the same continent. But the Atlantic-centric maps used in the Western hemisphere give an impression that England is in the centre and Japan on the periphery of the globe, while Pacific-centric maps of the Far East give the opposite impression. So, each and every civilisation develops its own 'objective' map based on its subjective imagination of the world.

A leading historian explains this fact through analysing the geographical world-image of the West:

It would be a significant story in itself to trace how modern Westerners have managed to preserve some of the most characteristic features of their ethnocentric medieval image of the world. Recast in modern scientific and scholarly language, the image is still with us; all sorts of scholarly arguments are used to bolster it against occasional doubts. The point of any ethnocentric world-image is to divide the world into moieties, the others and us, with us forming the more important of the two. To be fully satisfying, such an image must be at once historical and geographical. As in the Chinese image of the 'Middle Kingdom' and the Islamic image of the central climes, so also in Western image, most of this sleight of hand is performed through appropriate historical manoeuvers. Western Europe may be admitted to be small geographically, but all the history is made to focus there. But we must begin with the map. A concern with the map may seem trivial; but it offers a paradigm of more fundamental cases. For even in maps we have found ways of expressing our feelings. We divide the world into what we call 'continents'. In the Eastern Hemisphere, where more than four-fifths of mankind still live, there are still the same divisions as were used by medieval Westerners – Europe, Asia and Africa. As we know Europe west of the Russia has about the same population as historical India, now India and Pakistan; about the same geographical, linguistic and cultural diversity; and about the same area. Why is Europe one of the continents but not India? Not because of any geographical features, nor even because of any marked cultural breach at the limits we have chosen. [...] Europe is still ranked as one of the 'continents' because our cultural ancestors lived there. By making it a 'continent', we give it a rank disproportionate to its natural size, as a subordinate part of no larger unit, but in itself one of the major components of the world.[73]

This subjective geographical world-image became an effective means of civilisational hegemony with respect to the transformation of the colonial hegemony of Western civilisation into the monopolisation of human culture through a so-called process of globalisation. Scientific rhetoric and scholarly language have been used to create an image of global objectivity which is, in fact, just a new form of subjective and culture-bound ethnocentrism.

So, non-Western intellectual traditions and ways of life have been marginalised by the rising global forces led by the intellectual paradigm and power machine of Western civilisation. That is the reason why Toynbee

---

[73] Marshall G.S. Hodgson, *Rethinking World History: Essays on Europe, Islam and World History*, New York: Cambridge University Press, 1993, pp. 3-4.

underlines that non-Western civilisations are in their last agony, although he tries to show that there is a plurality in the history of civilisations.

The political and economic crisis in traditional civilisations defeated by Western colonialism has been transformed into a comprehensive psychological and intellectual crisis after the impact of the global educational paradigm based on the misconception of the unity of civilisation as a counterpart to the historical flow of Western societies. Societies of non-Western civilisations have been divided into two conflicting groups: those trying to integrate themselves into secular global/Western civilisation and those trying to reproduce the traditional parameters of their civilisation. The former try to use the educational machine as a force of transformation while the latter try to protect the continuity of the informal educational environment in families and societal networks.

The socio-cultural division leads to an individual crisis as well. The dogma of the unilinear and unified global/Western civilisation supported by educational means creates a psycho-ontological crisis in the individual personalities of the traditional civilisations because they are being taught that there are two forces in history; those which determine the flow of history, namely Western people; and the passive dependants of these history-makers; namely non-Western societies. This lack of reference in the education system to the integrity, continuity, consistency and contribution of non-Western civilisations creates a problem of self-confidence which accelerates the split from tradition.

Conclusion: civilisational self-perception and self-assertion

Islamic civilisation had to face three significant civilisational challenges in the course of its history: the Crusaders, the Mongol invasion and the colonial expansion of Western civilisation. The Crusaders had a limited objective in the conquest of the Holy Land although they aimed at destroying Muslim territory on their way to Jerusalem. Despite its aggressive rhetoric and brutal military practice, the challenge of the Crusader did not create a comprehensive internal crisis in the civilisational balance of the Muslim world. On the contrary, religious identity and its impact on political life were strengthened during this challenge. The crusaders had to withdraw from Muslim territory after being impressed by the supremacy of Islamic civilisation in all fields of this confrontation.

The Mongol invasion was a whirlwind that destroyed elements of the physical and written legacy of Islamic civilisation. The main spiritual, intellectual and cultural parameters of Islamic civilisation, however, continued to survive in strengthened form. The peak of Islamic civilisation in the sixteenth century and its political consequence in the form of Ottoman dominance in Europe and the Middle East, the Safavids in

Iran, the Uzbeks in Central Asia and the Mughals in India were part of the response to this invasion.

These two challenges were military threats. Therefore they did not create a civilisational crisis in the Muslim world. Contrary to these power-centric civilisational challenges of Crusaders and Mongols, the European challenge in the modern era, and its political consequence in the form of international colonial system, were a total challenge in all spheres of civilisational confrontation. Therefore, it created a comprehensive civilisational crisis in the Muslim world.

The basic parameters of traditional civilisations, including the Islamic, have been dissolved and re-shaped by the comprehensive influence of modern Western civilisation. The philosophical, spiritual, logical and institutional links between the substances and forms of traditional civilisations have been cut by this deconstructing influence. A disharmony emerged between the surviving substances of traditional civilisations and new superstructures of the political and economic institutions that were created by the leviathan of the colonial political system and the rising world-economy.

The transforming force of modern Western civilisation originates from its total character, which establishes a relationship of dependency between the power-centric structure of political economy and individual being-time consciousness. The process of secularisation has reformulated this dependency through restructuring institutional relations based on a new paradigm of time-being consciousness. Secularisation in Western civilisation has redefined the ontological and historic *stance* which guarantees the continuity of civilisational substance. The autocratic transfer of this process to non-Western societies, on the other hand, has destroyed the traditional stance without replacing it with a new one.

Thus, the most critical aspect of the process of secularisation is its impact on the *stance* of an individual human being related to his self-consciousness (ontological existence) and to his time-consciousness (historical existence). This *stance* has been redefined in the Western experience of secularisation through a process of continuity in a dynamic interaction of de-traditionalisation and re-traditionalisation. The institutional changes and transformations in Western civilisation have been natural consequences of the redefinition of this *stance*, which has been the intellectual, mental and historical foundation for the legitimacy of modernity.

However, the process of secularisation in non-Western societies, especially Muslim ones, created a break between two categories of *stance*: one modern/secular and the second traditional/religious. Autocratic modernisation strategies tried to impose on the masses a new self-consciousness and time-consciousness through institutional, political, economic and educational machinery. This has exacerbated the question of the 'divided self' in the sphere of self-consciousness and the question of historic existentiality in the sphere of time-consciousness. The revival of authentic civilisations is, in fact, a natural response to restore a 'new stance' which proves the ontological and historical existentiality of non-Western humanity. The answer to Ernest Gellner's question why Islam is secularisation-resistant lies in understanding the strong and consistent traditional *stance* of Islamic civilisation in defining being-time consciousness. The Muslim mind accepted the achievements of modern Western civilisation while it tried to resist changing this stance.

For example, the Muslim mind does not have any problem with a process of secularisation as a rational way of understanding nature and history without confining them to a dichotomic categorisation of profane and sacred. There is also no contradiction between the Islamic mentality and the egalitarian character of secularisation, which tries to eliminate the privileges of a clerical class because there has not been such a religious caste in Islamic ontological self-consciousness. There has never been a theologically justified religious caste in Muslim history.

The universalisation of the post-historic secular self and of the ego-centric secular history of Western civilisation in an age of globalisation has alienated the non-Western individual from his own self-perception and from the historical existentiality of his own society. Today, both the dynamic revival and extensive crisis in non-Western civilisational entities, especially in the Muslim world, are a product of the search for self-assertion in the sense of an 'existential program, according to which man posits his existence in a historical situation and indicates to himself how he is going to deal with the reality surrounding him and what use he will make of the possibilities that are open to him.'[74]

There is a clear difference between early generations of modernisers and contemporary revivalists in non-Western societies. Early modernisers tried to achieve national or civilisational self-preservation against the attacks of colonial powers and in response to the transforming force of modernity; civilisational revivalists at the end of the twentieth century aim at achieving self-assertion in the historic flow of mankind. Therefore early modernisers saw the process of modernisation as an irresistible and inevitable stage of historical existence, whereas civilisational revivalists attempt to revive their authentic *stance* in order to re-define their ontological and historical existentiality. The crisis of Western secular ontology accelerates this revivalist attempt to search for an alternative *stance*.

---

[74] This definition of self-assertion has been borrowed from Blumenberg's *Legitimacy of the Modern Age*, p. 138. The self-assertion in this definition 'does not mean the naked biological or economic preservation of the human organism by the means naturally available to it.'

An understanding which sees modernisation as a simple process of economic transformation to get the necessary means to survive can provide self-preservation, but can not create a feeling of self-assertion. Today, man's fundamental problem is self-assertion rather than simple self-preservation. The question of self-assertion necessarily leads to the question of self-perception. The process of secularisation has been seen as a direct threat to the self-perceptions of non-Western societies due to the fact it has shaken their self-assertion through identifying man's existence with the historical existence of Western civilisation. The search for a strong self-assertion based on a historical existence has led them to redefine their classical self-perception. This is the psycho-ontological foundation of the civilisational resistance of non-Western societies which injects a new impetus for civilisational revival at the beginning of the twenty-first century.

INDEX

Aaron, Raymond, 174
Abbas, Abdullah ibn, 166
Abbasids, 188
Abduh, Muhammad, 19, 21-2, 24, 25
abortion, 127
absolutism, 95
Abu Bakr, 156, 186-7
Adam, 59, 112
Adivar, Adnan, 7
Afghani, Jamal Al-Din Al, 19, 20, 21, 25
Afghanistan, 1, 5
Africa, 43, 49, 162
agnosticism, 33
Ajami, Fuad, 54
Alevi (Muslim minority), 6
Algeria, 3, 6 , 9, 16, 36, 97, 102-4, 116, 163
Al-Hilal, 22
alienation, philosophy of, 122
Al-Muqtataf, 22
altruism, 121
Amin, Husein, 26
Amin, Qasim, 24, 25
Amish, 40
Amnesty International, 103
Anatolia, 200
Andalusia, 188
Anglo-Saxon, 109, 110, 140
Ankara, 6
Antun, Farah, 22, 23
apartheid, 49, 105
Aquinas, St Thomas, 202-3
Arab socialism, 3
Arabisation, 101, 102
Arendt, Hannah, 33, 85, 86
Aristotle, 202
Arkoun, Muhammad, 106, 151, 154
Artaud, Antonine, 79
Atatürk, Mustafa Kamal, 2, 4, 7, 8, 16, 54,
   170, 200
atheism, 33, 81, 87, 118
Athens, 60
Audard, Catherine, 34
Augustine, St, 10
awqaf, 2, 107, 148
axiology, 178

Babylonia, 200
Balkans, 5, 35, 49
barbarism, barbarity, 111-12, 118, 121, 144
bay'ah, 112, 145
Bedouins, 108
Belfast, 49
Ben Ali, President, 105, 106
Bennabi, Malik, 114
Berger, Peter, 38, 192
Berlin, 118
Bernahardt, Reinhold, 37
Bersaglieri, 40
Bir, Gen. Cevik, 6
Bodin, Jean, 95
Bolsheviks, 141, 149
Bonhoffer, Dietrich, 1, 35, 82
Bosnia, 1, 175
Bourguiba, President Habib, 97, 101, 106
Bradlaugh, Charles, 15, 30
Braudel, Fernand, 203
Buddhism, 41, 89
Bulac, Ali, 36
Bustani, Butrus Al, 35

Cairo, 23
Caliphate, collapse of, 170
Caliphate, Rightly Guided, 123, 146, 147
Caliphate, Umayyad, 146
Caliphs, Rightly Guided, 144, 187
Calvinism, 14
capitalism, 3, 128, 137
Casanova, Jose, 124
Catholic Church, 111, 139, 141
Catholicism, 40, 41, 51, 47, 49, 185
Caucasus, 5
causality, 120
Central Asian Republics, 1, 4, 206
Charles X, King, 18
chauvinism, 165
Chicago, University of, 38, 46
China, 43, 199
'chosen nation', 190-1
Christendom, 93, 171
Cicero, 202
Ciller, Tansu, 5, 8

209